25-01-91

IN.

Advanced Prolog

International Series in Logic Programming

Series Editor
Keith Clark, Imperial College of Science and Technology

Associate Editors
Bob Kowalski, Imperial College of Science and Technology
Jean-Louis Lassez, IBM, Yorktown Heights, USA

Editorial Board
K Furukawa (ICOT, Japan)
H Gallaire (ECRC, Munich, FRG)
J W Lloyd (Bristol University, UK)
J Minker (Maryland, USA)
J A Robinson (Syracuse University, NY, USA)
S-A Tärnlund (Uppsala University, Sweden)
M H van Emden (University of Waterloo, Canada)
D H D Warren (Bristol University, UK)

Advanced Prolog

Techniques and Examples

PETER ROSS

University of Edinburgh

ADDISON-WESLEY PUBLISHING COMPANY

Wokingham, England · Reading, Massachusetts · Menlo Park, California
New York · Don Mills, Ontario · Amsterdam · Bonn · Sydney
Singapore · Tokyo · Madrid · San Juan

Cover designed by Marshall Henrichs
and printed by The Riverside Printing Co. (Reading) Ltd.
Typeset by the AMS from the author's L^AT_EX files.
Printed in Great Britain by Mackays of Chatham PLC, Kent.

First printed 1989.

British Library Cataloguing in Publication Data
Ross, P. M. (Peter Malcolm), *1950 –*
    Advanced Prolog: techniques and examples. –
    (International series in logic programming)
    1. Computer systems. Programming languages : Prolog
    I. Title   II. Series
    005.13′3

    ISBN 0–201–17527–4

Library of Congress Cataloging in Publication Data
Ross, Peter.
        Advanced PROLOG: techniques and examples / Peter Ross.
        p.   cm. – (International series in logic programming)
        Bibliography: p.
        Includes index.
        ISBN 0–201–17527–4
        1. Prolog (Computer program language)   I. Title.   II. Series.
    QA76.73.P76R67   1989
    005.13′3–dc20   89–6625
                                                                            CIP

QA
76
.73
P76
R688
1989

For Susan, Rebecca and Amy
without whom this book
would have been finished much sooner

Preface

Prolog has been in use for many years now, both for research in artificial intelligence (AI) and other fields and for commercial and industrial work. Recently interest in it has swelled dramatically, in part because of its role in the Japanese Fifth Generation project and in part because good implementations are becoming widely available. Special-purpose Prolog workstations such as the Japanese Personal Sequential Inference (PSI) machine are beginning to appear, and some mainframe manufacturers are producing Prolog accelerators for their machines. Nevertheless it remains a difficult language to learn; the gap between acquiring a reading knowledge and a writing knowledge of it is much wider than in almost any other programming language currently in use. From my own experience of teaching a postgraduate course in it for the past few years, it is clear that those who have considerable experience of more conventional languages such as Pascal or FORTRAN are handicapped by their instincts – they still thirst after 'for' loops and 'while' loops, type declarations and assignment statements and the many other features common to most languages. Many go so far as to try, elaborately and usually unsuccessfully, to recreate these features in Prolog rather than make the effort to explore the different idioms that it encourages.

Although there are a number of good introductions to the language now in print, only one or two books go beyond the elementary stage to suggest the range of what Prolog is good for or to discuss what it is bad for. This book is intended to fill such a role. It is not meant to be an introduction to the language, although in the interests of standardizing terminology the basics are covered in the first chapter. The rest of the book is built around a number of examples that provide contexts for discussing questions such as program design, efficiency and style, issues of data representation and control flow and so on. To generalize, it is aimed at a readership more interested in the practicalities than in the theoretical aspects of logic programming, who have mastered examples such as `member/2` and `quicksort/2` but do not yet have very much experience of creating larger programs.

It is a common observation in the educational world that a person who is learning some new skill tends to rise to a certain level of competence and then tends to stay there, on a plateau, for some while and perhaps for ever. Whatever the reasons, this is as true of people who are learning to program in Prolog. This book is an attempt to help lift people beyond the early plateaus, by providing some discussion of style and techniques and by showing some interesting examples of programs. In keeping with the excellent introductory book by Bratko [1986], the programs in this book are largely concerned with aspects of AI; indeed, I would like to think that this book could be used as an adjunct to that one.

Merely to read large programs will cure most kinds of insomnia; therefore none of the programs in this book is really large. However, they form a useful set for teaching purposes, to be extended or modified by students. Some suggestions for changes and improvements have been made for most of the examples included. In one or two places, the fact that the width of the published page, with a reasonable size of type, is significantly less than the width of an 80-character screen has meant that the layout of the programs has suffered a little. You may also find some parts of programs which you would have naturally written in a different way had you been inventing them. If you are a teacher, you can always ask your students why the author did it that way; if you are the student, do not automatically rule out the answer 'stupidity'.

Acknowledgements

My postgraduate classes of the past several years have contributed greatly to this book, usually in the form of good ideas and criticism of my early efforts and occasionally by looking at me blankly when my explanations have gone haywire. The classes have been too large to permit me to mention them all by name; thank you all, wherever you are now!

Richard O'Keefe was a great source of inspiration – he provided many excellent examples of Prolog programming during his years in the Department of AI at Edinburgh, and was also fun to disagree with. Michael Donat provided the ingenious 'stack to tree' example. Alex Thame thought up the heuristics used in the 'knight's tour' example in response to a class exercise, and first demonstrated their remarkable efficiency in comparison with the brute force approach. John Lewis discovered various bugs in early versions of the chart parser.

My family – Susan, Rebecca and Amy – provided the support and the kisses needed to finish it!

Contents

1
Introduction

This chapter sets the scene, discussing the basis of Prolog in logic and providing a short account of Prolog itself.

1.1 About Prolog and about this book

Prolog owes its origins to work in the early 1970s by Kowalski and Colmerauer. The former (see, for instance, Kowalski [1974]) showed that although first-order predicate logic was customarily viewed as a declarative language concerned with truths and falsehoods, a certain subset of it could also be viewed as the basis of a recursive programming language – something executable by machine. At the same time Colmerauer's group in Marseille were developing a theorem-proving system written in FORTRAN, based on Kowalski's ideas (see, for instance, Colmerauer [1974]). Both of these developments leaned heavily on Robinson's work in the mid-1960s on the resolution principle and a unification algorithm [Robinson 1965]. However, David Warren's efficient compiler and interpreter developed in the mid 1970s [Warren 1977] started the serious interest in Prolog as a real programming language. That implementation is still remarkably good despite its age, although it is by now far from being the fastest and many other versions have now appeared for hardware ranging from small micros and IBM PCs up to the largest mainframes. Some of these offer much more sophisticated environments than DEC-10 Prolog and many additional built-in predicates. For almost any computer you care to name, you can now probably find a reasonable Prolog that will run on it.

Many of these systems are modelled on what is now called 'Edinburgh Prolog', derived from DEC-10 Prolog [Warren *et al.* 1979]. Although these systems offer many idiosyncratic features, the existence of this Edinburgh Prolog 'standard' has helped to make books such as this one possible by providing a substantial common core that is almost the same in many different versions of Prolog. Alas, the core is not quite the same in all versions.

1

Systems can differ wildly in the semantics of the 'cut' and a few other predicates. Although many versions now provide features such as windowing, interfaces to routines written in other languages, hooks for term storage in hash tables and balanced trees and so on, the form of such features is usually unique to each of the systems that offers it. Appendix A describes the predicates offered by Quintus Prolog, one of the best-developed of the systems in widespread use. All the programs should run on any decent 'Edinburgh Prolog'-compatible system although a few of the PC-based Prologs without virtual memory may run into space problems with programs that consume a lot of space at run time, such as the chart parser. No doubt, devotees of any one particular Prolog will bemoan the fact that the special features they are used to do not get a mention. The range of such idiosyncratic extras is so wide that it is impossible to cater for them properly within a single volume. A list of suppliers of Prolog systems can be found in Appendix B, although this list will naturally be incomplete and will become less accurate as time passes.

This book is not meant to be a defence of Prolog. Just as LISP is not a true functional language, Prolog is far from being true 'programming in logic'. Like LISP, it is a good implementation language with special strengths and weaknesses. Nobody should learn just a single language and stick to it through thick and thin; the sensible course is to pick the language that suits the job, and perhaps even to work in more than one at once. Considering the versions of Prolog that are widely available at present, it is perhaps still best suited to small-scale tests of ideas, initial developments of commercial products and to research in fields such as AI where an experimental style of programming is more acceptable than it is in computer science. The single global space for term storage and the absence of any decent module system in most versions are not the products of any ideological purity or conceptual necessity; such oddities are just symptoms of the language's relative immaturity when compared to more conventional ones.

In order to give some feel for the particular strengths and weaknesses of Prolog as a programming language, it is necessary to give a short and informal account of first-order predicate logic. To set the rest of the book in context, it is also necessary to give a short account of the basics of the language itself. The rest of the chapter addresses these two goals. If you are really averse to logic you can skip to Section 1.6 – but try not to. Those who wish a more formal treatment of the foundations of logic programming and of Prolog in particular should consult Lloyd [1984].

1.2   The rudiments of logic

Omniscience is all very well, but it is quite taxing for the memory. In practice some method is needed for deducing, inducing or abducing new information from old. Deduction is essentially logic as most people know it, and AI has been leaning heavily on this for its needs. Induction is a matter of postulating generalizations from observing patterns in facts. For example, woodpeckers, swifts, eagles, falcons, finches all have four toes on each foot; maybe all birds have four toes on each foot? (This is nearly true, but runners such as partridges have only a stub for the fourth, for instance.) Abduction is a matter of postulating causes from results. For example, if the Prime Minister is seen to come into the House of Commons soaking wet, then maybe it is raining outside? If small men cast big shadows, maybe the sun is about to set? (This is an ancient Chinese saying!) The aim of this section is to convince you that even a machine can do some kind of logic, rather than to stun you with the full formalities.

1.2.1   First-order predicate logic (FOPL)

This is currently the most popular brand of logic in AI. It deals with the simplest notions of truth and falsehood, in a mechanistic way. It provides a language that can be used to reason about items and simple kinds of relationships between items. If you are philosophically inclined, you may start to sweat about what an item might be. Do not. As far as predicate logic is concerned, there is just a set of objects (referred to as the *universe*) which cannot be analysed individually, and could be meaningless for all that it concerns the logic, to be used as the atomic building blocks of everything else. The other ingredients are:

- A set of properties that an object may have, such as 'prime', 'Jewish', 'green'.

- A set of functions. Each function takes a certain (fixed) number of arguments – this is called its *arity* – and each argument is an object. The function identifies an object; think of it as another name for one of the objects. For example, the function 'eldest_son_of', given two parents, may identify another human being (or may not apply to those two parents). There may be some algorithmic way of figuring what the selected object is, or there may not be; as far as predicate logic is concerned, this does not matter.

- A set of relations between a certain number (the *arity* again) of objects. Given the right number of objects as its arguments, the relationship either holds (is true) or does not (is false). For example, given any three points on a plane, a relationship which tests whether they are the vertices of an equilateral triangle is either true or false.

- A method of composing formulae about relations and properties, which deal in their truth or falsehood and are themselves true or false. For example, 'if it swims in salt water and is caught off the British coast then it is edible' (is this true?), or 'every paperback has a price printed on it'.

All these can clearly be represented somehow in a standard computer programming language. The meaning of what you represent is only known to you, the computer will just be pushing symbols about. The knack lies in picking meanings in such a way that the symbol-pushing produces meaningful stuff. That is, your meanings for your relations and functions and properties should somehow mirror reality (assuming that reality is meaningful).

1.2.2 Syntax and terminology

The basic ingredients are names for the objects themselves, for variables which might stand for any object, for functions, relations and predicates. When talking of these last three, it is the name and arity together that identify them, the name alone is inadequate. Brackets are also used quite a lot, for grouping things together, indicating the arguments to a function and so on. There are also various special symbols, shown in Table 1.1. The names, brackets and special symbols are used to compose expressions of two kinds:

- *Terms*, which are essentially ways of referring to objects. Names of objects (alias constants), names of variables and functions are all terms. The expression $f(a, g(b, c, d))$ would be a term if f were the name of a function of arity 2 and g were the name of a function of arity 3 and a–d were names of constants (objects in some universe). The fancy symbols are not used when building terms.

- *Formulae*, which are essentially 'true' or 'false'. The simplest kind are called *atomic formulae*, alias *predicates*. Both properties and relations are expressed as predicates: a property is just a one-argument predicate such as *green(fred)* which is true or false depending on whether fred is green or not, and a relation is a predicate with more than one argument, for example *equilateral_triangle*(p_1, p_2, p_3), which, again, is just true or false. More complicated formulae are

Table 1.1   Special symbols used in first-order predicate logic.

spoken	*written*
for all	∀
there exists	∃
and	∧
or	∨
not	¬
implies	⇒ or →
equivalent to	≡

built up from these atomic types by using the special symbols in Table 1.1, in a very commonsense way. The formal definitions would bore you too much.

It is worth noting that, although functions and predicates appear here in the form $name(arg_1, arg_2, \ldots)$, there is no special reason why the name should appear before the opening bracket. In Prolog you will see notation like this, whereas in LISP and most LISP-based reasoning kits you will see something like $(name\ arg_1\ arg_2\ \ldots)$ instead. In fact micro-Prolog [Clark and McCabe 1984], a very popular dialect of Prolog for microcomputers, uses this kind of syntax.

Another important point is that the arguments to anything must be terms, *not* predicates or other formulae. This will be discussed further later on.

1.2.3   Manipulating formulae

Here are some points about formulae, to remind you. Greek letters are used here as a handy shorthand for formulae, and upper-case letters as variable names.

- $\alpha \vee \beta$ is true if either α or β is, or both are.

- $\alpha \wedge \beta$ is true if both are.

- $\alpha \Rightarrow \beta$ is identical to $\neg\alpha \vee \beta$. This does not quite fit the everyday sense. However, think of the cobra in Rudyard Kipling's story *Rikki-Tikki-Tavi*, which says 'if you move I will strike, and if you do not move I will strike'. This means 'I will strike'. This may help you to remember that if β is true, then the implication $\alpha \Rightarrow \beta$ is true even if α happens to be false.

- $\alpha \equiv \beta$ is just $(\alpha \Rightarrow \beta) \wedge (\beta \Rightarrow \alpha)$.

- Suppose the universe is the set of all people. Then $\forall X \exists Y\ likes(X, Y)$ might mean that everybody likes somebody. If this is true, it still does not mean that a particular person likes somebody *else*; maybe they only like themselves. However, given that such a formula is true, you can *specialize* it to get another true formula, by selecting an X: $\exists Y\ likes(peter, Y)$

- The objects are mere symbols. You might, for example, interpret the symbol *ronnie* as referring to an ex-President of the USA but equally it could be taken to refer to your grandfather, or Isaac Newton's favourite quill pen, or indeed anything else. The truth or falsehood of any formula is always relative to the *interpretation* of the objects, functions and relations that compose it.

- If there is some interpretation that makes a formula true, then the formula is said to be *satisfiable*. When talking of satisifiability one can make formal statements such as $\alpha \models \beta$ (α logically implies β), that is, for every interpretation in which α holds β also holds. Such a statement is *about* first-order predicate logic but not *in* it – an important distinction.

- Suppose you know that *likes*(*ronnie, nancy*) is true. Then you also know that $\exists Y$ *likes*(*ronnie, Y*) and $\exists X \exists Y$ *likes*(*X, Y*) and so on.

These last two are actually general-purpose rules of inference for FOPL. Here are some more (there are many others possible):

- Given α it follows that $(\alpha \lor \beta)$.

- Given $(\alpha \land \beta)$ it follows that α (likewise, β).

- Given α and $(\alpha \Rightarrow \beta)$ it follows that β.

- Given $\neg\beta$ and $(\alpha \Rightarrow \beta)$ it follows that $\neg\alpha$.

These last two are snappily referred to as *modus ponens* and *modus tollens*, respectively. Modus ponens is heavily used in computer reasoning systems, modus tollens less so, for some reason.

1.2.4   Getting started on reasoning

You, or your computer, get started on FOPL reasoning by taking certain formulae to be axiomatic (unilaterally declared to be true). The formal notation for 'α is an axiom' is '$\vdash \alpha$', if you want to know. Given some axioms, and some rules of inference, you can then start churning out new true formulae.

This is where you and your computer start to get into trouble. There are many ways of writing the same formula (such as $\alpha \Rightarrow \beta$ or $\neg\alpha \lor \beta$). There are also many rules of inference that might be applied, and a random choice is not likely to be satisfactory. For example, given one axiom α, you can generate an infinite number of possibly valueless new ones of the form $\alpha \lor \beta \lor \gamma \lor \ldots$. This looks like a search problem. What helped the topic of computer reasoning to get going were the discoveries that (a) the many variant forms of a formula can be transformed into one standard form by an essentially mechanical algorithm (no decisions needed) and (b) there is one single rule of inference that will let you deduce anything that could be deduced from a given set of axioms (so no decisions are needed about which rule to choose). Discovery (a), of course, can be used to decide whether two nasty-looking formulae are really the same one in different disguises – just standardize both and see if they give the same end product.

One standard form commonly employed is called *conjunctive normal form*. Formulae get transformed into a conjunct (that is, '...and...', or in formal notation '... ∧ ...') of *clauses*, where a clause is something that contains no explicit quantifiers (∀ or ∃) and is only a disjunction (that is, '...or ...', or in formal notation '... ∨ ...') of predicates and negations of predicates. For example, assuming that the Greek letters all stand for atomic predicates here,

$$(\alpha_1 \vee \neg\alpha_2 \vee \ldots) \wedge (\beta_1 \vee \ldots) \wedge \ldots$$

is in conjunctive normal form. This can be taken a step further, to *clausal form*, in which all the parts of such a conjunct are listed as being separately true. That is, the collection of formulae to be handled by the computer are all disjuncts: $(\alpha_1 \vee \neg\alpha_2 \ldots)$ and $(\beta_1 \vee \ldots)$ and so on. The next section describes how any formula can be transformed into such a clausal form.

The special rule of inference is called the *resolution rule*, originally discovered by J.A.Robinson [1965] and widely used in computational systems – see, for example, Kowalski and Kuehner [1971]. Section 1.2.6 gives a sketchy account; for better information see, for instance, Bundy [1985].

1.2.5   Standardizing formulae

Omitting the technical details, the process is:

(1) Get rid of ⇒, use the $\neg\alpha \vee \beta$ form instead.

(2) Move negation inside any quantifiers so that the negation is next to the actual predicate. For example, $\neg(\exists X(p(X) \vee q(X)))$ is $\forall X \neg(p(X) \vee q(X))$, which is $\forall X(\neg p(X) \wedge \neg q(X))$.

(3) Rename any variables so that each quantifier is using a unique name.

(4) You can now happily move all the quantifiers (∀ and ∃) to the front, that is, the left-hand end of the formula. The product of this step is called *Prenex Normal Form*.

(5) Get rid of all the explicit existential quantifiers (∃), merely by picking a name (or maybe a function will be needed) for each object whose existence is being asserted by such a quantifier. This may mean that some object in the universe has more than one name, it does not matter. This step is called *Skolemizing*, and the name or function is called a *Skolem constant* or *Skolem function*. The names or functions introduced must not, of course, conflict with any already in use.

(6) Rearrange the body of the formula so that it is expressed as a conjunct of simpler formulae (or maybe it is just a single disjunct already). For instance, $(\alpha \wedge \beta) \vee \gamma$ is just $(\alpha \vee \gamma) \wedge (\beta \vee \gamma)$. This is the Conjunctive Normal Form mentioned earlier.

(7) Erase those explicit universal quantifiers at the front, a handy nota-
tional change. Any variable in the formula is universally quantified
(the Skolemizing got rid of the existential variables), and the leftward
movement of the universal quantifiers handled any scope problems,
so this erasure does not affect the meaning at all.

(8) Now you have a formula that is just a conjunct of disjuncts. If it is
satisfiable, then each of the disjuncts is satisfiable, so you can happily
split the whole into a collection of true disjuncts.

So, at the end of all this, you are dealing with a collection of axioms and
deductions which are all disjuncts, and all satisfiable – that is, all in clausal
form. Here is an example of this process. Start with the doubtful assertion:

All Martians like to eat some kind of spiced food.

Let us suppose that Martians do not necessarily all like the same kind of
spiced food. In first-order logic, the assertion might be represented as

$$\forall X(martian(X) \Rightarrow$$
$$\exists Y \exists Z(food(Y) \wedge$$
$$spice(Z) \wedge contains(Y, Z) \wedge likes(X, Y)))$$

Getting rid of the explicit implication symbol, this becomes:

$$\forall X(\neg martian(X) \vee$$
$$\exists Y \exists Z(food(Y) \wedge$$
$$spice(Z) \wedge contains(Y, Z) \wedge likes(X, Y)))$$

and moving the quantifiers to the front it becomes:

$$\forall X \exists Y \exists Z(\neg martian(X) \vee$$
$$(food(Y) \wedge spice(Z) \wedge contains(Y, Z) \wedge likes(X, Y)))$$

There is no need to rename variables. To get rid of the existential quantifiers
it is not enough just to pick constants to stand for the Y and Z which are
claimed to exist. They might depend on the Martian, so functions must be
chosen instead – say $f(X)$ for the food in question and $s(X)$ for the spice
in question. This does point up a representational problem, of course: you
would suppose that the spice depends on the food rather than the Martian.
Let us ignore that and carry on. The formula is now:

$$\forall X(\neg martian(X)$$
$$\vee(food(f(X)) \wedge spice(s(X)) \wedge$$
$$contains(f(X), s(X)) \wedge likes(X, f(X))))$$

Rearranging the body into a conjunct and dropping the explicit quantifier,
this finally becomes:

$$(\neg martian(X) \vee food(f(X)))$$
$$\wedge(\neg martian(X) \vee spice(s(X)))$$
$$\wedge(\neg martian(X) \vee contains(f(X), s(X)))$$
$$\wedge(\neg martian(X) \vee likes(X, f(x)))$$

This can be split into the four disjuncts, all satisfiable if the whole conjunct is.

1.2.6   The resolution rule and unification

Suppose that all the formulae you are interested in are now in clausal form. The following *resolution* rule of inference will let you make deductions from your set (and so enlarge it). Find two formulae such that the same predicate appears in both, but in one of them it is negated. For example, $(\alpha \vee \beta \vee \gamma)$ and $(\neg\beta \vee \delta)$. A little thought will convince you that $(\alpha \vee \gamma \vee \delta)$ is also satisfiable – that is, strike out that predicate and its negation: the disjunct of the others is then satisfiable.

Actually, there is slightly more to this than might appear. These Greek letters are disguising what might be quite elaborate predicates. For example, you might have the following two formulae:

$$cheap(X) \vee likes(peter, whisky(X))$$
$$\neg likes(Y, whisky(laphroaig)) \vee drunkard(Y)$$

This means (if it is true in the obvious interpretation) that *peter* likes any expensive whisky, and that anybody who likes Laphroaig whisky is a drunkard. The likes-with-two-arguments predicate occurs, negated, in the second formula, but unfortunately the arguments are not the same. However, both formulae have more specific versions in which the arguments are the same – namely, take X to be *laphroaig* and Y to be *peter*. Then the resolution rule can be applied to deduce that $cheap(laphroaig) \vee drunkard(peter)$.

In looking for more specific versions of two formulae so that resolution can be applied, it makes sense to make the arguments only as specific as necessary rather than too specific. Fortunately, it turns out that there is a single most general substitution for the variables involved if there is any possible specialization that will do, and there is a simple algorithm for finding it (which is not stated in this book; try inventing it for yourself). The set of substitutions for the various variables involved is called the *unifier* of the predicate and its negated counterpart. The process is called *unification* of terms. Here is a further example. Consider the two terms

```
date(day(friday,13), Month, Year)
date(    D         ,   M  , 1901)
```

There are many possible unifiers, such as

```
{D=day(friday,13), M=coffee, Month=coffee, Year=1901}
```

but only a single most general one which subsumes all others:

```
{D=day(friday,13), M=Month, Year=1901}
```

In this, M and Month have been unified but nothing has been said about the value they might share; they are still uninstantiated. An algorithm for computing the unifier of two terms that is linear in space and time can be found in Paterson and Wegman [1978].

It is not obvious that the resolution rule of inference is what is needed, but such is the case. The original result is due to Robinson [1965]. It is not quite the whole story, either, because expressions of equality pose a special problem. For example, if we know that *peter = author* and also *scottish(peter)* then we know that *scottish(author)* is true too. As far as the resolution rule is concerned, there is nothing special about statements of equality. Clearly, it would be useful if there were; that is, it would be useful to have this way of expressing allowable rewritings of bits of formulae. The best-known is called *paramodulation* in the trade; see, for instance, Wos and Robinson[1970], Bundy [1985] or Loveland [1978]. Paramodulation provides a complete way to handle equality, but brings with it the problem of combinatorial explosion: there are usually a vast number of ways of applying rewriting using equality. If you can rewrite *peter* as *author* at one step, then you can reverse it at any later step. An alternative to paramodulation is e-resolution [Morris 1969].

1.2.7   Making use of resolution

As was noted above, it is still possible to conclude infinite amounts of rubbish. What you often want to get a computer to do, however, is to see if some given clause (say, δ) follows from some axioms (say, α, β and γ). The usual trick is to see if a contradiction follows from assuming α, β, γ and $\neg\delta$; that is, whether it is possible to resolve all the way down to a completely empty clause.

So now your computer does not have to decide which rule of inference to use. However, it still has to decide which formulae to apply it to, in the search for a way to resolve down to the empty clause. Various algorithms, called *resolution strategies*, are used by different systems. Some are cheap to apply, but do not guarantee to be able to come up with all the consequences that might follow from the original set of formulae. Such strategies are called *incomplete*. Completeness and slowness go together. Here are some examples of resolution strategies:

- *Unit preference.* Prefer formulae with just one predicate (or, maybe, insist).

- *Set of support.* Never try to resolve two formulae both taken from the original set (α, β and γ in the above example).

- *Lock resolution.* Given two formulae, tackle only one predicate at a time. It may not have occurred to you, from the above description of resolution, that you could resolve two formulae tackling two or more predicates in them at once.

There are many others.

1.2.8 How Prolog fits into first-order logic

Prolog is one example of a theorem-proving language, which restricts its efforts to handling a subset of possible formulae. The formulae it deals with are called *Horn clauses*; in a Horn clause there is at most one non-negated predicate. Consider the formula $\alpha \Rightarrow (\beta \vee \gamma)$. This is just $\neg\alpha \vee \beta \vee \gamma$, in which there are two non-negated predicates, so it is not a Horn clause. So it should be clear that Horn clauses are either single predicates or single negated predicates or implies-statements in which the conclusion is a single predicate rather than a disjunction of them. Clearly, restricting attention to Horn clauses does cut down the amount of decision-making required in the resolution strategy.

It would seem, therefore, that a language like Prolog cannot handle a problem such as this one:

> There are three books stacked on the table. The top one is black, the bottom one is not. Prove that there is a black book stacked on a non-black book.

Prolog is, in fact, often used as an implementation language, and it is possible to create an augmented reasoning system in Prolog that can handle such a problem. The key idea in just one of the possible approaches to this particular case is to add the 'general contrapositive' forms of the formulae too; the 'general contrapositive' form of a formula is logically equivalent to it, so nothing new is being added, life is just being made easier for a machine. The other important step is to augment the proof procedure to check whether the negation of any goal being sought was something that had been sought earlier. If so, that goal has been established, by a *reductio ad absurdum*. For example, suppose we start with:

$$\alpha \Rightarrow \gamma$$
$$\beta \Rightarrow \gamma$$
$$\alpha \vee \beta$$

It follows that γ is true, but ordinary Prolog will not do here. The idea is to transform this set of formulae to:

$$\alpha \Rightarrow \gamma$$
$$\neg\gamma \Rightarrow \neg\alpha$$
$$\beta \Rightarrow \gamma$$
$$\neg\gamma \Rightarrow \neg\beta$$

$$\alpha \vee \beta$$
$$\neg\alpha \Rightarrow \beta$$
$$\neg\beta \Rightarrow \alpha$$

and then a simple backward-chaining proof of γ will work, because it will devolve into an attempt to establish $\neg\gamma$. The *reductio ad absurdum* involved is as follows. If $\neg\gamma$ was in fact satisfiable, then forward chaining along the same path would eventually lead to showing that the original goal γ was satisfiable in the same interpretation. But $\neg\gamma$ and γ cannot be simultaneously satisfied. Thus it must be the case that $\neg\gamma$ cannot be satisifed, and so γ must be true in the interpretation. See Loveland [1978] for more details, and Poole *et al.* [1986] for some details of a system called Theorist which actually makes use of this. Another of the possible approaches is to somehow generate all the colours that the middle book might be (say, black and the ersatz colour 'non-black' in this case) and to check that it is impossible to fabricate a counter-example to the conclusion.

1.3   Some drawbacks of FOPL

Propositional logic (first-order predicate logic without the quantifiers, so to speak) has three useful attributes:

(1) Completeness. Theorems (true formulae) are provable.

(2) Soundness. Non-theorems (false formulae) are not provable.

(3) Decidability. You are able to classify any formula as true or false.

Propositional logic is a bit limited, since it does not allow you to represent statements such as 'all Spaniards eat paella' in any handy way (you would have to enumerate all Spaniards and give a statement about each). It does not let you represent 'all even numbers are the sum of two primes' at all (this statement is currently undecided, by the way).

First-order predicate logic does let you represent such statements, but does not have the property of decidability (as shown by Gödel's 1931 theorem). Nevertheless, it has been used as the basis of a great deal of machine reasoning work, partly because it is possible to do so. What are the problems of FOPL? It does not allow you to handle 'natural' deduction tasks very easily. For example, in FOPL, if a theorem can be deduced from a set of axioms, it can be deduced from any larger set containing the first set (this is a property called 'monotonicity'), whereas by 'natural' logic you might reason that, having a car, you could drive to the airport, even though it turns out the car has no petrol. A language like Prolog can be used to handle this kind of thing, but not in any straightforward way. FOPL does not let you treat the predicates as objects of the world (that's the 'FO' bit), so reasoning about reasoning can be cumbersome. In FOPL, you must rule out as malformed such 'Christmas-cracker' tricks as

If this sentence is true, then pigs can fly.

If you allowed it, you'd have something of the form 'formula α is $(\alpha \Rightarrow \beta)$', and so could reason:

> Suppose α. α is $\alpha \Rightarrow \beta$, so β follows. Thus, if α is assumed, β is so. Thus we have proved $\alpha \Rightarrow \beta$. Thus we have proved α. So we know α, and $\alpha \Rightarrow \beta$, so we know β.

In any logic, not just FOPL, the paradoxical sentence above should be ruled out on the grounds that you cannot assign a meaning to it. From the human point of view, you must assign meaning to formulae before you reason about them. From the computer point of view, there is no problem; the machine just pushes patterns about. If you have encoded your problem wrongly, or been inconsistent about interpretation (for example, a pidgin-French speaker and a pidgin-English speaker might make different assumptions about whether '(plus 3 2)' was a predicate or a function), the machine will not save you. Turning real-world knowledge into some logical form is normally tricky: consider the statement 'A horse has four legs'. You probably assume that this means that all horses have four legs rather than just a single unnamed horse. Compare 'A rich man has two credit cards' – what if I have three?

If you want practice in FOPL, or an entertaining route to the higher reaches of logic, books such as Smullyan [1981] are a good starting place. These start from simple problems of the form:

```
(1) If A is guilty, so is B
(2) If B did it, C is also guilty
(3) If C did it, then D is also guilty or B is innocent
(4) If A is innocent, B did it and D is innocent
(5) No-one other than A, B, C or D could be guilty
Who are guilty, who are innocent?
```

and take you up to Gödel's theorem and beyond purely by way of such puzzles.

1.4   MRS

Prolog is just one system that deals with a restricted subset of FOPL. A less familiar system, intended for work in expert systems, is MRS from Stanford University (MRS is an acronym for 'Metalevel Reasoning System'; see Russell [1985]). It is very briefly outlined here for the sake of contrast, to show that there are other well-developed systems based on logic. In it, formulae are expressed in a LISP-like way, and the system is written in LISP. For example,

```
(adjacent russia china)
(number daysofweek 7)
(population bolivia 470000)                      ; in 1976
......
(not (adjacent russia bolivia))
(or (british budd) (spanish budd))
(if (likes peter whisky) (drunkard peter)) ; not in 1976
......
(if (human $x) (hasheart $x)))
......
```

As in any other such system, it can be cumbersome to represent even simple things, such as 'More people smoke Bloodbaths than any other':

```
(if (and (number (smokers-of Bloodbaths) $N)
         (cigarette $F)
         (not (equal $F Bloodbaths))
         (number (smokers-of $F) $M)
    )
    (greater $N $M)
)
```

MRS provides tools for converting to conjunctive normal form and other standard forms, tools for forward-chaining, backward-chaining, linear-input resolution and a host of other features. The user has a high degree of control over representational and inference methods. The system can be set to record information about how deductions were made, in the same representational form as those deductions, so that MRS can be used to reason about the inferencing itself. There is a much wider range of facilities immediately available to the programmer than there is in many Prolog systems, although they could be replicated in Prolog. The cost, however, is in terms of space and speed; MRS is intended for research rather than for commercial development work.

In order to show the process of transformation to a standard form and the use of resolution in a language other than Prolog, consider this simple example:

> Cows eat more grass (per head) than sheep, and there is a
> Merino that eats more grass than any rabbit. Colin is a cow
> and Roger is a rabbit. Show that Colin eats more grass than
> Roger.

In MRS expressions such as $x denote object-level variables. Such a variable can stand for any object, but not for formulae; there is another kind of variable which can be instantiated to formulae and which is used in meta-level reasoning. The example becomes:

```
(if (and (cow $x)          ; 1
         (sheep $y))
    (eats-more $x $y))
(and (merino michael)      ; 2
     (if (rabbit $y)
         (eats-more michael $y)))
(cow colin)                ; 3
(rabbit roger)             ; 4
```

What we lack is that Merinos are sheep and the fact that 'eats-more' is a transitive relationship:

```
(if (merino $x)            ; 5
    (sheep $x)))
(if (and (eats-more $x $y) ; 6
         (eats-more $y $z))
    (eats-more $x $z)))
```

In clausal form, 1, 2, 5 and 6 become

```
(or                        ; 1a
    (not (cow $X))
    (not (sheep $Y))
    (eats-more $X $Y))
(merino michael)           ; 2a
(or                        ; 2b
    (not (rabbit $R))
    (eats-more michael $R))
(or                        ; 5a
    (not (merino $D))
    (sheep $D))
(or                        ; 6a
    (not (eats-more $A $B))
    (not (eats-more $B $C))
    (eats-more $A $C))
```

– here, `michael` is a specially introduced Skolem constant. Such a transformation can be done automatically by MRS. Applying the resolution rule of inference,

```
(sheep michael)            ; 7: from 5a and 2a
(or
    (not (sheep $Y))
    (eats-more colin $Y))  ; 8: from 1a and 3
(eats-more colin michael)  ; 9: from 7 and 8
(eats-more michael roger)  ; 10: from 2b and 4
(or                        ; 11: from 6a and 9
```

```
            (not (eats-more michael $C))
            (eats-more colin $C))
  (eats-more colin roger)      ; 12: from 10 and 11
```

which is what we wanted to prove. Note that we used all of the explicit and implicit given formulae. The fact that we are dealing with a monotonic logic means that from a theoretical point of view we do not have to worry about the order of generation of the consequences; the set of valid formulae just gets bigger and eventually includes what we want. In non-monotonic logics (which cannot be expressed directly in Prolog, but which can be handled by an interpreter implemented in it) the order does matter. Clearly, from a computational point of view the order also matters – we want to arrive at our desired result as fast as we can. See Genesereth and Nilsson [1987] for an introduction to non-monotonic logics.

1.5   Other kinds of logic

There are many other kinds of logic besides FOPL and its immediate derivatives. Here are just two examples of types.

Modal logics [Hughes and Cresswell 1969] try to get away from the absolute nature of truth and falsehood entailed in FOPL, which causes trouble when trying to represent ideas such as 'I believe X, you do not believe it, we are both reasonable people'. In a typical Kripke interpretation [Kripke 1963], modal logics are characterized by having a number of possible worlds $W_1 \cdots W_n$. In each, a set of axioms is given; the set depends on the world. Each world can 'view' a number of the others, not necessarily all of them. Then something is necessarily true(false) in a world if it is true(false) in all worlds viewable from it. Otherwise it is only possibly true. There have been fairly weak attempts to apply this to representing the notion that different people believe different things. Such attempts have run up against the problem of 'logical omniscience', namely that, according to this model, if a person believes a set of axioms he must therefore believe all the consequences of them. But are you convinced, knowing the basic rules of arithmetic and algebra, that there are infinitely many pairs of consecutive integers such that the two numbers in any pair have the same number of divisors (a proof appeared in 1984)?

Fuzzy logics try to get away from truth/falsehood altogether, by dealing in 'degree of truth'. The simple, now obsolete, formalism runs something like this. Given some object x and some set S, let Sx be a real number between 0 and 1 inclusive, denoting the degree to which x belongs to S. Merely by choice of definition, let us say that

$$(A \cup B)x = max(Ax, Bx)$$
$$(A \cap B)x = min(Ax, Bx)$$
$$(\backslash A)x = 1 - Ax$$

Let F be the set of all false propositions, T be the set of all true propositions. Then the 'truth of p' is chosen to be $(1 - Fp + Tp)/2$.

Suppose a has truth $t(a)$, and so on. Then, by the above chosen definitions,

if b is $(\neg a)$, then $t(b) = 1 - t(a)$
if c is $(a \wedge b)$, then $t(c) = \min(t(a), t(b))$
if c is $(a \Rightarrow b)$, then $t(c) = \max(1 - t(a), t(b))$

Problems arise in trying to square this with intuition. For example, if you are certain of the truth of $(a \Rightarrow b)$, then $t((a \Rightarrow b)) = 1$. But this means $t(a) = 0$ or $t(b) = 1$, which does not really follow. People have tried various other definitions of the truth of '$\Rightarrow$', such as:

$$t((a \Rightarrow b)) = \text{if } t(a) < t(b) \text{ then } 1 \text{ else } 0$$
$$\text{or } \min(1, 1 - t(a) + t(b))$$
$$\text{or } \min(1, t(b)/t(a))$$
$$\text{or if } t(a) < t(b) \text{ then } 1 \text{ else } t(b)$$

All these allow some truth to the proposition $(a \vee \neg a)$ in intuitively unreasonable circumstances.

Despite such problems, there is a lot of interest in fuzzy logics because they offer a possible escape from the absolute nature of true/false. Prolog-like systems based on fuzzy logic exist (for instance, see Baldwin [1983]). These and many other kinds of logic can easily be implemented using standard Prolog. See Mamdani and Gaines [1981] for a collection of papers on fuzzy reasoning.

1.6   The basics of Edinburgh Prolog

That short tour of first-order predicate logic, if you read it, should help you to appreciate that raw Prolog falls considerably short of being true programming in logic and that there are many other control strategies possible besides a simple depth-first search of the logical formulae. Fortunately it is possible to implement these in Prolog, as will become clear later.

This section outlines the syntax and terminology widely used in Prolog programming, which is unfortunately somewhat at odds with that of logic described above. Although Imperial College Prologs such as micro-Prolog and Sigma Prolog use a different basic syntax, most offer some kind of compatibility kit to allow users to adopt the Edinburgh Prolog syntax. From this point on, the word 'Prolog' will just refer to 'Edinburgh Prolog'.

1.6.1   Terminology and syntax

The language has a single basic data type used both for programs and for data – the *term*. This is a rather different use of the word from that described on page 4, since it also covers logical formulae expressed in Prolog. There are various subclassifications:

- *Atoms* are normally composed of alphanumeric characters, together
  with '_', beginning with a lower-case letter. Any sequence of characters from the set

  + - * / < > = ' ~ : . ? @ # $ &

  can also be used to form an atom. A sequence of any characters at
  all is acceptable as an atom if the whole is delimited by single quotes.
  The following are also, by convention, atoms:

  ! ; [] { }

  but be warned that the square brackets must occur as a pair, denoting
  the empty list. An isolated square bracket is not an atom unless
  wrapped in single quotes. Most versions of Prolog will tolerate space
  between the brackets. The Prolog use of the word 'atom' should not
  be confused with its use in logic as explained on page 4.

- *Numbers* tend to follow implementation-dependent rules. A few versions allow only integers, most allow decimals, many allow some kind
  of exponent notation. Integers can be often be expressed in bases
  from 2 to 9 too, like this: 5'132 represents 42. This overloading of
  the meaning of a single quote can sometimes cause trouble if the integer is mistyped so that the parser is fooled into hoping for a matching
  quote.

- *Variables* are normally composed of alphanumeric characters plus '_',
  beginning with an upper-case letter or '_'. The variable consisting
  of an underscore alone is called the *anonymous variable*, and every
  occurrence of it is distinct from every other. Any other variable name
  has as its scope the clause in which it appears, or to be more precise
  the instance of the clause in which it appears, and within a clause
  each occurrence of a variable name stands for the same (possibly not
  yet determined, or never determined) non-variable term.

- *Compound terms* are the structured objects of the language. A compound term is usually referred to by its principal *functor.* A functor
  is distinguished by two components, its name and its arity (alias
  number of arguments). The compound term is usually written as
  functor_name(arg1, arg2, ..., argN) and the principal functor is usually referred to in writing as *functor_name/N.* The arguments are also
  terms. Atoms are functors of arity 0. The one vital rule of layout
  is that there should be no space between the functor name and the
  opening left bracket.

Various forms of 'syntactic sugar' are catered for; these can make
input and output sweeter, but do not affect the internal representation of

Table 1.2   Associativity of operators.

fx or fy	prefix operator
xf or yf	postfix operator
xfx or xfy or yfx	infix operator

terms in any way. A functor of arity 1 can be declared, by use of the standard predicate op/3, to be a prefix or postfix *operator* – that is, the functor name comes before or after the argument, but the brackets can be omitted, although they need not be. Similarly, a functor of arity 2 can be declared to be an infix operator, with the functor name coming between the arguments. Each operator has an associated *precedence*, usually an integer in the range 0 to 1200, although it is very wise to stick to the range 1 to 999. Many systems reserve the use of 0 for a way of erasing an operator declaration. The higher the precedence, the less binding it is, so that the most significant functor in a term is the one with highest precedence. In some other computer languages the notion of precedence is akin to 'binding power', so that the scale of significance runs the other way. Each operator also has an associativity, which the input and output routines must resort to whenever there is a potential ambiguity because of the use of two operators of the same precedence. Associativity is expressed by one of the atoms in Table 1.2. In these atoms, the 'f' marks the position of the operator and the 'x' and 'y' mark the positions of the arguments. On the understanding that a term has the precedence of its principal functor, or zero if enclosed in brackets, an 'x' means that the corresponding argument must have strictly lower precedence than the operator and a 'y' means that that argument may have the same or lower precedence as the operator's. Some operators are pre-declared for you – consult Appendix A for the standard set. They can usually be redefined if, for some esoteric reason, you are unhappy with the provided declarations.

There is also a form of 'syntactic sugar' used for lists. The form

    [Head|Tail]

is equivalent to

    '.'(Head, Tail)

and the latter is virtually never used. Extensions to this notation are usually allowed, for example

    [E1, E2, E3, E4|Tail]

is equivalent to

    '.'(E1, '.'(E2, '.'(E3, '.'(E4, Tail))))

Also, [Term] is the same as [Term|[]] and ’.’(Term, []). It is easy to forget that [H|T] and [hello] will match. In many systems, life for the input parser is made harder by the fact that ‘|’ is acceptable as a synonym for a semicolon, for instance expressing a disjunction in a clause.

1.6.2   Terminology and syntax of programs

Programs are composed of sequences of terms, each term being delimited by a two-character sequence consisting of a full stop immediately followed by a 'layout' character such as a space, tab or newline (so the single quotes in ’.’(H, T) are not really necessary but are a defence against carelessness). Each of the terms in the sequence is referred to as a *clause*. If the principal functor of the clause is :-/2, a pre-declared operator, then the clause is a *non-unit clause*, and the first argument is called the *head*, the second is called the *body* of the clause. Otherwise the clause is called a *unit clause*; it is often handy to think of it as having a head but no body.

All the clauses whose heads have the same principal functor together make up the *procedure* for some *predicate* identified by that principal functor. Any *goal* is an instance of a predicate, and a goal – a term to be executed, so to speak – is sometimes referred to as a *procedure call*.

Most systems allow two styles of comments. The first follows the conventions of C, namely a comment begins with ‘/*’ and ends, perhaps many lines later, with ‘*/’. Everything between is ignored by the input routines. These delimiters, however, do not usually nest, so that the first ‘*/’ ends all comment. The second style, which a few systems do not accept, is that everything from a percent sign ‘%’ to the end of a line is ignored. Be warned that some systems permit the sequences ‘%(’ and ‘)%’ as synonyms for opening and closing curly brackets, a hangover from the days when many teletypes did not have these symbols. The percent style of comment is used in this book.

1.6.3   Semantics of program execution

It is common to distinguish between a *declarative semantics* and a *procedural semantics*. The former is recursively defined as follows:

> 'A goal is true if it is the head of some clause instance and each of the goals (if any) in the body of that clause instance is true, where an instance of a clause (or term) is obtained by substituting, for each of zero or more of its variables, a new term for all occurrences of the variable' Warren *et al.* [1979]

Although beginners are usually introduced to the declarative semantics first, it causes considerable conceptual problems at any stage beyond the elementary because it neglects considerations of the flow of control. Although it is possible to qualify the body of every clause with the details of the conditions under which it is the appropriate choice, so making clauses genuinely independent of one another, this can lead to horribly long clauses. From a practical standpoint it is probably better to start and stay with the procedural semantics, an informal account of which is as follows.

(1) To execute a goal, the system first searches the program clauses in order of appearance to find all those clauses for the predicate of which that goal is an instance. (In practice, the system will not search the whole program at run time: the clauses will already have been internally indexed to some degree when the program was first read in. The form and extent of such indexing can vary widely between systems.) Instances of the clauses are then tried in order, as follows.

(2) To execute a goal using an instance of a particular clause, the system matches (that is, attempts to *unify*) the goal with the head. (Again, in practice the load-time indexing of clauses may help the system avoid even trying to unify a goal with some clause heads.) If the unification cannot succeed, the system reverts to considering the next clause, or fails the goal if there are no more. If the unification succeeds, variable instantiations resulting from it are propagated throughout the body of the instance of the clause and the system attempts to execute each of the goals in the body in turn, left to right.

(3) If the system cannot execute one of the goals in the body, perhaps because all the possible clauses for it failed, the system then *backtracks* over the clause instances it has been considering, to find the most recent of the successful goals for which there might be another solution. If it can find another solution for that goal it reverts to 'forward tracking', otherwise it continues to backtrack chronologically through the goals looking for alternatives.

(4) Any goal is said to have succeeded when the system has found a matching clause instance head and successfully executed all the goals in the body. If the system has tried all the clause instances without success, the goal is said to have failed.

This account is oversimplified, of course, because it makes no mention of cuts or of the problems that may be caused by the lack of an 'occurs' check. The nature of the distinction between the two kinds of semantics can be rather baffling to those not especially interested in theoretical semantics issues. It lies in the nature of what is conveyed. To illustrate, consider the printing found on cardboard milk cartons. You will often see the 'procedural' inscription 'Open other side', which supposes that you are trying to open it and tells you that there is just one more side to consider. It implies that this is the wrong side. The 'declarative' milk carton might say 'Do not open this side', which makes no assumption about your active intention and suits even a stellated icosahedral carton (a sure loser in the packaging battle), although it does not tell you what to do to open it!

The following trivial example should serve to illustrate backtracking, should you need such a reminder. Consider the following program:

```
location(Person, Place) :-    % Clause 1: Person is at
    at(Person, Place).         % a known place
location(Person, Place) :-    % Clause 2: ..or they are
    visiting(Person, Another), % visiting another person
    location(Another, Place).  % - where is that person?


visiting(mohammed, faisal).
at(faisal, mecca).
```

The query

```
?- location(mohammed, Where).
```

first matches the head of clause 1, and leads to the subgoal

```
at(mohammed, Where)
```

but this fails, it matches nothing known. Backtracking therefore causes the system to try clause 2 instead for the location/1 goal, leading to two subgoals:

```
visiting(mohammed, Who), at(Who, Where).
```

The first suceeds, with Who = faisal. The second is now

```
at(faisal, Where)
```

which succeeds with Where = mecca. If the user rejects this solution, backtracking first seeks another match for at(faisal,Where); this fails. Backtracking therefore moves further back to seek another match for visiting(mohammed,Who), which also fails. Backtracking therefore moves further back to seek another match for the original top-level goal location(mohammed,Where), but since there are no further clauses to try this also fails and so the user is told that there are no more solutions.

The lack of an 'occurs' check in most Prologs can cause interesting problems. Here is a slightly more interesting example of the difficulties than is normally given:

```
?- f(X,Y) = f(g(Y), f(Y,X)).
```

Figure 1.1 illustrates the essence of what happens internally. In many systems this causes no trouble until the instantiations have to be printed, whereupon an infinite loop is entered if there is no limit set on the depth to which structures can be printed. It is sometimes possible to construct examples in which an infinite loop is entered while the system is attempting the actual unification, or while executing certain of the built-in predicates – for example:

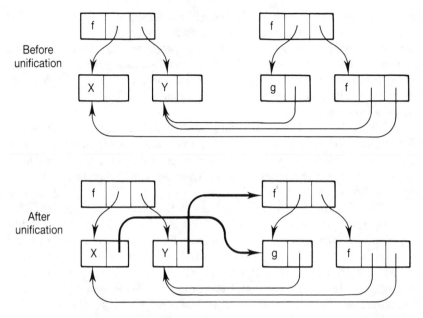

Figure 1.1   An 'occurs' check failure.

    ?- X = X+1, X is X+1.

will crash some systems with ease, and

    ?- X = f(X), Y = f(Y), X = Y.

will cause an infinite loop while attempting to unify X and Y. A few Prologs manage to avoid such looping in the unification algorithm at the cost of a little speed; that also calls for some other modifications, such as what the length of a list is deemed to be if it is part of a cyclic structure.

It is common to regard backtracking as a process of undoing the *instantiations* of variables caused by the process of unification with the head of a clause, and then reverting to consider earlier goals in the context of the newly undone state of variable instantiations. This suggests that there is considerable internal bookkeeping involved in the undoing, and that in this one special case the instantiations of variables can be updated. It is often conceptually better to think of backtracking as merely reverting to the earlier state in which those newly instantiated variables had not yet become instantiated.

1.7   The real prologue

Having sketched the rudiments of Prolog as a reminder, it will be assumed from here on that you already have at least a little familiarity with Prolog.

If you do not, texts such as Bratko [1986], Clocksin and Mellish [1987] and Sterling and Shapiro [1986] provide an excellent starting place. The aim of this book is to explore some of the power and flexibility of Prolog, mainly by discussion of examples. At various points open-ended exercises are suggested, some of which could occupy you for a long time. You are strongly encouraged to try them. Being open-ended, there are no 'correct answers' to give.

Those bits of Prolog that appear in captioned figures with a line above and below are meant to be the main anchors of the text. Other fragments of Prolog are merely part of the discussion, and are not intended to be good or bad examples in themselves. All the Prolog in this book is set in a distinctive typeface.

The text makes frequent reference to the *modes* of a predicate. This concerns the instantiation state of the arguments of the predicate, often but not always at the time when it is called. The commonly used shorthand is to use a '+' to indicate an instantiated argument, a '−' to indicate an uninstantiated argument, and a '?' to indicate an argument which might or might not be instantiated, and the choice is independent of the instantiation states of the other arguments. Thus you could say that `append/3` is typically called with mode `append(+,+,?)`. On the other hand, you would not want to say that the built-in predicate `functor/3` is used in mode `functor(?,?,?)`; the truth is that it is used in one of the modes `functor(+,?,?)` or `functor(?,+,+)`. The mode shorthand is sometimes conflated with actual argument names for the sake of providing short but useful program comments, for example:

```
% member(?Term,?List) checks whether the first argument
%    can unify with any member of the list.
 . . . . . .
 . . . . . .
% edit(+File) calls the editor to edit the given file
 . . . . . .
```

The idea of modes first appeared in DEC-10 Prolog in the form of mode declarations for the compiler, so that it could exploit the information about how a predicate might be called in order that it could generate more efficient and compact code. The built-in predicate `mode/1`, also predefined as an operator, was used for declaring modes to the compiler; the interpreter ignored the declaration.

The text of this book also assumes that your Prolog offers 'tail-recursion optimization' or TRO: that is, no internal stack remains in use for a procedure call when there are no remaining choices of clause for it. With this feature, a program such as

```
cpu(Address, RegSet) :-
    fetch(Address, Instruction),
```

```
    execute(Instruction, Address,     RegSet,
                          NewAddress, NewRegSet),
    cpu(NewAddress, NewRegSet).
```

should be able to cycle indefinitely. This trivial program, incidentally, suggests that Prolog can be used to implement almost anything but not necessarily in the most effective way. Without TRO you are forced into a convoluted and unpleasant programming style if you want to implement such indefinite control loops. With TRO the system's debugger may not be able to give a full account of the call sequence that gave rise to a particular goal, so in general you cannot win all round. Different Prologs with TRO also have different methods of spotting when it is possible to reclaim stack space, unfortunately – you just have to experiment to see what your Prolog really does in any given circumstances. You are very strongly encouraged to experiment with all other aspects of Prolog too.

Most Prologs provide a built-in predicate called `statistics/0`, or some near-equivalent. It provides useful information about the sizes of some internal data areas, and perhaps other information too. You can make good use of this information in trying to find out how your Prolog behaves in a variety of circumstances and which programming constructs it handles efficiently, or not. The output of `statistics/0` may, however, be couched in certain inscrutable terms which are often not explained in the system manuals. Typically, there will be references to:

- *Global stack*: this is customarily where all the data structures constructed at run time will live.

- *Local stack*: this is customarily where control information and information about current variable instantiations are held.

- *Trail*: typically holds data needed to manage backtracking, such as information about which variables became instantiated at each call. More generally, the word 'trail' is used to name a record of interesting events in the execution of a program so far. The execution of a cut will usually have effects on the local stack and on the trail.

Unfortunately there is no standardization of this terminology; thus the global stack is called the 'heap' in some systems, whereas others use that word to refer to the data area where atoms are stored.

SUMMARY

- This is not an introductory book on Prolog!

- It presupposes that you already know some of the language, but do not yet have much experience of using it in earnest.

- First-order predicate logic has its limitations.

- Prolog is based on the Horn clause subset of first-order predicate logic, but this is not a serious drawback.

- There are other kinds of logic than FOPL, and Prolog can be used to implement systems based on them.

- There are other logic-based languages, including excellent LISP-based ones.' Each has its strengths and weaknesses, as does Prolog.

- There is no 'best' language.

- It is a great asset if your Prolog has tail-recursion optimization.

2
On style and method

This chapter is concerned with questions of design and programming style, and layout.

2.1 Some Prolog idioms

Prolog is very simple, although beginners who can only see it in the context of more traditional languages may take a good while to realize this. At the most general level there are only a very few basic techniques to consider, although with many variations. Recursion and failure-driven 'loops' account for 99% of all programs, with special cases such as ingenious run-time modification of the program accounting for the rest. However, the imprecise but widely used vernacular of Prolog helps to obscure things. Consider, for example, append/3 as shown in Figure 2.1.

It is entirely reasonable to speak of this, when used in the mode append(+,+,-), as 'appending the two lists' or 'appending the second list to the end of the first', which hides the point that an entirely new term is being constructed as a result. The new term(s) may, internally, consist wholly of copies of parts of the original terms or may include pointers to parts of existing structures; it depends on the implementation. Nevertheless, the point remains that the program does not alter existing structures, although it is common to talk loosely as though it did.

```
append([], L, L).
append([H|T], L, [H|T2]) :-
    append(T, L, T2).
```

Figure 2.1   append/3.

Recursion is normally used for nearly all the control constructs found in other languages, such as 'while', 'for' and 'do/until'. The basic flavours of the use of recursion are:

- To dismantle a term, often a list, looking for the appearance of some kind of condition. The familiar member/2 in Figure 2.2 is an example.

- To dismantle a term while building another using copies of selected parts of the original and perhaps other terms too. The normal use of append/3 is an example; if the third argument is a variable when it is called, then that variable is instantiated to a list structure which is progressively 'filled out', from the outside in, as the recursion proceeds.

- Variants of the above in which more than one term is dismantled, perhaps not even in synchrony, and maybe more than one term is constructed at the same time. For example, the merging of two lists that are already both ordered is illustrated in Figure 2.3. (This presupposes the existence of a user-defined predicate less/2.)

It is difficult to enumerate the uses of recursion at a more specific level of detail, since there are many subtle variations on these themes. Examples will occur throughout this book. You can replicate something like a 'for' loop pretty closely using a failure-driven loop, as in Figure 2.4. But it is better to use recursion directly, say by constructing a specific analogue of between/3 for the purpose, unless you must be pragmatic because your Prolog has no good provision for tail-recursion optimization. There are two main reasons, besides any question of aesthetics. The first is that, especially in more elaborate examples, it can be quite hard to read the program and even harder to appreciate what an interactive debugger is implicitly telling you about it. The second is that it is uneconomic to have to do both the 'Low < High' and the 'Number > N' for each number. Before abandoning this bad example, there is an unrelated point worth mentioning. The predicate between/3 is defined in a slightly sloppy way, since the goal between(5,1,X) will succeed once rather than not at all. Succeeding five times would be better than just once, but let us suppose

---

```
member(Thing, [Thing|_]).
member(Thing, [_|Tail]) :-
    member(Thing, Tail).
```

Figure 2.2   member/2.

```
merge([], List, List) :-
    !.
merge(List, [], List).
merge([Head1|Tail1], [Head2|Tail2], [Head1|Rest]) :-
    less(Head1, Head2),
    !,
    merge(Tail1, [Head2|Tail2], Rest).
merge([Head1|Tail1], [Head2|Tail2], [Head2|Rest]) :-
    merge([Head1|Tail1], Tail2, Rest).
```

Figure 2.3   Merging two lists.

```
% between(+,+,-) instantiates its third argument, on
% successive backtrackings, to all numbers from its first
% argument to its second.
between(Low, High, Low).
between(Low, High, Number) :-
    Low < High,
    NewLow is Low+1,
    between(NewLow, High, Number).

% squares_to_N/1 is somewhat tacky - try to avoid this...
squares_to_N(N) :-
    between(1, N, Number),
    NumSquared is Number*Number,
    write(Number), write(' squared is '),
    write(NumSquared), nl,
    Number > N.
```

Figure 2.4   An ersatz 'for' loop (poor style).

that it should not succeed at all. This could be fixed by inserting a goal
Low =< High as the body of the first clause: but this is again uneconomic
since that goal is subsumed by the goals executed in the second clause if
the predicate is used as intended, yet will be executed once each time the
system backtracks to the call of between/1. There are three courses of
action open to you:

- Tolerate this odd behaviour, either because you are working alone and
  do not need to justify your idiosyncratic code to others, or because
  the intended users are a forgiving lot, experienced in Prolog, who will
  understand.

- Pay the price and include that extra goal. It is a tiny price in practice,
  although such things have a way of ganging up against your CPU.

- Do it right: introduce another layer that checks the cleanliness of the
  call just once and then invokes your defenceless code:

```
enumerate(Low, High, Number) :-
    integer(Low),    % NB fails if Low is a variable
    integer(High),
    Low =< High,
    between(Low, High, Number).
```

  This is good software engineering, but can be bad logic programming
  since another part of the program may want to read the clauses of
  your sloppy predicate but be unaware of the implied calling conventions. It is also less efficient than the first answer.

The best answer is a combination of the third of these and a decent module
system which will prevent other parts of the program from poking about
where they should not. In practice all three answers are defensible in a
just world, if you arm yourself with the right evidence by commenting your
program properly. (Of course, if you are a paid programmer you will know
that life is not fair.) A purist might maintain that all clauses should be able
to stand independently, so that each should include checks on any calling
conventions, but this is hideously inefficient in general.

2.2   Commenting and layout

Get into the habit of adding comments as you go along, and try to adopt
a single style that you like. I happen to like the following:

```
% member/2: check whether first argument is a member of
% the list given by the second. But any mode is OK.
.....
```

but others prefer to be more heftily formal:

```
% *****************************************************
% Predicate: member(Element, List)
% Types:    argument 1: any term
%           argument 2: list
% Modes:    any
% Purpose: Is the first argument a member of the second?
%           Can be used to enumerate members, or to
%           enumerate all most general lists of which the
%           first argument is a member
% Intended use: normally member(+,+) or member(-,+)
% Created: Fri May 15 16:40:20 GMT 1987 by D.Reference
% Updated: Fri May 15 16:42:59 GMT 1987 by D.Reference
  . . . . .
```

With really detailed comments, the code can get lost against this background. It is a matter of balance, of giving the reader enough useful information to make the code understandable without swamping the forebrain in the process. It is possible to make the actual code more readable too. You can go overboard:

```
append([], List, Answer) :-
    Answer = List.
append([Head|Tail], List, Answer) :-
    append(Tail, List, PartOfAnswer),
    Answer = [Head|PartOfAnswer].
```

This is perhaps better for complete beginners since it gives a sense of each argument's role, but it is mildly inefficient not to make good use of the unification that happens when a goal is matched against a clause head. That is such a commonplace idiom that beginners should be urged to get used to it quickly. There is a happy medium:

```
append([], List, List).
append([Head|Tail], List, [Head|RestOfResult]) :-
    append(Tail, List, RestOfResult).
```

in which the subgoal in the second clause betrays what is supposed to be going on even if the first clause is a little inscrutable.

Incidentally, the imposition of structure on a variable in the calling goal by the form of the head of a clause can cause problems. Consider the example of Figure 2.5, which at the time of writing was still available in one of the best-known of the publicly accessible Prolog libraries. What is wrong with it? The answer is in Section 2.4.

Returning to the topics of commenting and layout, it is also wise to adopt a standard form of header for source files, giving useful basic

```
% intersect/3: given two lists, finds their intersection.
%    That is, find all the members of the first list
%    which also appear in the second. If the lists
%    contain no duplicates (are set-like) then this
%    does the job of set intersection.
:- mode intersect(+, +, ?).

intersect([], _, []).
intersect([H|T], L, [H|Rest]) :-
    member(H, L),
    !,
    intersect(T, L, Rest).
intersect([_|T], L, L1) :-
    intersect(T, L, L1).
```

Figure 2.5   The (flawed) intersection of two lists.

information. This is a trivial point, but it is surprising how many people forget it. The following is an example:

```
% File:     prolog.rc
% Created:  7 Jan 1985
% Updated:  13 May 1986
% Author:   Peter Ross
% Purpose:  useful utilities, to be loaded at startup
% Needs:    no external predicates
    . . . . . . . . . .
```

Many good text editors can be persuaded to amend the 'Updated' line automatically whenever the file is edited. A header such as this helps the reader to grasp quickly what the file is about, and is particularly useful when looking at a printed copy that has been lying on a messy desk top for weeks. If your Prolog source has to spread over several files you might want to have a single file whose sole job is to load the others, and to mention this in each of the others that is specific to the one program. A simple alternative is mentioned in the next chapter.

Sensible layout can make a huge difference to the reader's comprehension. Having seen many styles I have come to prefer one, in which each goal in the body of a clause appears on a line by itself and each is indented by a standard amount, such as one tabstop. Some people like to indent the entire clauses for subsidiary predicates, so that the amounts of indentation give some sense of the calling hierarchy of the predicates. However, the width of a screen or of line-printer paper is not only finite but usually too small. The one-goal-per-line dictum is more important. It often permits a little room for percent-style comments about the goal on the same line instead of on an adjacent line. Moreover, although many written languages expect the reader to work left to right and top to bottom, Prolog programs that have several goals per line can be awkward to read because of the need to scan backward to trace the occurrences of variables in a clause. A scan that is always up and down is usually easier to handle.

This should not be regarded as a rigid rule, of course. Goals that are simple and very closely related in purpose might appear on the same line, for example a `write/1` and the `nl/0` that ends the line of output. Vertical alignment of disjunctions, with the semicolon at the left-hand side, helps the reader too, as the rewrite of `merge/3` shown in Figure 2.6 suggests. To remind you about disjunctions: `(P->Q;R)` behaves as though defined by

```
(P->Q;R) :-
    P,!,Q.
(P->Q;R) :-
    R.
```

and is the equivalent of 'if/then/else'. The '->/2' is an operator and built-in predicate, and allows 'else if' constructs such as `(Test1 -> Act1; Test2 -> Act2; ...; Default)`. Arity Prolog users must use the `case/1` construct instead, but the translation is trivial. The most crucial point is that you should be consistent about your layout rules.

```
merge([], List, List) :-
    !.
merge(List, [], List).
merge([Head1|Tail1], [Head2|Tail2], [First|Rest]) :-
    ( less(Head1, Head2) ->   % If Head1 is smaller,
        First = Head1,        % it comes first in result,
        merge(Tail1, [Head2|Tail2], Rest)
    ;   First = Head2,        % else Head2 does.
        merge([Head1|Tail1], Tail2, Rest)
    ).
```

Figure 2.6   Merging two lists – layout of a disjunction.

2.3   Some design observations

This section lists a collection of points about the design of a Prolog program. First, it is important to *have* a design stage. You should design the data structures that are to be handled by the program, and design the algorithms to handle them on paper first. Common sense and thorough checking at this stage can save a great deal of time later, and can help you to avoid ever using a debugger. Three examples of simple design are given in Chapter 4. The form of the data structures often dictates the structure of the program, so it pays to do the job well.

It is usually an excellent idea to have data structures passed around as arguments rather than making heavy use of `assert/1`, `recorda/3` and the like. There are various reasons:

- If you use assertions, and interrupt your program at some point, you will probably not know exactly what clauses exist at that moment. This means that you have to have some clean-up routines which erase any left-over assertions at the start of a program. These ought to be at the start, since the possibility of interrupting means that there is no guarantee of the program's reaching any later point.

- These predicates are typically slow. Indeed, in many Prologs, the built-in predicates `recorda/3` and `recorded/3` are implemented in Prolog itself by means of `assert/1` and `retract/1`, and the vendor's claims of relative efficiency are still so much hot air. In other systems, the compiled code must call an interpreter to handle clauses asserted at run time, and this is usually an appalling overhead.

- You risk modifying the flow of your program if you are careless.

- If you use assertions or the recording database to stash data piece-meal, then when you want to gather up the set of data to determine certain properties of it, such as how many items there are, you are forced to use something like the built-in `setof/3`. This is itself often implemented in Prolog and has to use assertion or recording for intermediate results, and so can be very slow if the set involved is large. See Section 5.2 for more about `setof/3`, `bagof/3` and `findall/3`.

Note that assertion may behave subtly differently in different versions. Look at this situation:

```
go :-
    assertz(go), fail.

go2 :-
    assertz(go3), go3.
```

Suppose that these are initially the only clauses. It is reasonable to suppose that **go** will fail, since the presumed sequence of events is that, when it is first called, clause information is extracted from some 'clause store' and this is used to set up choice information. No further reference to the 'clause store' is made for this call, so the newly added clause is not found. In a few systems there is no initial setting up of choice information for a call, it just refers back to the 'clause store' whenever backtracking dictates that it is worth looking for further clauses to try. This can be less horribly inefficient than it might at first appear. In such a system, **go** will succeed. Similarly, it is reasonable to suppose that **go2** will succeed, but in some Prologs it fails, perhaps because the entire clause body is preprocessed before execution. The situation can even differ between the interpreted and the compiled code from the one vendor's software.

The order of arguments of a predicate matters. You should contrive that those arguments that are normally instantiated when the predicate is called are the first arguments, and those that are variable come last. Sometimes ergonomic or pragmatic considerations will go against this. Nevertheless it is a good principle. More and more Prologs construct sub-indexes of clauses when they are read in, and for any given predicate the only universally available sub-indexing keys are the functors of the arguments. Since the system cannot know in advance how many arguments a predicate will have, if any, the implementor can only arrange for sub-indexing to be done on the functor of the first argument if there is one, and then perhaps on the functor of the second argument if there is one, and so on. If the predicate is then called with a variable as its first argument, potentially all the clauses might match, rather than just those having a first argument with some given functor. For instance, if `merge/3` above is called with an empty list as its first argument, no attempt need be made to match the goal against the head of the third clause. If it is called with a variable as first argument, all the clauses must be considered. So, try to stick to this style; even if your Prolog does not have these features your program may be ported to one that does.

Lists can be overused. They are useful constructs for handling unknown numbers of terms in a single structure, but any functor of arity 2 would do for that purpose; it is the available syntactic sugar that makes them so appealing, together with the fact that you are unlikely to use the functor name '.' for any other purpose by mistake. However, when dealing with collections of fixed numbers of terms in a single structure it is far better to use a more meaningful functor name. Sometimes another functor name – such as 'and' or '&' – is better even when handling unknown numbers of terms together. Use the flexibility that Prolog offers rather than sticking with LISP habits.

Try to minimize the occasions on which control is passed into a predicate, never to return, rather than being passed along the body of a clause, perhaps to a final recursive goal. For example, the trivial program in

```
go :-
    read(Term),
    report_on(Term).

report_on(end_of_file) :-
    write('bye bye'), nl.
report_on(Var) :-
    var(Var),
    write('that''s a variable'), nl,
    go.
report_on(Other) :-
    write('that''s not a variable'), nl,
    go.
```

Figure 2.7   An example of bad flow of control.

Figure 2.7 is badly designed, for several reasons. If you add further clauses
for `report_on/1` you must remember to add the final call to `go/0`, and it
is not obvious at first glance how the loop ends. Note that this program
also does not do what it suggests. If the user enters a variable in response
to the `read(Term)`, the head of the first clause of `report_on/1` will match;
the second clause will never be used. It is easy to forget the symmetrical
nature of the unification algorithm. A better version would be as given in
Figure 2.8 in which the only control requirement for `report_on/1` is that
it succeeds. The 'cut' is very often abused. Unfortunately many Prolog
implementors have made a mess of providing it, as Moss [1986] shows. For
example, consider this trivial example using \+/1, which may be provided
as 'not/1'in your Prolog:

```
test :- \+ \+ !, fail.
test.
```

The \+/1 is supposedly (maybe even actually, in Prolog itself) defined as
though by the clauses

```
\+ Goal :- Goal, !, fail.
\+ Goal.
```

so that the goal `test` should succeed. In many systems this is true, but
in some systems such as Expert Systems International's Prolog-2 and in
compiled DEC-10 code (but not interpreted DEC-10 code) the test fails
because the cut acts 'through' the negation and cuts the `test` goal so that

```
go :-
    read(Term),
    ( nonvar(Term),
      Term = end_of_file,
      write('bye bye'), nl
    ; report_on(Term),
      go
    ).

report_on(Var) :-
    var(Var),
    write('that''s a variable'), nl.
report_on(Other) :-
    write('that''s not a variable'), nl.
```

Figure 2.8   Better flow of control.

the second clause does not get tried. On the other hand, manuals tend to say also that disjunction is defined as though by:

```
(P;Q) :- P.
(P;Q) :- Q.
```

but if it is actually so defined, with explicit clauses for it, then the test

```
test2 :-
    ( !
    ; write('bad news'), nl
    ),
    fail.
test2.
```

will succeed because the cut cuts the clauses for the disjunction, not the clauses for test2/0. In most Edinburgh Prologs the test fails, and a cut in a disjunction is assumed to behave this way in this book. In Imperial College Prolog dialects the equivalent test will succeed – that was an explicit design choice.

Arity Prolog provides an extra construct, called *snips*, which saves you defining an auxiliary predicate. A snip is a pair of 'decorated' square brackets like this:

```
a :- b, [! c, d, e !], f, g.
```

```
replace(_, _, [], []).                           % clause 1
replace(Old, New, [Old|Rest], [New|Tail]) :- % clause 2
    replace(Old, New, Rest, Tail).
replace(Old, New, [H|Rest], [H|Tail]) :-     % clause 3
    replace(Old, New, Rest, Tail).
```

Figure 2.9   `replace/4` (buggy).

Once control flows onward from e to f, then any later backtracking from f will omit the 'snipped' trio of goals and go straight back to b. If you want to translate an Arity Prolog program into a dialect that lacks this, you can just rewrite it as:

a :- b, ((c, d, e) -> true), f, g.

which behaves in exactly the same way, although it is bad style because the intention is obscure at first glance.

There are widely varying practices about the use of the cut. Figure 2.9 is a flawed version of a procedure to replace all occurrences of some given term by a new term in a given list. This is bad mainly because there is nothing in the third clause to require that H should fail to match Old. Therefore, on backtracking, this procedure will come up with a list in which not all the occurrences have been replaced because clause 3 will be mistakenly used for clause 2's job. A simple fix is to put a cut in the body of clause 2, since if a goal matches the head of that clause then that is the one to be used. This is cheaper than being purist and inserting a goal '\+ Old = H' at the start of the body of clause 3. My own preference is for the cut to be inserted into clause 2 before the `replace/4` sub-goal, since that is the point where it is known that clause 2 is the one and only one to be used. Not only does this get choices thrown away as soon as possible, but also it alerts the reader of your program to the fact that something has been settled by that point. However, some people have acquired the habit of adding the cut to the end of the body instead, perhaps in the mistaken belief that the discarding of choice information happens when control backtracks to the cut so that the cut should be placed where it is met soonest upon backtracking. Others add the cut at the end because they view this use of the cut as committing to a discovered solution, so that the cut should be placed at the point where the one desired solution has been found. In this example it makes no difference, although having the cut at the end of clause 2 does assume that the predicate is going to succeed; in a predicate that might fail, it makes sense to place the cut where it will eliminate unnecessary backtracking. As a final point on this subject, a few Prologs handle clauses that have a cut as the first goal of the body in a special way for efficiency, at load time. In these systems, choices are never set up to be thrown away moments later if such a clause is selected at run time, and there may be a resultant speed gain. Try some experiments on your own Prolog to see how it behaves. For more on the use and abuse of cuts, see O'Keefe [1985]. Unary predicates whose job is to vet the argument, to ensure that it has some specified type, can often be eliminated by making good use of compound terms. By way of illustration, consider this problem, which was posed as a challenge for automated theorem-proving systems:

> Wolves, foxes, birds, caterpillars and snails are animals and there are some of each of them. Also there are some grains, and grains are plants. Every animal either likes to eat all plants or all animals much smaller than itself that like to eat some plants. Caterpillars and snails are much smaller than birds, which are much smaller than foxes, which in turn are much smaller than wolves. Wolves do not like to eat foxes or grains, while birds like to eat caterpillars but not snails. Caterpillars and snails like to eat some plants. Therefore there is some animal that likes to eat a grain-eating animal.

It is known as 'Schubert's Steamroller' because it was first proposed by Lehnart Schubert of the University of Alberta in 1978; at that time, it could flatten the existing theorem-provers because the search space involved seemed so large. Since then various kinds of prover have been built which can handle it with ease – see, for example, Cohn [1985]. Figure 2.10 shows a simple-minded encoding of the problem, which takes some liberties with the interpretation and violates the conditions of the challenge by introducing cuts.

```
% Type information:

animal(X) :-
    wolf(X).
animal(X) :-
    fox(X).
animal(X) :-
    bird(X).
animal(X) :-
    caterpillar(X).
animal(X) :-
    snail(X).
plant(X) :-
```

```
        grain(X).

% ".. and there are some of each of them":
wolf(william).
fox(ferdinand).
bird(brian).
caterpillar(clive).
snail(stephen).
grain(wheat).

% eats/2: this is assumed to be of mode eats(+,+); it
%    cannot be used to generate instantiations for its
%    arguments. This assumption allows the use of cuts.

eats(X, Y) :-
    bird(X),
    caterpillar(Y),
    !.
eats(X, Y) :-
    caterpillar(X),
    plant(Y),
    !.
eats(X, Y) :-
    snail(X),
    plant(Y),
    !.
eats(Animal, Thing) :-
    wolf(Animal),
    grain(Thing),
    !, fail.
eats(Animal, Thing) :-
    animal(Animal),
    plant(Thing),
    !.
eats(Animal, Thing) :-
    bird(Animal),
    snail(Thing),
    !, fail.
eats(Animal, Thing) :-
    wolf(Animal),
    fox(Thing),
    !, fail.
eats(Animal, Thing) :-
    animal(Animal),
```

```
        animal(Thing),
        much_smaller(Thing, Animal),
        plant(Plant),
        eats(Thing, Plant).

% animal_sizing/2 and much_larger/2 are another cheat,
% avoiding a recursive definition of much_larger/2.

animal_sizing(Thing, 1) :-
        caterpillar(Thing).
animal_sizing(Thing, 1) :-
        snail(Thing).
animal_sizing(Thing, 2) :-
        bird(Thing).
animal_sizing(Thing, 3) :-
        fox(Thing).
animal_sizing(Thing, 4) :-
        wolf(Thing).

much_smaller(X, Y) :-
        animal_sizing(X, ScaleOfX),
        animal_sizing(Y, ScaleOfY),
        ScaleOfX < ScaleOfY.

% This is the question:

question(Animal, OtherAnimal) :-
        animal(Animal),
        animal(OtherAnimal),
        eats(Animal, OtherAnimal),
        grain(Thing),
        eats(OtherAnimal, Thing).
```

Figure 2.10   A simple, poor solution of Schubert's Steamroller.

The program in Figure 2.11 is a reworking of the one above, using nested terms to replace the type checks. Thus a fox will appear as the term animal(fox(ferdinand)) rather than merely as the atom ferdinand, and wheat appears as the term plant(grain(wheat)), and both are part of the universe of objects of this problem. For purposes of generating candidates, the objects have to be enumerated explicitly – the universe/1 predicate does this job. The potential advantage of this is that the type of an object (e.g. `ferdinand`) gets passed around with it, so there is no need for Prolog to search through clauses to check whether it has the right type. The simple-minded approach illustrated here is only appropriate when the type hierarchy is a tree rather than a lattice; in the latter case, you need something a bit more sophisticated unless you can cheat by 'unfolding' the lattice to form a tree through duplication of parts of the hierarchy. For more on types in Prolog, see Mycroft and O'Keefe [1984].

```
universe(animal(wolf(william))).
universe(animal(fox(ferdinand))).
universe(animal(bird(brian))).
universe(animal(caterpillar(clive))).
universe(animal(snail(stephen))).
universe(plant(grain(wheat))).

eats(animal(bird(_)), animal(caterpillar(_))) :-
    !.
eats(animal(caterpillar(_)), plant(_)) :-
    !.
eats(animal(snail(_)), plant(_)) :-
    !.
eats(animal(wolf(_)), plant(grain(_))) :-
    !, fail.
eats(animal(_), plant(_)) :-
    !.
eats(animal(bird(_)), animal(snail(_))) :-
    !, fail.
eats(animal(wolf(_)), animal(fox(_))) :-
    !, fail.
eats(animal(A), animal(B)) :-
    much_smaller(animal(B), animal(A)),
    universe(plant(Plant)),
    eats(animal(B), plant(Plant)).

% animal_sizing/2 and much_smaller/2 are a cheat,
% intended to avoid the need for a recursive definition
% of the size ordering.

animal_sizing(animal(caterpillar(_)), 1).
animal_sizing(animal(snail(_)), 1).
animal_sizing(animal(bird(_)), 2).
animal_sizing(animal(fox(_)), 3).
```

```
animal_sizing(animal(wolf(_)), 4).

much_smaller(X, Y) :-
    animal_sizing(X, ScaleOfX),
    animal_sizing(Y, ScaleOfY),
    ScaleOfX < ScaleOfY.

% This is the question:

question(animal(A), animal(B)) :-
    universe(animal(A)),
    universe(animal(B)),
    eats(animal(A), animal(B)),
    universe(plant(grain(G))),
    eats(animal(B), plant(grain(G))).
```

Figure 2.11   Using terms for type classification.

This solution of the Steamroller is roughly twice as fast as the other one. They produce the same answers. Speed gain obviously depends on the implementation, for example whether there is any form of secondary indexing in the clause store. To explain this last point, consider the initial candidate generation by the goal `universe(animal(A))`. Will your Prolog ever try to match this with `universe(plant(grain(wheat)))` and fail? With some forms of secondary hashing, the goal `universe(animal(A))` will set up choices only within clauses whose principal functor is `universe/1` and whose argument has principal functor `animal/1`, so that `universe(plant(grain(wheat)))` is never even among the choices to reject. The secondary hashing would have been done at load time rather than at query time, of course. It is possible to build special features for taxonomic reasoning into the Prolog system itself. See, for example, Monti [1987].

By the way, this use of nested terms to represent a type hierarchy is likely to cause heartburn in logical purists. They might well worry about what a `fox/1` term (say) really 'meant', because it only has a meaning when used in a certain context, namely as an argument to an `animal/1` term. There is nothing to say, as they might wish, that a term such as `universe(plant(fox(joe)))` was ill-formed. The smart man in a hurry will deflect such arguments by claiming that 'fox' here is short for 'foxglove', so earning intellectual credit to boot by implying that context is everything.

2.4   The promised answer

The `intersect/3` predicate in Figure 2.5 looks good – the terminating case is handled by the first clause, the two recursive clauses handle the separate cases and the cut prevents confusion between which clause to use. The flaw is in the mode declaration made for the compiler. It should be

```
:- mode intersect(+, +, -).
```

As stated, the goal

```
?- intersect([a,b,c], [a,b,d], []).
```

would succeed, as would any goal in which the third argument is instantiated to a suitably ordered subset of the actual intersection. The problem lies in the head of the clause

```
intersect([H|T], L, [H|Rest]) :-
    member(H, L),
    !,
    intersect(T, L, Rest).
```

because if the third argument is instantiated, but not to the full and correctly ordered intersection, then the match with the head will fail and so the `member/2` goal will not be tried. However, a match with the head of the third clause, in which the first element of the first argument is deemed irrelevant to the eventual success or failure, will succeed. A simple repair is as follows:

```
intersect([], _, []).
intersect([H|T], L, Result) :-
    member(H, L),
    !,                      % OK this is the right clause
    Result = [H|Rest],      % So the Result starts with H,
    intersect(T, L, Rest).  % find the rest of it.
intersect([_|T], L, L1) :-
    intersect(T, L, L1).
```

This still requires that, if the third argument is instantiated, it must be in the 'correct' order if the call is to succeed. The following slightly more elaborate and slower version does not have such a restriction:

```
intersect([], _, []).
intersect([H|T], L, Result) :-
    member(H, L),
    !,                      % OK this is the right clause
    includes(Result, H, ResultMinusH),
    intersect(T, L, ResultMinusH).
intersect([_|T], L, L1) :-
```

```
        intersect(T,L,L1).

    includes([H|T], H, T) :-
        !.
    includes([X|T], H, [X|Rest]) :-
        includes(T, H, Rest).
```

The cut in this definition of includes/3 is very important – why? This predicate, like every other, can be rewritten so as to avoid using any cuts. The following version comes close:

```
    includes(List, Element, ListMinusElement) :-
        append(This, [Element|That], List),
        append(This, That, ListMinusElement).
```

If you are tempted by this sort of rococo programming style, then you should at least ask yourself these questions. Is this version of includes/3 more or less efficient than the preceding version? Why does this version not work properly when it is called in mode includes(-,+,+)? Will the readers of your program be able to answer these questions as well as you?

SUMMARY

- The two principal types of programming idiom in Prolog are recursion and failure-driven loops.

- Proper commenting of programs is essential if the programmer or anyone else is going to be able to read them in the future.

- You should try to adopt a consistent and legible style of layout.

- It is important to have informative headers in files.

- Design a program before writing it.

- There are many subtle differences between different versions of Prolog. It is worth investigating how your own system behaves, thoroughly.

- The order of arguments of a predicate can affect efficiency.

- Try to avoid using assert/1, recorda/3 and so on where possible; there are often easier, faster and cleaner ways that do without them.

- Lists can be overused. If some structure has a fixed number of arguments, use an informative functor name rather than a list to represent it in your program.

- Nested terms can often be used instead of unary predicates for the job of type-checking. This can improve performance significantly.

- It is easy to abuse the 'cut'.

- Calling modes matter.

EXERCISES

2.1   Devise a predicate that writes out a given clause according to the layout conventions suggested in this chapter.

2.2   Conduct experiments to see what difference the ordering of arguments in the head of clause makes on your Prolog system.

2.3   It was mentioned in Section 2.3 that the behaviour of `assert/1` is system-dependent. Find out how your system behaves.

2.4   Similarly, do tests to find out how the 'cut' behaves.

2.5   Investigate whether the idea of using nested terms for type tests can be extended to examples in which the types form a lattice and not just a hierarchy, and still save time. For example, you could start with a very simple type lattice with a most general type 'object', two subordinate types 'vehicle' and 'consumer goods', a subtype of 'vehicle' named 'train' and a subtype of both 'vehicle' and 'consumer goods' named 'car'.

2.6   A theoretical exercise: if you know the calling mode of some top-level predicate, then in what circumstances is it possible to make deductions about the calling modes of the predicates that it calls?

3

The working environment

If you intend to do any large-scale or long-term work with Prolog, then you should build yourself a set of tools that will make life much easier for you. There is a wide selection of such tools available over computer networks or from system vendors. This chapter introduces a few of the simpler tools, which you can easily customize to your own ends.

3.1 Working with Prolog

Although, in general, good LISP systems can provide a much better environment to support the programmer than good Prolog systems do, the Prolog world is catching up fast. Logic Programming Associates' MacProlog [Clark *et al.* 1988] on the Apple Macintosh offers a full Edinburgh Prolog and many extensions for making full use of the Macintosh screen; the program development environment it offers is outstanding. On IBM PCs and the like some Prologs now provide window-based tools coupled with a mouse interface. Even if your PC-based Prolog does not have such features, if you are an industrious programmer it is not too difficult to build your own in some other language such as C or assembler; this does require that your Prolog offers a way of calling such routines. On SUNs many Prologs already offer a window-and-mouse-based interface. For example, Figure 3.1 shows NIP Tool, an interface to the NIP version of Prolog. The panel of buttons near the top of the main window is currently showing those buttons that can be used with the built-in debugger; the set of buttons changes according to what the user is currently doing with Prolog. Further examples of good environments can be found in Eisenstadt and Brayshaw [1987] and Numao and Mariyama [1985] among others.

Whether or not you have access to such glamorous interfaces, you can make life much easier for yourself by developing a set of predicates to aid your use of Prolog. For example, you probably still need to use an editor to write your programs and you probably still need to work repeatedly through the cycle of

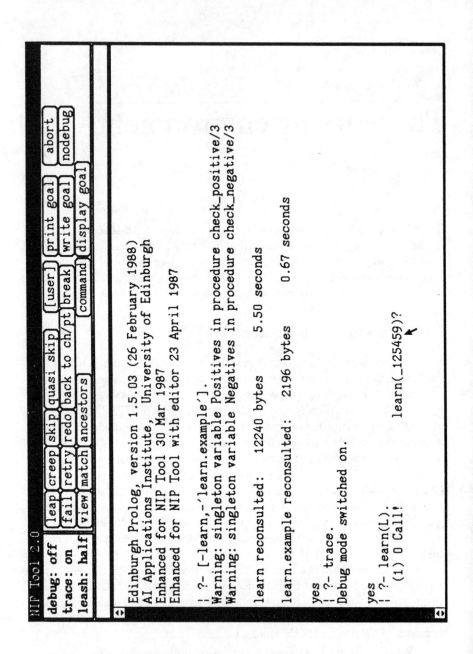

Figure 3.1   NIP Tool: a snapshot of a window-and-mouse interface.

- edit some file(s)

- (re)consult some file(s)

- do some tests

All but the simplest Prologs let you call other programs without having to exit first, even if they provide no way for Prolog to communicate directly with another program. Suitable predicates can cut down the amount of typing you have to do drastically. Some examples are described in the following section.

3.2   A simple toolkit

For the sake of standardization, let us suppose that there is a built-in predicate `sys_command/1` which can be used to call any other program. The predicate fails if the program cannot be run, and otherwise it succeeds but only when the called program finally finishes. The argument, let us further suppose, is to be a list of ASCII character codes; thus

```
?- sys_command([100, 97, 116, 101]).
```

calls the program named 'date'. Often, the syntactic sugar `"date"` is usable instead of that explicit list of character codes.

In a toolkit, there is a need for some way of keeping certain flags and useful 'constants' around and of modifying them from time to time. While this can be done by a process of assertion and retraction, it makes good sense to provide a uniform mechanism for the purpose. The following predicate `flag/3` does just this. The first argument must be given, although it can be any term at all. The other two correspond to an old value and a new value to be stored as the 'value' of the flag identified by the first argument. Thus, a flag `printer_type` (which might not yet exist, and if not is created by this) can be given a new value `epson(mx80)` by

```
:- flag(printer_type, _, epson(mx80)).
```

and the value can be accessed without changing it by the simple device of

```
:- flag(printer_type, Value, Value).
```

A suitable definition is given in Figure 3.2. There is an explicit check as to whether the old and new values are meant to be the same, since this is a special and simpler case. If the user asks for the value of some unknown flag it is returned as 'undefined'. The `var(Ref)` test handles the case where the flag is as yet unknown, so that the earlier `recorded/3` failed. Users who call

```
recorda(Flag, '$flag'(Flag, Value), Ref)
```

```
flag(Flag, OldValue, NewValue) :-
    nonvar(Flag),
    ( recorded(Flag, '$flag'(Flag, OldValue), Ref)
    ; OldValue = undefined   % .. if recorded/3 fails
    ),
    ( OldValue == NewValue   % If true, no change needed
    ; ( var(Ref)             % True if recorded/3 failed
      ; erase(Ref)           % ..else clobber record.
      ),
      recorda(Flag, '$flag'(Flag, NewValue), _)
    ),
    !.
```

Figure 3.2   `flag/3`: a simple mechanism for global 'flags'.

without using this `flag/3` mechanism deserve all they get; the idea of picking a functor name such as '`$flag`' is that the user should stay away from
using atoms beginning with a dollar sign. It would be better if the system
could enforce such a convention rather than relying on the improbability
of users employing such a functor name in just the wrong way in their own
programs, say by means of a proper module system – the fact that most
systems cannot do this is merely a sign of the relative immaturity of Prolog
as a commercial language.

3.2.1   Calling external programs

Suppose that you are using the UNIX operating system, and that your preferred editor is /usr/local/gnuemacs, and that you often use /usr/ucb/more
to browse through files. A goal such as

```
?- sys_command("/usr/local/gnuemacs graphsearch").
```

is tedious to type, and offers a lot of scope for finger troubles. The tools
described in Figure 3.3 are considerably handier. These allow you to do
the following, among other commands, which is easier and safer:

```
?- edit graphsearch.
```

The predicate `redo/1` calls the editor to edit the named file, then reconsults
it. Using 'edit', 'redo' or 'more' with no argument causes the last argument
used with any of these to be used by default. The parentheses in a clause
such as

```
(more) :-
    .....
```

are there solely because a few Prologs have input parsers that might be
fooled upon seeing 'more' immediately followed by a space, into expecting
an argument and then complaining when it is not found. The operators
were declared to have a fairly high precedence, just greater than that of
=/2, for no better reason than that you might carelessly type

```
?- redo master=file.
```

and it is nicer to be told

```
master=file needs to be atomic - please quote it
```

than to be told only 'no'.

```
:- op(701, fx, [more, edit, redo]).

more File :-
        update_file_record(File, FileCharList),
        give_command("/usr/ucb/more", FileCharList).
(more) :-
        access_file_record(FileCharList),
        give_command("/usr/ucb/more", FileCharList).

edit File :-
        update_file_record(File, FileCharList),
        give_command("/usr/local/gnuemacs", FileCharList).
(edit) :-
        access_file_record(FileCharList),
        give_command("/usr/local/gnuemacs", FileCharList).

redo File :-
        update_file_record(File, FileCharList),
        give_command("/usr/local/gnuemacs", FileCharList),
        reconsult(File).
(redo) :-
        access_file_record(FileCharList),
        give_command("/usr/local/gnuemacs", FileCharList),
        name(File, FileCharList),
        reconsult(File).

update_file_record(Name, NameList) :-
```

```
        atomic(Name),
        !,
        name(Name, NameList),
        flag('$current_file', _, NameList).
update_file_record(Name, _) :-
        write(Name),
        write(' needs to be atomic - please quote it'), nl,
        fail.


access_file_record(NameList) :-
        flag('$current_file', NameList, NameList).


give_command(CommCharList, FileCharList) :-
        append(CommCharList, [32|FileCharList], Command),
        sys_command(Command).
```

Figure 3.3   Basic tools for development work.

3.2.2   Files everywhere

It pays to build a library of generally useful Prolog programs, and to load what is needed rather than copying fragments from the library into your current work. It saves disk space as well as your hair. After a short while, this raises the problem of keeping track of the bits, since presumably your library will be kept in a standard directory or set of them and you will be working elsewhere in the file system. Particularly if you are using MS-DOS, you may also choose to adopt naming conventions such as ending Prolog file names with the extension '.pl', and perhaps identifying useful library files by the extension '.plb', for example.

What follows is a minimal toolkit to find files, and perhaps load them. It rummages around a specified set of directories, considering a specified set of extensions. It consists of:

- dirsearching(+YesNo): turns the automatic searching of the specified directories on or off.

- dirsearching: succeeds if automatic directory searching is on.

- directories(?Old,?New): lets you inspect or alter the set of directories to search.

- extending(+YesNo): turns the automatic consideration of the specified set of name extensions on or off.

- **extending**: succeeds if automatic file name extending is on.

- **extensions(?Old,?New)**: lets you inspect or alter the set of extensions to consider.

- **which(+Name,?FileFound)**: finds a full file name given the name without directory or extension information. It backtracks through all candidates.

- **lib(+NameOrList)**: tries to locate the specified file(s) and reconsults what it finds, if it has not been loaded already.

```
:- flag('$dirsearching', _, yes).
:- flag('$directories', _,
        ['/usr/lib/prolog', '/usr/fred/prolib']).
:- flag('$extending', _, yes).
:- flag('$extensions', _, ['.pl', '.plb']).

dirsearching(YesNo) :-
    ( YesNo == yes    % Check that it's 'yes'
    ; YesNo == no     % .. or 'no'
    ),
    flag('$dirsearching', _, YesNo).

dirsearching :-
    flag('$dirsearching', YesNo, YesNo),
    YesNo = yes.       % Tests that it's 'yes'

directories(OldValue, NewValue) :-
    flag('$directories', OldValue, NewValue).

% .... the extension predicates are similar ....
% ....      and so have been omitted        ....

which(Name, FileFound) :-
    ( dirsearching ->
        directories(Dirs, Dirs)
    ;   Dirs = []
    ),
    ( extending ->
        extensions(Exts, Exts)
    ;   Exts = []
    ),
```

```
            rummage_about(Name, Dirs, Exts, FileFound).

% rummage_about/4 always tries current directory
%    first, and always tries no extension first.
rummage_about(Name, Dirs, Exts, FileFound) :-
    name(Name, NameList),
    ( PossFoundList = NameList
    ; member(Dir, Dirs),
      name(Dir, DirList),
      append(DirList, [47|NameList], PossFoundList)
    ),
    ( FullNameList = PossFoundList
    ; member(Ext, Exts),
      name(Ext, ExtList),
      append(PossFoundList, ExtList, FullNameList)
    ),
    name(FileFound, FullNameList),
    exists(FileFound).

lib([File|Files]) :-
    !,
    lib(File),
    lib(Files).
lib([]) :-
    !.
lib(user) :-
    !,
    reconsult(user).
lib(File) :-
    which(File, FileFound),
    !,     % To stop a backtrack to another file
    ( flag(FileFound, '$now_loaded', '$now_loaded') ->
      true
    ;   flag(FileFound, _, '$now_loaded'),
        reconsult(FileFound)
    ).
```

Figure 3.4   Predicates for finding and loading files.

The program given in Figure 3.4 is very straightforward. The '47' that appears in the clause for rummage_about/4 is the ASCII code for a slash; change it to 92 for MS-DOS purposes. From the engineering point of view, it is more efficient to stash away each directory and extension to consider in the form of a list of ASCII codes rather than as an atom. However, that would make this program harder to understand, and the extra time taken to convert an atom to a list of ASCII codes is likely to be dwarfed by the time taken to actually reconsult a file.

Notice how `lib/1` notes what it has already loaded, in the form of the full name of the file lest you refer to the same file by two different names inadvertently. For instance, you refer in one place to a file called 'sets' (meaning 'sets.pl') and in another place to 'sets.pl' explicitly. This is still not foolproof, since the 'full name' of a file might not be unique if you employ relative rather than absolute path names for the directories to be searched. However, the program represents a good balance between idiot-proofing, size and comprehensibility. Although there are rare occasions on which you might want to load more than one copy of the same library file, the anti-duplication check is extremely useful. It permits you to put something like

```
:- lib([utilities, sets, graphsearch]).
```

at the start of each file whose contents use those materials, and then to load several such files without getting multiple copies of your library files loaded at the same time. Notice that setting of the '`$now_loaded$`' marker for a file must happen *before* reconsulting it, to prevent accidental loops in which file A calls for loading file B first, and file B calls for loading file A first, or worse. Of course, `lib/1` is meant to be explicitly for loading proven code; there is an assumption here that you will not use it for loading the files in your current directory that you are still developing.

3.3   A simple timing harness, and the LIPS rating

This book cannot hope to advise you on how to optimize your code for speed, since versions of Prolog differ greatly in implementation details. What you should do is time different ways of doing things for yourself. Many systems provide a moderately accurate way of assessing the amount of CPU time used by Prolog, but since the amount of time taken up by activities such as internal garbage collection can vary significantly between consecutive calls of exactly the same goal, it is usually necessary to make many calls to a goal to be timed and then average the result. The short program in Figure 3.5 provides a simple way of doing this and getting the results printed out. Personal experience with various Prologs on SUNs and VAXes suggests that it is often wise to call a goal several hundred times or more in order to obtain a stable average.

```
% testcode(K) calls your predicate. The timing test calls
% it N times, with K in the range 1..N, and fails back
% over it each time.

testcode(K) :-
     % INSERT YOUR CODE TO BE TIMED AFTER THIS COMMENT
     % Add a final cut if you do not want to include the
     % time taken to backtrack over it. K will be
     % instantiated to successive integers at each call.
     .... place your goal(s) here ....

% between(Lower, Upper, Var) successively instantiates
%     Var to all the numbers from Lower to Upper inclusive

between(A,Z,A) :-
        A =< Z.
between(A,Z,N) :-
        A < Z,
        B is A+1,
        between(B,Z,N).

% test(N) does your test (fit it into the spot mentioned
%     above) N times, prints out the average timing of it,
%     having deducted the time taken in extraneous code.

test(N) :-
            %% Use the next line for C-Prolog
            % X1 is cputime,
            %% Use the next line for Quintus Prolog or NIP
            statistics(runtime, [X1|_]),
            dummy(N),
            %% Use the next line for C-Prolog
            % X2 is cputime,
            %% Use the next line for Quintus Prolog or NIP
            statistics(runtime, [X2|_]),
            do_it(N),
            %% Use the next line for C-Prolog
            % X3 is (cputime+X1-2*X2)/N,
            %% Use the next line for Quintus Prolog or NIP
            statistics(runtime, [X4|_]),
            %% Use the next line for NIP (uses centiseconds)
            X3 is (X4+X1-2*X2)/(N*100),
```

```
%% Use next line for Quintus (uses milliseconds)
% X3 is (X4+X1-2*X2)/(N*1000),
  write(N), write(' calls took '),
  write(X3), write(' secs each on average'), nl.

dummy(N) :-             % This does nothing N times;
        between(1,N,K), % the cost of this is to be
        do_nothing(K),  % subtracted from the ..
        fail.
dummy(_).

do_nothing(_).

do_it(N) :-             % .. cost of doing your goal(s)
        between(1,N,K), % N times, the result divided
        testcode(K),    % by N in test/1 above.
        fail.
do_it(_).
```

Figure 3.5 A timing harness.

Different Prologs are often compared by their 'LIPS rating', that is, a figure for the number of 'logical inferences per second' that they can do. A 'logical inference' is deemed to be a successful match between a goal and the head of a clause for it. The LIPS figure depends very strongly on the program being run, so a standard program is normally used for the purpose. It is the naive version of reversing a list. When this is used to reverse a list consisting of the numbers 1 to 30 inclusive, there are 496 logical inferences involved, assuming that the standard form of append/3 is being used. For reference, the derivation of that number 496 goes like so. A successful match with append([],L,L) is a single logical inference. A

```
nrev([],[]).
nrev([H|T],L) :-
    nrev(T, RevT),
    append(RevT, [H], L).
```

Figure 3.6 Naive reverse, used for measuring LIPS ratings.

successful use of the other clause for append/3 involves one logical inference to match the head, plus all those needed in the body. Thus if it takes a_N logical inferences to append a list of length N to something, we know that

$$a_0 = 1$$
$$a_N = 1 + a_{N-1}$$

and therefore

$$a_N = N + 1$$

Similarly, if r_N is the number of logical inferences needed to reverse a list of length N, then

$$r_0 = 1$$
$$r_N = 1 + r_{N-1} + a_{N-1}$$

and therefore

$$r_N = (N+1) + N + (N-1) + \cdots + 1$$
$$= (N+1)(N+2)/2$$

Such a calculation is simple for a predicate like nrev/2 when it is used deterministically – that is, when there is no doubt about which goals will be run at any stage. In more complicated cases the best you might be able to do is to set lower and upper bounds on the number of logical inferences required.

You can therefore use something like the timing harness above to work out a LIPS rating for your own system. Figures around 200,000 have been quoted for one system on a SUN-3/200 and around 900,000 for another on an IBM 3090. Figures in the low thousands are not uncommon on IBM PCs, usually for compiled code.

Exercise 3.1   Compute the LIPS rating for the Prolog system you use. Experiment to see how much the rating depends on how many times you run nrev/2 and on the length of the list reversed. If you work on a time-shared system, experiment to see whether the rating is affected by the system loading.

Exercise 3.2   Try using append/3 rather than nrev/2 as the basis for calculating a LIPS rating, to see if you get a significantly different result.

However, the LIPS rating is no more meaningful than 'instructions per second' for a CPU. Some Prologs are engineered to run this particular benchmark very fast, yet will run other programs fairly slowly. LIPS tables are useful only for comparison purposes, and even then are very questionable. Do your own tests if you can, and not just on short and/or deterministic

programs – try something big too, and test individual aspects such as some
of the built-in predicates. Comparative tests remain a poor guide: the
only moral is that a LIPS rating of 'enough' is more than good enough for
development work.

3.4   Devising other utilities

There is an endless variety of useful utilities that can be constructed. Whenever you write a Prolog program you should consider whether any of it
might be useful to you later on, perhaps after being suitably generalized.
A particularly useful example is the 'formatted-write' package developed
principally by Lawrence Byrd and Richard O'Keefe. If you make much use
of `write/1` you should very swiftly see the need for such a tool. It offers a
convenient way of hiding the many variants of code such as this behind a
single goal:

```
report_score(Task, N)  :-
    write('You have had '),
    report_tries(N),
    write(' at '), write(Task),
    write(' so far'), nl.

report_tries(1)  :-
    write('1 try').
report_tries(N)  :-
    write(N), write(' tries').
```

Having to examine more than one predicate in order to get a sense of what
will be printed can strain the brain, and offers a golden opportunity to put
the wrong number of spaces between words.

The Byrd/O'Keefe formatted-write utility is easy to replicate, although the source code is omitted here because the details are not especially interesting. The basic ingredient offered to the user is a predicate
`writef(+FormatAtom, +List)` which is similar in spirit to a much-used C
language routine. The `FormatAtom` is an atom consisting of a sequence of
characters to be printed out, with embedded control sequences specifying
either that some special character is to be output at that point or that
something else, according to the next term(s) in the given list, should appear at that point. Some ideas for useful control sequences are given in
Table 3.1 – all are taken from the existing package. The `%i` ('i' for 'indi-
rect') is useful for an error message package. The `%j` sequence comes in two
flavours. Normally it swallows three elements from the given list – an integer and two terms. If the number is 1, the first term is output; otherwise
the second is. For example:

```
writef('%j %j guilty\n', [N, 'He', 'They', N, is, are])
```

Table 3.1   Some `writef/2` control sequences.

Sequence	Action
\n	output a newline
\t	output a tab
\e	output ESC (for terminal control sequences etc.)
\%	output an &
\nnn	output the character with the given ASCII code
%w	use write/1 to output next item of list
%p	use print/1 to output next item of list
%i	next item of list is a format atom, followed by a list
%j	singular/plural indication (see below)

The other flavour is `%Nj` which swallows just one item, an integer, from the list and outputs a word ending according to whether the integer is 1 or not. Table 3.2 lists some common singular/plural combinations. Using this, the `report_scores/2` predicate might be rewritten as

```
report_scores(Task, N) :-
        writef('You have had %w tr%3j at %w so far\n',
                        [ N,    N,    Task]).
```

If you create your own version rather than picking up a publicly available one, remember to warn other users that it is your own version. The publicly available versions have many more options than are given here. The basic idea is very simple: transform the format atom into a list of ASCII codes using name/2, and then work down this list recursively printing out the characters or taking appropriate action whenever a control sequence is found.

Table 3.2   Some singular/plural possibilities.

Form	Singular	Plural	Example
%1j	blank	's'	dog%1j
%2j	blank	'es'	go%2j
%3j	'y'	'ies'	tr%3j
%4j	'fe'	'ves'	li%4j
%5j	's'	blank	think%5j
%6j	'es'	blank	do%6j
%7j	'ies'	'y'	fr%7j
%8j	blank	'j'	(Esperanto)

SUMMARY

- It pays to build yourself a good working environment.

- You should not have to keep exiting from Prolog as you work. A good toolkit should make it possible and convenient to remain within Prolog.

- Build libraries of useful tools, and build tools to help you access the libraries.

- The LIPS rating of a system is easy to determine but is usually an unreliable indicator of overall performance.

ADDITIONAL EXERCISES

3.3 Devise a predicate that examines a file or a list of files and outputs information about which predicates are defined in each file, either to your screen or to a file. The built-in predicate **read/1** should be sufficient for reading the file; it reads a complete Prolog term, such as a clause, however that term is laid out. It skips comments and it aborts with an appropriate error message if it encounters anything which does not look like a term. Some commercial Prologs already provide a tool similar to the one suggested in this exercise.

3.4 Devise a tool that calls your favourite editor to edit whichever file happens to contain the definition of a predicate specified by you. Use the results of the previous exercise as a starting point. Be careful: what if a predicate happens to be defined in more than one file (presumably because of carelessness)?

3.5 Devise a tool that reads a file or a set of files looking for **lib/1** commands (as defined in Section 3.2.2). If it finds any it should recursively look at the files that would be loaded by that command. The aim is to output a complete set of the file-names that collectively contain a program. This information is useful when writing the final documentation, when shipping or archiving the source of a large program or when trying to find out what files did not get loaded but should have been.

4

Three studies of program design

This chapter contains three examples of the process of designing a Prolog program, to show how a program might evolve from the initial idea and to give you some feeling for the different ways in which they might be tackled. The first example is an old 'chestnut', chosen for its familiarity; nevertheless it is all too often done badly. The second example is a short but very powerful procedure useful in many situations. The third is most suitable for micro-based Prologs; it turns an input line of characters into a list of words, allowing you to use the backspace key to erase mistakes as you type. There are suggestions for extending each of them.

4.1 Alphabetic sums

Puzzles that give a sum of two numbers, but with digits replaced by letters, frequently appear in papers and magazines. Different letters in these puzzles are meant to denote different digits. For example,

```
      CROSS
  +   ROADS
  ─────────
      DANGER
```

The problem here is to write a Prolog program to solve such puzzles. The initial strategy is, in general terms, that of brute force and ignorance – try assigning letters to digits, starting with the right-hand column, until a valid answer turns up or there are no more possibilities. Turning this into Prolog requires a little thought; it is the aim of this section to show you the thoughts.

4.1.1 Solving it

The first question is how to represent the problem. Since we want to deal with individual letters, it seems at first sight sensible to represent each row as a list, such as `[C,R,O,S,S]`, `[R,O,A,D,S]` and `[D,A,N,G,E,R]`. The reason is that we are going to want to deal with columns: a letter from the top row, a letter from the bottom row and a letter from the answer, and (implicitly) a carry digit from the previous row. We could represent each column as a list, of course – but that would mean having as many lists as columns, and dealing with an unknown number of arguments is usually slightly more awkward than dealing with a fixed number (such as three). Here each element of the list is a variable, so that, provided the three lists are part of the same term, whenever a variable in one of the lists is assigned a value it will be instantiated to the same value in the other two lists. However, there is one point against this: the user would find it rather cumbersome to have to enter the three lists just like that. It would be more natural to have a top-level goal of the form

```
?- alphasum(cross+roads=danger, Ans).
```

(remember, `cross+roads=danger` is a perfectly good Prolog term, equivalent to `=(danger,+(cross,roads))`, assuming the standard operator declarations of many Prologs). A top-level goal of the form

```
?- alphasum(CROSS+ROADS=DANGER, Ans).
```

would be a terrible idea, of course – in most Prologs, when such a term is read in, the actual names of the variables (`CROSS`, `ROADS` and `DANGER`) are lost at once. This means that the letters that make up these names are also lost. The first argument to `alphasum/2` could be a quoted atom instead:

```
alphasum('CROSS+ROADS=DANGER', Ans)
```

but that is slightly more tedious to type in and slightly more work to decompose into something handy than the first suggestion of having a term of the form `...+...=...` as the first argument.

So, in the interests of making some decision, we shall opt for the first form of top-level goal. The atoms in this term have to be broken up into letters. The built-in predicate `name/2` will do part of this:

```
name(cross, TopRow)
```

will instantiate `TopRow` to the list `[99, 114, 111, 115, 115]` – the elements being the ASCII codes of the characters in 'cross'. Ideally, we want to work with a list containing the letters rather than the ASCII codes. At this point, if not sooner, you will realize that it would be a good idea to have the list of letters in a row in reverse order, because sums are (usually) done from right to left, and it is easier to work with the first element of a list (using the `[Head|Tail]` syntactic sugaring) than to work with the last. So, we will decide that we are going to want to deal with three lists, such as `[s,s,o,r,c]`, `[s,d,a,o,r]` and `[r,e,g,n,a,d]`.

```
rev_and_char([], []).
rev_and_char([Code|MoreCodes], Result) :-
    rev_and_char(MoreCodes, PartResult),
    name(Char, [Code]),
    append(PartResult, [Char], Result).
```

Figure 4.1   Solving alphabetic sums: part 1.

Given a list of the character codes, the Prolog predicate in Figure 4.1 will do the necessary job of reversing it and producing a list of letters, although this is far from being the most efficient way to do it.

The idea here is this:

- The first argument is the list of ASCII codes; the second is the result (a list) that we want.

- If the given list is empty, then the result is empty.

- To process a list such as [99, 114, 111, 115, 115], first process the tail (in this case [114, 111, 115, 115] – what the variable MoreCodes will be instantiated to in the first call of rev_and_char/2) to get the intermediate result [s, s, o, r]. Then use name/2 to turn a list containing just the code (99) of the first character into an atom ('c'), then use append/2 to glue that atom onto the end of the intermediate result to get the final answer.

Now we can start to write a definition for alphasum/2 – see Figure 4.2. What form should the answer take? There are many equally good choices. We shall opt for a list containing elements of the form

```
<letter> = <digit>
```

```
alphasum(TopRow + BottomRow = Result, Ans) :-
    rev_and_char(TopRow, Top),
    rev_and_char(BottomRow, Bottom),
    rev_and_char(Result, Res),
    ... go on to solve it ...
```

Figure 4.2   Solving alphabetic sums: part 2.

such as [s=9, a=3, o=7, ...etc...]. The basic algorithm for the solution will be something like this:

- Generate a suitable substitution for the (next) letter of the top row.

- Generate a suitable substitution for the (next) letter of the bottom row.

- Try adding them together, remembering any carry, and see whether the result leads to a suitable substitution for the letter in the bottom row. If so, carry on with the next column to the left. If not, backtrack to try to generate other suitable substitutions.

The meat of this is likely to look something like this in Prolog:

```
solve([T|RestTop], [B|RestBottom],
            [R|RestRes], ...etc...) :-
    generate(T,DigitForT, ...etc...),
    generate(B,DigitForB, ...etc...),
    DigitForR is (DigitForT+DigitForB+Carry) mod 10,
    generate(R,DigitForR, ...etc...),
    NewCarry is (DigitForT+DigitForB+Carry) div 10,
    solve(RestTop, RestBottom, RestRes, ...etc...).
```

This presupposes that the generator can also be used to check that the substitution for the letter in the result (R in this case) by the appropriate digit (namely DigitForR) does not conflict with any already chosen substitution. Note the use of div/2 here – Prologs differ about the actual name of the integer division operator. Experience of using Prolog suggests that this dual usage of the predicate named **generate** should be easy to cater for.

What arguments does the predicate named **solve** require? These seem reasonable:

- a list of letters representing the untackled part of the top row;

- a list of letters representing the untackled part of the bottom row;

- a list of letters representing the untackled part of the answer row;

- a list of the <letter>=<digit> substitutions made so far;

- a note of any required carry from the earlier column;

- a variable that will, at the end of the day, be instantiated to the answer, namely the final value of argument 4.

The predicate named **generate** needs the following arguments, at least:

- a letter – the first element of one of the first three arguments above;

- the digit, or a variable to be instantiated to a suitable digit;

- a list of the substitutions made so far;

- a variable to be instantiated to a new list of substitutions, which may be exactly the same as the previous list (if a substitution had already been chosen for the letter) or may be the old list plus the new substitution.

The first and the third arguments will definitely be instantiated at the time the predicate is called. The second might or might not be. The fourth definitely will not be. Here is a start at defining **generate/4**:

```
generate(Letter, Digit, List, List) :-
        member(Letter=Digit, List),
        !.
```

This clause (not the only one – more to come) is meant to cope with the case in which a choice of substitution for the letter has already been made. The predicate **member/2** is used to look for a term **Letter=Digit** in the list given by the third argument. If a match is found, **Digit** will then be instantiated if it was not already, the **member/2** will succeed, and thus **generate/4** will succeed. The cut will ensure that no further clauses for **generate/4** will be considered if execution backtracks to here – assuming, of course, that other clauses do in fact come after this one and not before it. Provided that is so, this cut is needed, because if execution does backtrack to **generate/4** and a substitution did exist for that letter, then there is no point in considering other digits for that letter.

Having tackled the case in which there already exists a substitution for the letter, we shall now look at the case in which there is not yet one:

```
generate(Letter, Digit, List, [Letter=Digit|List]) :-
        member(Digit, [0, 1, 2, 3, 4, 5, 6, 7, 8, 9]),
        \+ member(Something=Digit, List).
```

This says: find a digit, and succeed if we cannot find a term of the form **Something=Digit** in the list of substitutions. (That is, that digit is not already assigned to another letter. Nothing in the semantics of this clause stops it being the given letter either – but in that case the earlier clause would have picked it up, and the cut at the end of that earlier clause would stop backtracking to this one.) If it is already assigned, control will backtrack to the **member/2**, which will instantiate **Digit** to the next element of [0, ..., 9] until an unused digit is found. If no unused digit is found, the call to **generate/4** will fail.

Unfortunately, **generate/4** does not do quite what we want. Look at the case in which both the letter and the digit are given – for example, consider

```
generate(Letter, Digit, List, List) :-
    member(Letter=N, List),    % We've seen that letter..
    Digit = N.                 % ... so assign or compare
generate(Letter, Digit, List, [Letter=Digit|List]) :-
    \+ member(Letter=_, List), % Haven't seen that letter
    member(Digit, [0,1,2,3,4,5,6,7,8,9]), % ...so find a
    \+ member(_=Digit, List).  % digit we have not seen.
```

Figure 4.3   Solving alphabetic sums: part 3.

```
?- generate(d, 5, [d=3], NewSub).
```

The term d=5 is not a member of the list [d=3], so the first clause will
fail. In the second clause, member(5, [...]) will succeed, and then
member(Something=5, [d=3]) will fail, so the call of generate/4 will succeed with NewSub instantiated to [d=5, d=3]. The trouble is that the first
clause now does not check to see whether d has been assigned any value,
just whether it has the given value. This is good enough when that value
is a variable, but not when it is a specific digit. If you do not have much
experience of using Prolog, you probably would not spot this flaw for quite
a while. In general, it is a good idea to examine the definition of each
predicate as soon as you have defined all its clauses to see whether it does
what you want in all the cases that you want.

A workable replacement for that first clause might be:

```
generate(Letter, Digit, List, List) :-
    member(Letter=Anything, List),
    !,
    Digit = Anything.
```

– that is, find out whether the letter has been assigned any value. If so, this
is the correct clause to be using, and the entire success or failure of the call
of generate/4 depends on whether Digit and the discovered Anything
can be unified. They can if Digit is still a variable, or if it is instantiated
to the same thing as Anything; otherwise not.

That completes generate/4 (but check...). You might feel that this
subtle bit of patchwork to make generate/4 do the right thing suggests
that Prolog is going to spring other nasty surprises on you in due course. In
fact, you can always avoid trouble by not trying to be too smart (a flaw well
illustrated here). Just make things explicit. A straightforward alternative
form of generate/4 is shown in Figure 4.3. As you see, comments help!

Now, look at solve/6. The main clause, as suggested above, is going
to be as shown in Figure 4.4.

```
solve([T|RestTop], [B|RestBottom], [R|RestRow],
                            Subs, Carry, Ans) :-
    generate(T, DigitForT, Subs, NewSubs),
    ( RestTop = [] ->
            DigitForT =\= 0
    ; true
    ),
    generate(B, DigitForB, NewSubs, NewerSubs),
    ( RestBottom = [] ->
            DigitForB =\= 0
    ; true
    ),
    DigitForR is (DigitForT+DigitForB+Carry) mod 10,
    ( RestRow = [] ->
            DigitForR =\= 0
    ; true
    ),
    generate(R, DigitForR, NewerSubs, NewestSubs),
    NewCarry is (DigitForT+DigitForB+Carry) div 10,
    solve(RestTop, RestBottom, RestRow,
                    NewestSubs, NewCarry, Ans).
```

Figure 4.4   Solving alphabetic sums: part 4.

Notice how the fourth argument of each call of **generate/4** becomes the third of the next – that is, the 'output' of one forms the 'input' for the next. Notice also that there has to be a test to ensure that the final (leftmost) digit in each row is not 0.

So far, **solve/6** is just recursive. How does it stop? There are various cases:

- There are no letters left in any row, and there is no carry left over (Figure 4.5). The sixth argument is finally instantiated, to be the fourth argument. By this means, all the sixth arguments in every call of **solve/6** get instantiated at the same time – including the top-level call. Thus the answer is now available at the top level.

- There is no digit left in the top or bottom rows, but one left in the answer. The digit in the answer must just be the carry, which must be 1 (Figure 4.6).

```
solve([], [], [], Subs, 0, Subs).
```

Figure 4.5   Solving alphabetic sums: part 5.

- There are digits left over in the top or the bottom row, but not both, and so there must also be one (at least) left in the answer. There may be more than one left in the answer, of course; consider cases such as $9 + 91 = 100$ or $99993 + 7 = 100000$. There has to be a check that the final digit in either top or bottom row is not 0. This case is shown in Figure 4.7. Figure 4.8 shows the analogous case when it is the top row that is exhausted. The body of this is exactly the same as in the clause above. The only difference is that the first and second arguments of the head are swapped round.

Provided the standard **member/2** and **append/2** are available, that seems to complete the job. What order should the various clauses for **solve/6** come in, and are any cuts needed in them to control backtracking behaviour between (rather than within) the clauses? If you look at the first three arguments of **solve/6**, you will see that the appropriate choice of clause to call is uniquely determined by which of these three is an empty list and which is not. Therefore, there is no doubt about which clause to use in any given situation, and no cuts are necessary. Some may be desirable, for efficiency's sake – the cut usually causes some information about choice points, for the predicate within whose definition it appears, to be discarded, with consequent benefits in space and speed. However, efficiency is a separate topic, and that will not be considered just yet.

On a VAX-11/750, using C-Prolog version 1.5a, the program described above took about 3 seconds of CPU time (but about a minute of user time) to solve the given example.

```
solve([], [], [X], Subs, 1, Ans) :-
    generate(X, 1, Subs, Ans).
```

Figure 4.6   Solving alphabetic sums: part 6.

```
solve([X|RestTop], [], [Y|RestRow],
                    Subs, Carry, Ans) :-
    generate(X, DigitForX, Subs, NewSubs),
    ( RestTop = [] ->
            DigitForX =\= 0
    ; true
    ),
    DigitForY is (DigitForX+Carry) mod 10,
    ( RestRow = [] ->
            DigitForY =\= 0
    ; true
    ),
    generate(Y, DigitForY, NewSubs, NewerSubs),
    NewCarry is (DigitForX+Carry) div 10,
    solve(RestTop, [], RestRow,
            NewerSubs, NewCarry, Ans).
```

Figure 4.7   Solving alphabetic sums: part 7.

4.1.2   Doing better

Try it. Once you are satisfied that you understand what is going on, improve it. For example, if the result is longer than either top or bottom, then it can only be one letter longer. If it is, the leftmost letter must be 1. If the answer is two or more letters longer than top or bottom, then there can be no answer. You can build this and other such observations into your suitably modified version of the program.

Exercise 4.1   If you know any two of the three digits in a column, and you know the carry, then there is no doubt about the third digit, so you do not need to do any generation-and-test for it. Implement this change.

Exercise 4.2   The program can be made a little faster, too. For instance, as it stands, generate/4 uses member/2 to select a digit to try from the same list of the ten digits each time. It might be better to pass an extra argument from one call of solve/6 to the next, listing those digits that have not yet been chosen. Thus generate/4 would become

```
solve([], [X|RestBottom], [Y|RestRow],
                        Subs, Carry, Ans) :-
    generate(X, DigitForX, Subs, NewSubs),
    ( RestBottom = [] ->
            DigitForX =\= 0
    ; true
    ),
    DigitForY is (DigitForX+Carry) mod 10,
    ( RestRow = [] ->
            DigitForY =\= 0
    ; true
    ),
    generate(Y, DigitForY, NewSubs, NewerSubs),
    NewCarry is (DigitForX+Carry) div 10,
    solve([], RestBottom, RestRow,
        NewerSubs, NewCarry, Ans).
```

Figure 4.8   Solving alphabetic sums: part 8.

generate/6, the extra two arguments being a list of the unselected digits from which it is to select one, and a variable to be instantiated to the list of all that remains, which can then be passed on to the next step of the recursion. Implement this change and test whether it does improve the speed.

Exercise 4.3   Go on to solving sums involving three or more numbers. This involves a substantial rethink of the representation.

Exercise 4.4   Try subtraction and multiplication puzzles.

4.1.3   More general comments

It is possible to improve a little on the program given above, with very little extra thought. The definition of rev_and_char/2 is extremely simple; in particular, the goal

```
append(PartResult, [Char], Result)
```

causes it to be pretty inefficient. To process a list in that way involves $O(N^2)$ goals, where N is the length of the first argument. There are neater, faster ways. For example, to digress, consider the improvement on the naive way of reversing a list shown in Figure 4.9. This is akin to the notion of reversing the carriages of a train by shunting them one by one from one siding to another. To understand what it does, look at an example, say the goal rev([a,b,c], A). This calls rev([a,b,c], [], A), which calls rev([b,c], [a], A), and this calls rev([c], [b,a], A), which calls rev([], [c,b,a], A). This succeeds, instantiating A to the third argument [c,b,a].

The clauses for the predicate rev/3 could be described in English like this:

- The first argument is the raw material being reversed. The second is an 'accumulator', or 'partial answer' or 'stack' (sort of). The third is going to be the ultimate answer.

- The first clause says that if there is nothing left of the first argument, then the second argument IS the answer.

- The second clause says that, to reverse the list whose first element is Head, put the Head onto the 'accumulator'/'partial answer'/'stack' and carry on with the Tail. It is a terser form of this clause:

```
rev([Head|Tail], Stack, Ans) :-
    NewStack = [Head|Stack],
    rev(Tail, NewStack, Ans).
```

Unfortunately, many Prolog programs in print use the terse and idiomatic forms. Obviously, therefore, it is a very good idea to give variables sensible names, such as Ans at least, rather than short names such as X and to include large quantities of comments. Regrettably, it is easily possible to disguise even a program as simple as this one, in such a way that its true nature is not immediately obvious – see Figure 4.10.

```
rev(List, Ans) :-
    rev(List, [], Ans).

rev([], Ans, Ans).
rev([Head|Tail], SoFar, Ans) :-
    rev(Tail, [Head|SoFar], Ans).
```

Figure 4.9   Improving on 'naive reverse'.

The predicate `rev/2` above involves only $O(N)$ goals. A version of `rev_and_char/2` based on this would be:

```
rev_and_char(Atom, Ans) :-
    name(Atom, List),
    rev_and_char(List, Ans, []).

rev_and_char([], Ans, Ans).
rev_and_char([Head|Tail], Ans, SoFar) :-
    name(Char, [Head]),
    rev_and_char(Tail, Ans, [Char|SoFar]).
```

There are other improvements that can be made to the problem solution. As in other domains, it is experience and planning that count the most.

One final point: the program above relies heavily on Prolog's depth-first flow of control to do a depth-first search of the possible assignments of digits to letters. This is acceptable in this specific problem, because there is clearly a limit to the depth of search, and the search space is reasonably small. In practice, search spaces are usually big, and depth-first searching needs careful control even if it is an appropriate thing to do. In general it is better to make the searching strategy explicit rather than, as in this case, relying on the happy chance that the search strategy and Prolog's flow of control overlap so much.

4.2   A special-purpose matcher

It is often useful to be able to see whether a given list conforms to a given simple pattern. The most commonly cited example in AI literature seems to be that of Joseph Weizenbaum's ELIZA, a conceptually trivial program that emulates the reactive style of a Rogerian psychotherapist [Weizenbaum 1966]. For example, the user's utterance 'I hate using personal computers' might be reflected back as 'Why do you hate using personal

---

```
odd_reverse(X,Y) :-
    odd_rev(X,[Y]).

odd_rev([],[Z|Z]).
odd_rev([Head|Tail],[Z|Temp]) :-
    odd_rev(Tail,[Z,Head|Temp]).
```

Figure 4.10   The same reversing algorithm, travelling *incognito*.

computers?' in an attempt to get the user to pick up this particular con-
versational ball and run with it. In the simplest form of reconstruction of
ELIZA, a user's input – transformed into a Prolog list – might be checked
against patterns of the form

```
[i, hate, <<..sequence of words..>>]
```

where such a pattern might have an associated response

```
[why, do, you, hate, <<..same sequence..>>, ?]
```

There are many other applications in which it is useful to be able to check
a sequence of items for certain characteristics, but to do the checking in
some order other than plain left-to-right. One example might occur in a
simple rule-based expert system shell, in which the rules were required to
be of the form

```
Tag : if  <<premises>> then <<conclusions>>.
```

Given a sequence representing a single utterance in the language of the
shell, it might make sense to check for the ':', 'if' and 'then' keywords
first rather than attempting a depth-first parse. If found, these keywords
strongly suggest that – however mangled the other parts are – the user was
intending to give a rule here. This information is very useful when trying
to give appropriate feedback.

4.2.1   A simple form of matcher

Let us suppose that we wish to have a predicate match/2, which accepts
some form of pattern as its first argument and a list to be checked against
that pattern as its second argument. The pattern ought to be a list, containing a sequence of various kinds of item. There need to be items that
stand only for themselves, and others that stand for some subsequence
of indeterminate length. A 'natural' choice would be to use variables to
indicate where unknown subsequences occur, and to let all other Prolog
terms stand only for themselves. It remains to be seen whether it is a good
choice in practice. With this convention, the list [a,X,d] will match the
list [a,b,c,d], although not in the normal Prolog sense; the lists are even
of different lengths. A good reason for using a Prolog variable as a 'segment
matcher' is that it is obviously useful to be able to get hold of the matched
subsequence somehow – why not just contrive that the variable gets instantiated to a list containing just that subsequence? This means that in the
example, X should be ultimately instantiated to [b,c] somehow. Here are
some further examples of what should happen:

```
?- match([X, a, Y], [here, is, a, duck]).
X = [here, is]
Y = [duck]
```

```
?- match([X, a, X], [a, joke, is, a, joke]).
no

?- match([X, is, X], [a, joke, is, a, joke]).
X = [a, joke]
```

It also remains to be seen whether this is easy to implement. If not, perhaps the design choices need to be adjusted.

The next stage is to create a suitable algorithm, in English. Recursing down the pattern and the 'target' would seem to be the key. There are various cases to worry about:

- If both the pattern and the target are empty, the match has succeeded.

- If the first element of the pattern is not a variable, then the first element of the target must be the same, or at least must unify with it. If so, then all depends on whether the tails match. If the two first elements do not unify, then the whole match has failed.

- This leaves the case in which the first element of the pattern is a variable. There are two sub-cases to consider:

  - The tail of the pattern matches the tail of the target. In this case, we should (try to) instantiate the variable that is the head of the pattern to a list containing only one element, the head of the target.

  - The tail of the pattern does not match the tail of the target. In this case, the only hope of success is if the variable should happen to represent a sequence of length greater than 1. This needs a very little thought. Consider an example: the pattern is [Var,pile], the target is [the, wrong, pile]. This match should succeed but the two tails do not match. However, notice that [Var,pile] and [wrong,pile] would match according to our algorithm so far. The trouble is that it would instantiate Var to [wrong], whereas what is wanted is [the,wrong]. That is, we want Var to be instantiated instead to something that actually is [the|Var]. This is the key observation: we can compose a brand new pattern, namely [NewVar,pile] and try to match this to the tail of the target. This will succeed with NewVar instantiated to [wrong]. So we need only (try to) instantiate Var to [the|NewVar], as the last step.

This algorithm looks good, and it turns easily into Prolog, with one clause per case – look at Figure 4.11. There are, however, some subtle points lying in wait for you. There are several ways to get this wrong. Suppose that the second clause had been written thus:

```
match([], []).                    % Terminating case.
match([Head|Tail], [First|Rest]) :-
    nonvar(Head),                 % If Head is non-variable,
    !,                            % this is the only clause.
    Head = First,                 % Check that they unify.
    match(Tail, Rest).            % Now all depends on this.
match([Var|Tail], [First|Rest]) :-
    match(Tail, Rest),            % Var is a variable here,
    Var = [First].                % matching sequence of one.
match([Var|Tail], [First|Rest]) :-
    match([NewVar|Tail], Rest),   % Want Var to match
    Var = [First|NewVar].         % just 1 more than NewVar.
```

Figure 4.11   A simple list matcher.

```
match([Head|Tail], [Head|Rest]) :-    % WRONG!!
    nonvar(Head),
    !,
    match(Tail, Rest).
```

This seems more economical, but a goal match([X,it], [blast,it]) will unify with the head of this clause, instantiating X to the atom blast rather than a list containing it. Thus the nonvar/1 test succeeds, despite the fact that this clause was not intended to handle this case.

Suppose that the third clause had been written as:

```
match([Head|Tail], [First|Rest]) :-
    Head = [First],
    match(Tail, Rest).
```

This is also a mistake. The nonvar/1 and cut in the second clause do ensure that if the flow of control gets to this clause, then Head is a variable. However, it might appear more than once in the pattern; the goal match([X,and,X], [bye,and,bye]) will match the head of this clause. However, the recursive subgoal will be match([and,[bye]], [and,bye]), which will eventually fail. The point is that the algorithm makes a distinction between variables and non-variables, and so nothing must alter the instantiation states of any variables in the pattern until after it is clear that the match is going to succeed.

The cut in the second clause could, of course, be disposed of by putting a var(Head) goal at the start of the bodies of the third and fourth clauses. Nevertheless, this program might help to dissuade you from relying too much on the declarative reading of Prolog, because it is rather delicate here. Although `Head` will be still a variable on entry to the body of the third or fourth clauses, it might not be by the time control gets to the `=/2` goal in either clause. The recursive subgoal might have instantiated it if that same variable had appeared in the tail of the pattern. Thus, the `=/2` subgoal actually reads 'either instantiate `Head` or check that it is already consistently instantiated'.

Exercise 4.5 In this program a variable stands for a subsequence of one or more elements. What changes are needed if it is to stand for zero or more elements? What is the effect of swapping the third and fourth clauses around?

Exercise 4.6 If you are already fairly comfortable and experienced with Prolog, you may have spotted that the last two clauses of `match/2` could be replaced by one like this:

```
match([Var|Tail], Target) :-
    append(Front, Back, Target),
    match(Tail, Back),
    Var = Front.
```

which does handle the case in which the variable may stand for zero elements too. This makes use of the generative powers of `append/3`. It is indeed shorter to write, but it is not so direct an encoding of the English version of the algorithm (nor does it provide such an easy link to the next section of this chapter). What else is wrong with it?

Exercise 4.7 Here is a rudimentary version of ELIZA; improve it. The predicates for input and output need to be defined.

```
eliza :-
    input(Input),
    stimulus_response(InputPattern,
                      OutputPattern),
    match(InputPattern, Input),
    output(OutputPattern),
    eliza.

stimulus_response([i,hate,X],
```

```
                                    [why,do,you,hate,X,?]).
           ...etc...
```

This provides another cautionary tale about declarative readings. If you look at `eliza/0` in isolation, there is no overt connection between the
input and the output. It is the variables buried in
each clause of `stimulus_response/2` that communicate phrases of input to the output.

4.2.2   A better matcher

Although the idea of using a Prolog variable to stand for a subsequence
turned out to work well, it is sometimes more convenient to be able to get
some kind of list of the subsequences identified by the process of matching.
It can also be useful to allow the pattern list to contain other lists, so that

```
[[X,is,X],is,X]
```

matches

```
[[a,joke,is,a,joke],is,a,joke]
```

Here the use of Prolog variables does cause problems because, as noted
above, it is important that any variable in the pattern remains uninstantiated until the success of the match is established. However, in this example,
the heads of the pattern and target cannot be matched first, for then the
tails will be `[is,[a,joke]]` and `[is,a,joke]` which will not match. This
is because X will have been instantiated to `[a,joke]` by the process of
matching the heads. For the same reason, the tails cannot be matched
first, for then the heads will fail to match, when they should do.

Therefore, it would be sensible to abandon this use of variables altogether. An alternative is to reserve some functor for the job of signifying
where subsequences of one or more elements may appear. Let us use `?/1` for
the purpose – the argument can be some atom, and the matching predicate
should therefore provide a list of terms, say of the form

```
Atom = Subsequence
```

as a result of a successful match. So what is now wanted is something like
this, a `match/3`:

```
?- match([?x,is,?x],is,a,?y],
          [[a,joke,is,a,joke],is,a,saying],
          Bindings).
Bindings = [y=[saying], x=[a,joke]]
```

The basic algorithm remains the same as before, but the 'bindings list' needs to be built during the recursion somehow.

There is another, more subtle issue as well. In the last clause of the simple matcher above, a new pattern was used, involving a variable `NewVar`. This variable was of course local in scope to the particular instance of the clause that was used, and so could not conflict with any other pattern variable. If compound terms are to be used instead, then there seems to be a need to invent unique new terms for the same purpose. How can uniqueness be guaranteed?

One way is to require the user not to use subsequence indicators of some special form, such as `?(X-Y)` – that is, the user must not use `-/2` as the principal functor of the argument of a `?/1` term in the pattern. Then the program can create such terms for its own use. For example, the program might then be written so that

```
1:  matching [?x, ?x] with [a,b,c,a,b,c]
    leads to matching
2:          [?x-a, ?x] with   [b,c,a,b,c]
    and so to matching
3:      [?x-a-b, ?x] with      [c,a,b,c],
    so that
3:          x-a-b = [c] and x = [a,b,c],
    so that
2:          x-a = [b,c] and x = [a,b,c],
    so that
1:          x = [a,b,c] and x = [a,b,c],
    that is, x = [a,b,c].
```

This seems like a fairly reasonable idea. If need be, another predicate could be provided to scan the pattern recursively and check that the user has obeyed the requirements before attempting the match.

For this purpose, it is sensible to define `?/1` to be a prefix operator with a precedence higher than that of `-/2`. This should let the user put patterns in code in a fairly natural way. (LISP programmers do not have such an operator declaration mechanism but they can employ 'read macros' – input rewrite rules – for the same purpose.) This new matcher is shown in Figure 4.12.

```
:- op(650, fx, ?).

match(Pattern, Target, Bindings) :-
    match(Pattern, Target, [], Bindings).
```

```
match([], [], Bindings, Bindings).
match([Head|Tail], [First|Rest], BindSoFar, BindFinal) :-
    Head = [_|_],  % If a list, try recursive match first
    match(Tail, Rest, BindSoFar, SomeBind),
    match(Head, First, SomeBind, BindFinal).
match([Head|Tail], [Head|Rest], BindSoFar, BindFinal) :-
    match(Tail, Rest, BindSoFar, BindFinal).
match([?X|Tail], [First|Rest], BindSoFar, BindFinal) :-
    match(Tail, Rest, BindSoFar, SomeBind),
    ( member(X=[First], SomeBind), % Seen in tails?
      BindFinal = SomeBind           % ..no new bindings.
    ; \+ member(X=_, SomeBind),      % No binding known?
      BindFinal = [X=[First]|SomeBind] % ..add one.
    ).
match([?X|Tail], [First|Rest], BindSoFar, BindFinal) :-
    match([?X-First|Tail], Rest, BindSoFar, SomeBind),
        % If that worked, there will be an entry of the
        % form X-First = List within the list SomeBind.
        % We must now replace it by X = [First|List]...
    modify(X-First, SomeBind, BindFinal).

modify(X-Element, OldBindings, NewBindings) :-
    del_bind(X-Element=List, OldBindings,
                             ShorterBindings),
    ( member(X=[Element|List], ShorterBindings),
      NewBindings = ShorterBindings
    ; \+ member(X=_, ShorterBindings),
      NewBindings = [X=[Element|List]|ShorterBindings]
    ).

del_bind(A=B, [A=B|Rest], Rest) :-
    !.
del_bind(A=B, [One|Rest], [One|NewRest]) :-
    del_bind(A=B, Rest, NewRest).

member(X,[X|_]).
member(X,[_|T]) :-
    member(X,T).
```

Figure 4.12   A better list matcher.

There is an interesting point about the last clause for match/4, which
may have caused you some worry. It introduces a subsequence indicator

of the form ?X-First – might this not clash with an identical one created deeper in the recursion, say as a result of trying to handle another ?X later in the pattern? In fact this is a needless worry, although an understandable one until you are thoroughly conversant with the design of such recursive programs. It will not conflict with any that is brought into existence deeper in the recursion. That is, there will never be a second ?X-First on the 'bindings list', provided that the user has obeyed the conventions of use. The reason is that whenever a binding for X-First is put onto the list, that is the last thing done before the match succeeds – and then modify/3 removes it from the bindings list as the very next operation. The artefactual term ?X-First does not 'live' long enough on the bindings list to cause trouble. So the hypothesized 'scope clashes' cannot occur.

4.3   An essential tool: line input

One of the tools that you will have to have, if your Prolog is one of the many that do not provide it, is a predicate that reads a line of input and turns it into a list of words. For example, the input line

```
What do I know?
```

might be turned into the list

```
['What',do,'I',know,'?']
```

Most introductory texts give some sort of program for doing this, in which the input is read character by character using the built-in predicate get0/1. The programs tend to assume that any necessary input processing is carried out by the operating system, which treasures up the input until the return key is pressed, whereupon the entire cleaned-up line is made available to Prolog. However, many microcomputer operating systems do not do this for you; a call of get0/1 succeeds as soon as any key is pressed, and the backspace key does not erase the most recent character on the screen. Instead, when (say) the backspace key is pressed the cursor just moves leftwards by one place and get0/1 succeeds, instantiating its argument to the ASCII code for a backspace, 8.

A program that does the necessary 'rubout processing' is shown below in Figure 4.13. It requires a little care to make such a program reasonably efficient. For instance, a simple-minded method might be:

(1) Recursively read in the whole line of characters up to the end-of-line character and gather them into a list. It is easy to ensure that the order of ASCII codes in this list is the order in which the characters were typed in.

(2) Recursively work through this list, doing the necessary 'rubout processing'.

(3) Recurse down the resulting list, gathering those characters that make up each word into a list and converting each such list into a word by using the built-in predicate **name/2**.

This effectively takes three complete passes through the input and is therefore likely to be unacceptably slow if the input line is long. It also means that no rubouts happen until the whole line has been typed, a phenomenon that would worry the most hardened user. In any case, it would seem that not much work can be done towards dividing the list into the character groups representing the words until the user has typed the end-of-line character. Until then, there is still the chance the user will type a large number of backspaces, forcing the system to undo whatever grouping into words it had already done.

However, it is possible to do some useful processing while the user is still typing. The program below builds an 'input stack' as the user types, consisting of a list containing lists of ASCII codes to represent the words and numbers to represent the number of erasable 'white space' characters between each word. For instance, if the user types in these characters:

a b c space space space d e

then the program will build the following list (remember, 'a' has ASCII code 97):

```
[[101,100],   % the 'e' and the 'd'
 3,           % the three spaces; could be erased later
 [99,98,97]]  % the 'c', 'b' and 'a' .
```

This makes it easy to do the necessary processing of backspaces as soon as each is typed. When the user finally presses the return key, the input is already grouped into the lists of characters in each word: it is only necessary to reverse each such list and then use **name/2** to construct the word itself. Most of the input processing is thus done in between the user's key presses!

Of course, if your Prolog allows you to call routines written in some other language, such as C, then you would probably do better to write all this in that language. Nevertheless, a Prolog version is very useful at the prototyping stage because it is so easy to change it to suit your specific needs.

```
% sentence/1: instantiates its argument to a list
%    of words on the current line of input, doing
%    any necessary processing of backspaces
sentence(L) :-
    gather_char_list([], List),
```

```
        turn_lists_to_words(List, [], L).

    gather_char_list(Stack, Final) :-
        get0(C),
        ( end_of_line(C),
          Final = Stack
        ; deal_with_it(C, Stack, NewStack),
          gather_char_list(NewStack, Final)
        ).


% deal_with_it/3: given a character, modify the stack of
%    input characters, as follows.
% case 1: a backspace, no input, so ignore it
deal_with_it(Backspace, [], []) :-
        backspace(Backspace),
        !.
% case 2: a backspace, something potentially erasable,
%    so do it on screen and on stack
deal_with_it(Backspace, Stack, SmallerStack) :-
        backspace(Backspace),
        !,
        do_actual_rubout,
        pop_char_stack(Stack, SmallerStack).
% case 3: a white space character: just note it.
%    BY THE WAY: if you backtrack to sentence/1, the
%    end-of-line character will next be caught here, being
%    treated as white space (and therefore erasable). But
%    do_actual_rubout/0 does not cope with erasing off the
%    left edge of the line, so beware.. (easy to fix)
deal_with_it(Space, Stack, NewStack) :-
        space(Space),
        !,
        push_space(Stack, NewStack).
% case 4: a single-character word. Follow it with 0 white
%    spaces, this will stop a non-space following
%    character from being associated with it to make some
%    multi-character word.
deal_with_it(Char, Stack, [0,[Char]|Stack]) :-
        single_char_word(Char),
        !.
% case 5: an ordinary character. Just deal with it..
deal_with_it(Char, [], [[Char]]).
deal_with_it(Char, [N|More], [[Char],N|More]) :-
        integer(N).
deal_with_it(Char, [[H|T]|More], [[Char,H|T]|More]).
```

```
pop_char_stack([0|More], NewStack) :-
    pop_char_stack(More, NewStack).
pop_char_stack([1|More], More).
pop_char_stack([N|More], [NewN|More]) :-
    integer(N),
    N > 1,
    NewN is N-1.
pop_char_stack([[_]|More], More) :-
    !.
pop_char_stack([[H|T]|More], [T|More]).

push_space([N|More], [NewN|More]) :-
    integer(N),
    !,
    NewN is N+1.
push_space(Stack, [1|Stack]).

% turn_lists_to_words/3: given the stack of input, use
%    an ordinary accumulator/result pair to build up the
%    list of words. The order gets reversed again as the
%    result is built, so restoring the correct order.
turn_lists_to_words([], Result, Result).
turn_lists_to_words([N|More], Words, Result) :-
    integer(N),
    !,
    turn_lists_to_words(More, Words, Result).
turn_lists_to_words([H|T], Words, Result) :-
    rev(H, [], RevH),
    name(Word, RevH),
    turn_lists_to_words(T, [Word|Words], Result).

single_char_word(C) :-
    member(C,"!$%^&*()_-+=[{]};:@#~<>,.?/").
% Many micro-based systems will be consistent with the
% system-specific definitions given below. Some Prologs
% and operating systems will need different forms of
% these predicates.

end_of_line(10).    % <NL>, alias control-J
end_of_line(13).    % <CR>, alias control-M

backspace(8).       % Backspace or 'rubout'

space(Char) :-      % A lazy definition of 'space'
```

```
    Char < 33,        % Note: end_of_line characters count!
    \+(backspace(Char)).

% do_actual_rubout/0 does whatever is necessary to
%    erase the last character from the screen. This
%    version is suitable for an ANSI-compatible terminal:
%    the backspace will put the cursor on the last
%    character, so put out a space (32) and then an ANSI
%    'cursor back' sequence.
do_actual_rubout :-
    put(32),                        % space
    put(27), put(91), put(68).  % ESC [ D
```

Figure 4.13   Line input with 'rubout processing'.

The predicate **rev/3**, which efficiently reverses a list, was defined in Figure 4.9.

In theory, any program to read in a sequence of N characters and build a list of W words from it is going to require $O(N + W)$ logical inferences to do the job. This program does no worse; indeed the number of logical inferences per character is small, typically 4 or 5, and most of those are done between key presses. The main work done after the return key has been pressed is to reverse the list of characters in each word and to call **name/2** on each result.

As you will have noticed from the program comments, if control backtracks into a call of **sentence/1** then the end-of-line character will be treated as a space instead and the call will return a list of the words in the already entered line and the next line typed in as well. This can be exploited:

```
    . . . . ,
    sentence(Input),
    parse(ResultStructure, Input, UnparsedRemains),
    . . . . ,
```

If the user's first line of input proves to be unparsable, say by some definite clause grammar, then control can just backtrack to **sentence/1** to collect some more input. This enlarged input might then be parsable. Any unparsed remains could be given to a slightly modified form of this **sentence/1** that attaches it to the front of the next list of input words.

It was also pointed out in the comments that there is a potential problem if control is allowed to backtrack to a call of **sentence/1**. The end-of-line character is then treated just like a space and so, if the user tries to backspace past the left-hand end of the line, it will not be possible to see characters on the previous line being erased but the program will act as though they had been.

Exercise 4.8   Fix this so that backspacing past the end of a line that is in the middle of some input is not allowed. You can also adapt the program so that a control-W (ASCII code 23) erases the last word and a control-U (ASCII code 21) erases the entire current line.

SUMMARY

- The first question is how to represent the problem to be solved.

- Create the necessary algorithms before starting to write the Prolog code.

- You should consider carefully what information a predicate needs to be given in its arguments: either for itself or for it to be able to pass on to those it calls.

- A careful analysis of cases in the logic of an algorithm will help you to write correct programs.

- Calling modes matter.

- Improvements are always possible.

- Use expressive names for variables rather than very short ones.

- Prolog can be used to implement other forms of matching than simple unification.

- Always worry about how your predicates will behave if control backtracks to them.

ADDITIONAL EXERCISES

4.9   Test to see whether the line input routine described in this chapter is fast enough to read a reasonably sized file in a reasonable time. If so, you have the basis of tools such as a simple interface to spreadsheet files or a binary code analyser.

4.10   Use the line input routine to implement a simple fill-and-justify program that accepts lines of input and tries to create output lines of a fixed length by inserting extra spaces as necessary.

5
Some general issues

The two studies in the last chapter were both fairly straightforward. This chapter aims to make several points:

- that Prolog's standard flow of control is not the limitation that people often claim it to be;

- that the notion of a variable in Prolog is one of the great strengths of the language;

- that the 'obvious' way of writing something in Prolog is often far from being the most efficient way.

5.1   Searching in general

It was mentioned at the end of the 'alphabetic sums' study that you should not normally rely directly on Prolog's depth-first search and chronological backtracking as a means of doing a search of some kind. There are better and more general ways of managing searches. Figure 5.1 shows a simple directed graph that will be used as an illustration.

Suppose that the purpose of some search is to find a route from 'start' to 'end'. For the sake of simplicity, such a graph might be represented as a sequence of unit clauses of the form

```
successors(start,  [a]).
successors(a,       [b,c,i]).
successors(b,       [a]).
successors(i,       []).      % or maybe just omitted?
...etc...
```

Each node of the graph appears just once as the first argument of such a unit clause. Although it would make no difference to the searching process if there were no clause for the successors of 'i', it is better practice to include one as shown. This way, it is easy to determine the set of all nodes in the

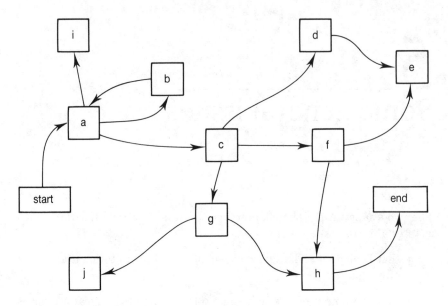

Figure 5.1   A very simple example of a directed graph.

graph, if that is to be needed at any stage. Of course, the list of successors
might not be available in this explicit form: it might be generated instead,
according to circumstances. In that case, you must take care to avoid
infinite or circular lists – for instance, something as horrible as

```
successors(r, List) :-
    List = [s,t,y,x|List].
```

which most Prologs will cheerfully accept, instantiating `List` to a circular
structure – that is, one which contains a pointer to itself. If the graph is
instead represented by the individual arcs rather than sets of them, such
as in:

```
arc(start, a).
arc(a, b).
arc(a, c).
arc(a, i).
...etc...
```

then `findall/3`, a predicate that is usually not built in but is available in
many libraries, can be used to replicate `successors/2`. This can be much
better than using the allied built-in predicates `setof/3` or `bagof/3`, since
these two are potentially resatisfiable, whereas `findall/3` does what its
name implies and succeeds precisely once, perhaps returning an empty list.

In what follows, it will be assumed that `successors/2` succeeds at most
once, for any given first argument. Section 5.2 contains a digression on the
distinction between `setof/3` and its friends.

A simple depth-first search of a graph such as Figure 5.1 is obviously
a poor idea unless there is some check against the route looping back on
itself. It is easy to include such a check in the naive form of search:

```
% search(+,+,-) expects a node, a list of the nodes on
%    the current path so far (so initially []), and a
%    variable to be instantiated to the final path. The
%    path list is in reverse order.
search(Node, PathSoFar, [Node|PathSoFar]) :-
    final_node(Node).
search(Node, PathSoFar, FinalPath) :-
    successors(Node, ListOfSuccessors),
    member(NextNode, ListOfSuccessors),
    \+ member(NextNode, PathSoFar),
    search(NextNode, [Node|PathSoFar], FinalPath).
```

If the graph is generated rather than defined by a flock of unit clauses, it
may turn out to be infinite. This brings the risk that such a depth-first
search may never terminate despite there being finite paths to an end point.

5.1.1   Using an agenda

It is much better to make the search strategy explicit somehow, by using a
'search list' or 'agenda' of the nodes known about but still awaiting consideration. An accompanying 'visited list' of nodes considered and dealt with
is used to collect up nodes that have come off the agenda. A depth-first
search of the graph in Figure 5.1 could go like this:

The agenda	The visited list
[start]	[]
[a]	[start]
[b,c,i]	[a,start]
[c,i]	[b,a,start]
[d,f,g,i]	[c,b,a,start]
[e,f,g,i]	[d,c,b,a,start]
[f,g,i]	[e,d,c,b,a,start]
[h,g,i]	[f,e,d,c,b,a,start]
[end,g,i]	[h,f,e,d,c,b,a,start]

The process starts with an agenda containing all the start nodes and an
empty 'visited list'. Thereafter, these steps are done repeatedly until an
end node appears: add the head of the agenda to the visited list, find
the list of successors to that node, construct a list consisting of all those
successors that are not on the visited list (that is why the node was added

to the visited list as the very first step), and add this list to the front of the agenda.

To get a breadth-first search, just add the unvisited successors to the back of the agenda instead:

The agenda	The visited list
[start]	[]
[a]	[start]
[b,c,i]	[a,start]
[c,i]	[b,a,start]
[i,d,f,g]	[c,b,a,start]
[d,f,g]	[i,c,b,a,start]
[f,g,e]	[d,i,c,b,a,start]
[g,e,h,e]	[f,d,i,c,b,a,start]
[e,h,e,h,j]	[g,f,d,i,c,b,a,start]
[h,e,h,j]	[e,g,f,d,i,c,b,a,start]
[e,h,j,end]	[h,e,g,f,d,i,c,b,a,start]
[h,j,end]	[h,e,g,f,d,i,c,b,a,start]
[j,end]	[h,e,g,f,d,i,c,b,a,start]
[end]	[j,h,e,g,f,d,i,c,b,a,start]

Obviously it may pay to check whether any of the unvisited successors of a node are end nodes before adding them to the agenda, and it may pay to check whether any are already on the agenda. Doing both of these would cut down on the number of recursive steps in the search but increase the running time because of the extra checks involved, since some of them are unproductive. If you understand the idea, the Prolog program in Figure 5.2 should be clear.

```
search([First|RestOfAgenda], _) :-
    final_node(First).
search([First|RestOfAgenda], Visited) :-
    successors(First, Successors),
    get_unvisited(Successors, [First|Visited],
                                    Unvisited),
    append(Unvisited, RestOfAgenda, NewAgenda),
        % Swap first two argument of append/3
        % if you want breadth-first instead.
    search(NewAgenda, [First|Visited]).
```

Figure 5.2   A 'general' search program.

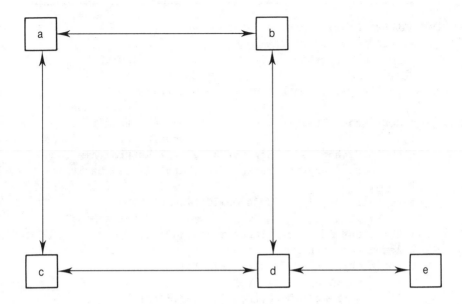

Figure 5.3   An example of a problem with a 'visited' list.

Other flavours of search – best-first, once-then-best, heuristic and so on – can be implemented purely by replacing that **append/3** goal by something else that blends the unvisited nodes into the agenda in some appropriate way. Note that if **successors/3** succeeds precisely once, then this program is essentially iterative rather than recursive and a good compiler could turn it into very fast-running code.

The program as it stands does not provide any useful information, such as the path found. There is a more subtle problem too: it finds a solution, but it may not find them all even by backtracking. The source of this problem is that the 'visited' list is treated as something that is a property of the complete search. Thus a node once visited from one direction and then rejected can never be visited from any other direction. Figure 5.3 shows an example. In this, the search starting at **a** and looking for **e** might proceed depth-first, from **a** to **c** to **d**, and then take a wrong turning to **b** before backtracking and finding its way to **e**. But by this time **b** will be on the global 'visited' list, so that the program cannot later backtrack and find the equally good route from **a** to **b** and then onward.

A simple cure for this, which also returns each path, is given in Figure 5.4. Rather than having a global 'visited' list, the idea is to keep each developing path together with the node it currently reaches – say in a term of the form **path(Node,PathToNode)**, where a path is simply a list of the nodes traversed, most recent first. The agenda can now consist of

```
search(StartNodes, Targets, AFinalPath) :-
    member(Node, StartNodes),
    do_search(Targets, [path(Node,[])], AFinalPath).

do_search(Targets, [path(Node,HowIGotThere)|More],
                                        AFinalPath) :-
    member(Node, Targets),      % If Node = a target do not
    !,                          % use other search/3 clause
    ( AFinalPath = [Node|HowIGotThere]    % Return this path
    ; do_search(Targets, More, AFinalPath) % ... backtrack
    ).                          % ... for any more
do_search(Targets, [path(Node,HowIGotThere)|More],
                                        AFinalPath) :-
    % NOTE: cut in above clause means Node is
    % not a target here
    setof(path(Succ,[Node|HowIGotThere]),
        ( arc(Node,Succ),
          \+(member(Succ,[Node|HowIGotHere]))
        ),
        NewItems),
    !, % If setof/3 succeeded, this is the right clause
    add_to_agenda(NewItems, More, NewAgenda),
    do_search(Targets, NewAgenda, AFinalPath).
do_search(Targets, [_|More], AFinalPath) :-
    do_search(Targets, More, AFinalPath).
```

Figure 5.4   A better 'general' search program.

---

a set of such terms, and the 'no-loop' check consists of making sure that any potentially interesting successor of a given node does not appear on the path to that node.

It is left to you to define add_to_agenda/3, say as just a call to append/3 if you only want depth- or breadth-first search. It is possible to represent the agenda as something more elaborate than a list, say as a difference pair – difference pairs are explained later in this chapter, in Section 5.3.1. The agenda could have been represented as a difference pair in order to save the cost of recursion in such an append/3, but using a difference pair will not save significantly if you are employing some fancier search method (such as one that is guided by properties of the whole agenda) and anyway you can make the changes needed for using a difference pair with little trouble. Also, the HowIGotHere terms could be difference pairs, if you need to have the paths ordered so that the start node comes at the front of the list. In this case you need a minor variant of member/2, of course, for use in the setof/3 call.

There are numerous other ways to code this, which change the surface form and the efficiency but are not doing anything radically different. Here are some of the points you might think about. In the above program there are three clauses for do_search/3. The first checks whether the 'current' node of interest is a target. If it is, there's a cut so that we do not have to put a goal

```
\+(member(Node, Targets))
```

at the start of the second clause. Doing that would be logically attractive because each clause could then be read in complete isolation and would make sense by itself. But the result would be run-time inefficiency, since the bulk of the second clause is executed only after *two* complete recursions down the Targets list – once for the member/2 in the first clause, which must have failed to let control get into the second clause, and then once for the \+(member(...)) as well. Having the cut in the first clause, as above, spares us the second traversal of Targets. But that cut does have another unfortunate effect. In the first clause there is a disjunction, so that initially the third argument gets instantiated to one of the possible paths that the search is looking for. If the user or the application wants to backtrack to look for other paths, then the thing to do is to abandon the 'current' node (since presumably we do not want paths that go through a target node to another one) and just continue the search using the rest of the agenda. But the cut stops backtracking to another clause, so we need a disjunction in the first clause because of that cut.

In the second clause, we use setof/3 to generate a list of new items to put on the agenda. We do not want to use bagof/3, because it might give duplicate entries if you have carelessly allowed duplicate arcs. A problem with setof/3 is that it will never return an empty list; if there are no suitable successors to a node, the setof/3 will fail – in which case, we need to abandon that node and continue with the rest of the agenda. So now we need the third clause, to handle the case in which the 'current' node has no acceptable successors. We also need a cut after the setof/3, because we do not want to backtrack to the third clause if there are successors.

And now we have arrived at what seems like another inefficiency because the third clause is doing just what the second part of the disjunction in the first clause is doing. Is there no way to eliminate this apparent repetition? Yes: in the first clause, rather than having a disjunction, we pass the rest of the agenda back to the caller as well as passing back the path found: for instance, using a do_search/4 instead:

```
do_search(Targets, [path(Node,Path)|More],
          [Node|Path], More) :-
```

```
            member(Node,Targets),
            !.
do_search(Targets, [path(Node,Path)|More],
                   FinalPath, EndAgenda) :-
        setof(......, ......, ......),  % as before
        add_to_agenda(NewItems, More, NewAgenda),
        do_search(Targets, NewAgenda, FinalPath, EndAgenda).
```

and then we can restart the search using that returned tail end of the agenda. For this we need an extra layer in the calling sequence:

```
    search(StartNodes, Targets, OneFinalPath) :-
        member(Node, StartNodes),
        run_search(Targets, [path(Node,[])], OneFinalPath).

    run_search(Targets, Agenda, Result) :-
        do_search(Targets,Agenda,OnePath,RemainingAgenda),
        ( Result = OnePath
        ; run_search(Targets, RemainingAgenda, Result)
        ).
```

However, we still have an extra clause (the clause for **run_search/3** rather than the third clause for **do_search/3**) and at the expense of needing an extra argument for the **do_search** predicate. Such an extra argument usually costs very little in speed, and a little in space, but overall the new program is not really any better than the old one.

Note that both the new and the old program rely on backtracking to the goal

```
    member(Node, StartNodes)
```

in order to consider each of the start nodes, whereas one could easily just have made an agenda item for each start node and avoided the backtracking. In some systems this might be a good thing to do if it lets the system avoid keeping that information about choice points, or if you have some other reason to have all that extra information tacked onto the agenda. But it would mean bigger agendas, of course (bigger by just the size of the StartNodes list, so if that is large you might not want to make the agenda so big; it makes debugger output messy, for example).

The moral is that there are lots of trade-offs to be considered, and usually it is a good idea to include lots of comments about why you did it the way you did. At least another reader of your code will know why, and maybe avoid trying something you already thought of and rejected.

If you wanted to obtain the set of all shortest paths, you would only need to do a breadth-first search and, when a complete path has been found, look through the agenda to find any other paths that are complete or are just one step short of completion. There may be some of the latter, since this search program recurses once per entry on the agenda, not once per increment in the path length. A breadth-first search that is based more closely on path length is almost as easy to implement, however. In Figure 5.5, the predicate traverse(Start,End,Paths) finds all the shortest paths that connect the given Start and End.

```
% traverse/3: find all shortest paths from node given
%    by the first argument to that given by the second.
%    Instantiate the third argument to a list of these.

traverse(Node, Node, []).
traverse(Start, End, FinalPaths) :-
    step([[Start]], End, FinalPaths).

step(PathsSoFar, End, FinalPaths) :-
        % Now collect all (perhaps none) paths starting
        % with End:
        complete_paths(PathsSoFar, End, [], FinalPaths),
        % Finished if there are any:
        \+ FinalPaths = [],
        !.
step(PathsSoFar, End, FinalPaths) :-
    expand_each_path(PathsSoFar, NewPathsSoFar),
    step(NewPathsSoFar, End, FinalPaths).

complete_paths([], _, F, F).  % No more paths to check.
complete_paths([[End|T]|Rest], End, Paths, Ans) :-
    !,
    complete_paths(Rest, End, [[End|T]|Paths], Ans).
complete_paths([_|Rest], End, Paths, Ans) :-
    complete_paths(Rest, End, Paths, Ans).

% expand_each_path/2 takes the given paths. For each,
% it builds the collection of paths one step longer. Note
% that [N|MorePath] is the path explicitly handled here,
% and we need to get hold of N to find the successors.
% Other paths are handled by the recursive subgoal.

expand_each_path([],[]).
expand_each_path([[N|MorePath]|MorePaths],
                                      NewPathsSoFar) :-
    expand_each_path(MorePaths, PartAnswer),
```

```
        successors(N, SuccessorsOfN),
        add_to_part_answer(SuccessorsOfN, [N|MorePath],
                            PartAnswer, NewPathsSoFar).

% add_to_part_answer/4: given a list of nodes one step
% beyond current end of a given path, add all the new
% paths so formed to a given collection being built up.

add_to_part_answer([], _, Result, Result).
add_to_part_answer([S|MoreS], PathToN, SoFar, Answer) :-
    member(S,PathToN),
    !,
    add_to_part_answer(MoreS, PathToN, SoFar, Answer).
add_to_part_answer([S|MoreS], PathToN, SoFar, Answer) :-
add_to_part_answer(MoreS, PathToN,
                        [[S|PathToN]|SoFar], Answer).
```

Figure 5.5   A search for shortest paths.

The member/2 subgoal in add_to_part_answer/4 means that paths
that return to themselves are ignored. New paths that join already known
ones, so that the new one cannot be a shortest path, are not detected by
this program. The cost of the detection is, in general, too high but if it
were very cheap it would be worth doing.

Exercise 5.1   Try implementing a version of this 'general' search
program that does test to see whether a new path
joins a known one, so that the new path can be
discarded in the search for the shortest. Can it
be made cheap enough to be worthwhile?

5.2   About setof/3 and related predicates

This section is something of a digression from the main themes of this
chapter. The predicates setof/3 and bagof/3 and the allied findall/3,
which is not normally built-in, often cause trouble to start with because
most manuals seem to be bad at explaining their behaviour.

The simplest is findall(Thing, Goals, ListOfThings). It calls
Goals, records an instance of Thing for that solution of Goals, then backtracks to do the same for every other solution of Goals. When there are
no more to be found, it proceeds to gather up all those recorded instances
of Thing, and instantiates ListOfThings to a list of them. This means, of

```
findall(Thing, Goals, List) :-
       % In recorda/3 below, the second arg is irrelevant!
       % It's the Ref that matters in the ensuing code.
       recorda('$findall', '$findall', Ref),
       '$findall'(Thing, Goals, Ref, [], List).

'$findall'(Thing, Goals, _, _, _) :-
       call(Goals),
       recorda('$findall', Thing, _), % even if var(Thing)
       fail.
'$findall'(_, _, Ref, SoFar, Result) :-
       '$sweep_up'(Ref, SoFar, Result).

'$sweep_up'(Ref, SoFar, Result) :-
       recorded('$findall', Term, RecordRef),
       erase(RecordRef),
       !,
       ( Ref == RecordRef ->  % Reached end of sweep
             Result = SoFar
       ;     '$sweep_up'(Ref, [Term|SoFar], Result)
       ).
```

Figure 5.6   One way of defining findall/3.

course, that you will be in trouble if Goals is member(a, X) or some such
goal which has infinitely many solutions if X is uninstantiated.

A typical definition of findall/3 is given in Figure 5.6. The instances of Thing are all recorded under a suitably obscure key. The first
recorda('$findall', '$findall', Ref) is only a marker whose discovery by the later recorded/3 indicates that the sweeping-up process should
end. Such a marker is needed; if you relied instead on the eventual failure
of recorded/3 to find more terms under the key '$findall', you might
run into trouble when you want to have findall/3 invoked as one of the
goals involved in another findall/3. Moreover, it is the unique database
reference that the sweeper tests for, rather than some test such as Term
== '$findall'. This is a defence against the clown whose Goals lead to
trying to include a term '$findall' in the final list. As you should be able
to see, this means that another findall/3 can be invoked by the Goals
without causing any trouble.

When using the more elaborate setof/3 and bagof/3, there are a
few simple points worth remembering:

- `setof/3` is really no more than `bagof/3` followed by a sort of its result. This sort should behave just like the standard `sort/2`, sorting the given list into the 'standard order' for all Prolog terms. To remind you, the order is: variables first (in some implementation-defined sub-order), then numbers in number order, then atoms in alphanumeric order, then terms sorted first by arity, then by name of principal functor, then by arguments left to right. Duplicates, as judged by the `==/2` predicate, are *removed*.

- Neither will ever return an empty list; they will fail instead.

- Both are potentially resatisfiable if control should backtrack to them. This may happen if there are uninstantiated variables in the second argument that do not also feature in the first argument.

To understand these two, it is sufficient to grasp what `bagof/3` does. Consider the goal

```
    ...., bagof(Thing, Goals, ListOfThings), ....
```

The essence of what happens is this. First, Prolog finds all those uninstantiated variables that occur in `Goals` but not in `Thing`. If `Goals` is of the form `Var1^Var2^...^MyGoals`, then `Var1`, `Var2` and so on are ignored in this hunt for 'free variables'; these variables are regarded as being existentially quantified. Then it constructs a 'key term' (say `KeyTerm`) involving just those free variables, and proceeds to do a `findall/3` of the form

```
    findall(KeyTerm-Thing, Goals, ListOfKeyTermMinusThings)
```

In the list of instances of `KeyTerm-Thing`, any of those free variables might have been instantiated as a result of some call of `Goals`. The list is key-sorted (for example, by `keysort/2`, another built-in predicate) and the result contains runs of terms such that within a single run the key is identical. The first run, with the keys stripped off, is returned by the first success of `bagof/3`; later runs are returned whenever control backtracks to it. For example, in

```
    ?- bagof(Y, member(X=Y, [a=1, a=2, b=7]), List).
```

there is an implicit call to something like this:

```
    ....,
    findall('$free'(X)-Y, member(X=Y, [a=1,a=2,b=7]), L),
    keysort(L, NewL),
    ....
```

so that `NewL` is

```
    ['$free'(a)-1, '$free'(a)-2,'$free'(b)-7]
```

Thus List will first be instantiated to [1,2] and, on backtracking, to [7]. Your Prolog may not have bagof/3 implemented in Prolog itself, but it should function in essentially this way. The result is required to be non-empty; an empty list would have meant that Goals had failed for some instantiation of the free variables, but since the form of bagof/3 offers no convenient way of finding out those instantiations, it is more appropriate to require a non-empty result. For example, would you like this?

```
?- my_bagof(Y, (member(X=Y,[a=1,a=2,b=7]), X=b), List).
X=_125505
List=[] ;   % due to the case X=a

X=b
List=[7]
```

In a realistic situation, there might be many such vacuous solutions to discard. If you really do want this behaviour, you can of course define my_bagof/3 for yourself.

Despite the apparent usefulness of these three predicates, it is important to realize that they are very often not needed. Consider the problem of generating a list of all the subsets of a given list. The word 'subset' is meant to indicate that ordering is irrelevant here – [a,b] and [b,a] are the same subset of [a,b,c]. The naive approach is to create a predicate subset/2 that, through backtracking, can be used to enumerate all subsets of a given list by choosing whether any given element is included or excluded from the subset being formed. The result looks like this:

```
pset(L, S) :-
    bagof(Subset, subset(Subset, L), S).

subset([],[]). % NB NOT subset([],_),
               % which would over-generate.
subset(Subset, [H|X]) :-
    subset(T,X),
    ( Subset = T
    ; Subset = [H|T]
    ).
```

The empty subset appears just once, as a result of choosing to leave out every element. However, look at the definition in Figure 5.7. On my currently preferred Prolog system, this is around fifteen times faster than the version that uses bagof/3! On the few other Prologs on which it was tested, the performance ratio was similar or even more in favour of the second version.

```
% powerset/2: given a list, returns a list of all the
% subsets of the list.
% Example:
%    ?- powerset([a,b], L).
%    L = [[], [a], [b], [a,b]]

powerset([], [[]]).
powerset([H|T], L) :-
    powerset(T, PowerSetOfT),
    extend_pset(H, PowerSetOfT, L).

% extend_pset/3: given an element, and a powerset,
% construct a new set twice as big: the old sets, plus
% new sets formed by adding the given element to each.

extend_pset(_, [], []).
extend_pset(H, [List|MoreLists], [List,[H|List]|More]) :-
    extend_pset(H, MoreLists, More).
```

Figure 5.7   Generating a 'power set' without **bagof/3**.

5.3   Some uses of variables

There are various ways in which variables can be put to particularly good use in the design of efficient Prolog programs. This section gives three examples.

5.3.1   Difference structures

The crunch idea here is that of building a term (such as a list) from the outside in; have a variable deeply buried inside the term, which can later be instantiated to your chosen inner bit. This looks like something you can do only once, but why not instantiate that variable to a term representing the inner bit, but with yet another variable inside it too?

How can one 'get hold of' this variable? Simple, in fact – unify some other explicit variable with it, so that instantiating that explicit variable also instantiates that part of the inside of the term. This idea is most often used when the terms in question are lists. In this case one speaks of 'difference lists', although 'difference structures' is the more general expression. The genesis of these names will be explained below. The phrase 'difference structures' was first used by Clark and Tärnlund [1977].

```
% rotate/2: given a difference list, rotate it one step
%    leftwards

rotate([Head|Tail]-[Head|NewVar], Tail-NewVar).
```

Figure 5.8   Rotating leftward by one step.

To see it in practice, first consider a list such as [a,b,c,d|Z]. You can attach e to this list by instantiating Z to [e], or rather – in order to preserve usefulness – by instantiating it to [e|Y] so that now Y is the variable at the end of the list. Remember, you will always be wanting to instantiate that variable to a list – perhaps the empty list – in order to turn the list into a fully instantiated one. The variable is often referred to as the 'tail variable'.

Suppose you need to 'rotate' a list – that is, keep the cyclic order but bring new elements to the front. For instance, given the list

[a,b,c,d,e,f,g,h]

you might want to 'rotate' it by 3 (leftwards) to get

[d,e,f,g,h,a,b,c]

First, add a 'tail variable' if there is none, or rather build a new list just like the given one except that there is a tail variable too:

append([a,b,c,d,e,f,g,h], Z, Result)

to get a **Result** of

[a,b,c,d,e,f,g,h|Z]

Now, the predicate in Figure 5.8 can be used to do a leftward rotation by a single step. Isn't that mysterious? What are those minus signs doing there? The answer is, one commonly chooses to deal with the term

[a,b,c,d,e,f,g,h|Z]-Z

rather than just

[a,b,c,d,e,f,g,h|Z]

since the former can be matched with

List - Variable

```
rotate(N, List, Answer) :-
    append(List, Var, ListWithVar),
    rot(N, ListWithVar-Var, Answer-[]).

rot(0, X, X).
rot(N, List-Var, NewList-NewVar) :-
    N > 0,
    rotate(List-Var, MidList-MidVar),   % one step, as above
    N1 is N-1,
    rot(N1, MidList-MidVar, NewList-NewVar).
```

Figure 5.9   Rotating a list leftward by N steps.

and now you have `Variable` unified with that variable hidden inside whatever term `List` is instantiated to.

So, consider the goal

```
?- rotate([a,b,c,d,e,f,g,h|Z]-Z, Answer).
```

Now this matches the unit clause above, with

```
Head=a
Tail=[b,c,d,e,f,g,h|Z]
Z=[a|NewVar]
Answer=Tail-NewVar=[b,c,d,e,f,g,h,a|NewVar]-NewVar
```

and, by design rather than chance, the `Answer` is of the same general form as the 'input' to `rotate/2`.

Thus, to rotate leftward by N steps, we just need a predicate such as is shown in Figure 5.9.

Thus in the execution of the goal

```
?- rotate(3, [a,b,c,d,e,f,g,h], Ans).
```

the `append/3` instantiates `ListWithVar` to `[a,b,c,d,e,f,g,h|Var]` and then calls

```
rot(3, [a,b,c,d,e,f,g,h|Var]-Var, Ans-[])
```

You will appreciate that a goal of the form

```
rot(3, [a,b,c,d,e,f,g,h|Var]-Var, Thingie)
```

will do `rotate/2` three times, and by the end `Thingie` will be instantiated to `[d,e,f,g,h,a,b,c|V]-V`; and that if `Thingie` is required to be of the form `Ans-[]`, this forces `V` to be `[]` and so `Ans` is `[d,e,f,g,h,a,b,c]`.

Was this worth it? Yes, especially for big lists. The `append/3` goal recursively works down the given list once, to attach that variable at the end. Thereafter each single step of the rotation is done just by a match with the single, unit clause for `rotate/2`. If you had

```
rotten_rotate(0,L,L).
rotten_rotate(N,[H|T],Answer) :-
    N > 0,
    append(T,[H], OneStepRotated),
    N1 is N-1,
    rotten_rotate(N1, OneStepRotated,Answer).
```

this would be much more inefficient since that `append/3` works recursively down past all but one element of the list once for each step of the rotation. There are $O(N)$ goals in the 'difference list' version and $O(N^2)$ in the rotten version. It is possible to improve on the version in Figure 5.9, by contriving to take the trouble to collect up the first N elements of the list to be rotated while recursing down it towards the end, where those collected elements will ultimately be appended. However, since it is sensible to collect them into a list in the same order as they appear in the given list, so that this can just be appended to the remainder, it makes sense to use a 'difference list' again, this time as the structure in which they are collected. Figure 5.10 shows this version; compare it closely to Figure 5.9. The syntactic similarities are striking, despite the fact that the rationales given for these two versions seem to be so different. There is one more point to notice about this list rotation problem. The `collect_rotate/3` version can be used to do rightward rotations too, by calling it with the third argument instantiated and the second a variable. The other two cannot be so safely used. Both will provide the answer, but on backtracking will enter an infinite loop when control backtracks to an `append(-,?,-)` goal. This will succeed, but in infinitely many ways, each with inappropriate instantiations of the arguments. Suitable cuts can repair both versions.

The name 'difference list' is a racy bit of terminology that arises out of thinking of a list such as

`[a,b,c,d,e,f,g,h]`

as being 'represented by' the 'result of the difference'

`[a,b,c,d,e,f,g,h|Var] - Var`

despite the fact that Prolog does not evaluate any terms except in very special circumstances. The list and the difference list are of course completely different terms, they cannot be matched, but the terminology is suggestive,

```
% collect_rotate/3: same arguments as rotate/3, but
% works by recursing down the list, collecting up the
% N elements to be transplanted to the end.

collect_rotate(N, List, Ans) :-
    collect_rot(N, Var-Var, List, Ans).

collect_rot(0, FirstN-[], Rest, Ans) :-
    append(Rest, FirstN, Ans).
collect_rot(N, Some-[H|NewTailVar], [H|T], Ans) :-
    N > 0,
    N1 is N-1,
    collect_rot(N1, Some-NewTailVar, T, Ans).
```

Figure 5.10   Rotation by collecting during recursion.

since the plain list can be extracted from 'difference' form at any moment
of your choosing, by instantiating Var to [] so that the first argument of
the -/2 here is what you wanted to extract. Even the empty list has a
natural counterpart in such differences. This is how one might handle an
agenda that is represented by a difference list rather than just a list:

```
% Get a new, empty agenda:
new_agenda(A-A).

% Add item to front of given agenda, get new agenda:
add_to_agenda_front(Item,
                    Agenda - TailVar,          % Old one.
                    [Item|Agenda] - TailVar).  % New one.

% Add item to end of given agenda, get new agenda:
add_to_agenda_end(Item,
                  Agenda - [Item|NewTailVar],  % Old one.
                  Agenda - TailVar).           % New one.
```

Thus, given the goals

```
?- new_agenda(X), add_to_agenda_front(reset, X, NewX).
```

the variable NewX will be instantiated to an agenda of the form

```
[reset|Var]-Var
```

Using agendas that are difference lists will save the cost of the appending in the general-purpose search methods outlined earlier, in Section 5.1.1. In particular, the cost of adding to either end of the agenda is trivial, and the same in both cases. This idea will be illustrated in the general-purpose chart parser in Chapter 8.

Sometimes you will see a difference list expressed not as a compound term such as `List` - `Var` but as two separate, usually adjacent arguments of some predicate. My own view is that this tends to make a program less readable: it is better to keep intimately linked terms together by wrapping them up in a single term. There may, of course, be other reasons for separating them which override this consideration.

There is a final point that is worth making here. Often, you do not need to pay the price of recursing down an ordinary list in order to add a variable to the end for 'differencing' purposes. For example, look again at the definition of `findall/3` in Figure 5.6. It is `'$findall'/5` which does all the work, and in the call of it in the single clause for `findall/3`, the tail of the returned list is given explicitly as an empty list. You can just define a `findall/4` instead, in which that tail end of the result is given as a user-defined term – such as a variable. The result returned will be a list with that variable already in the right place for your subsequent 'differencing' purposes.

5.3.2 'Updatable arrays'

Very occasionally you will find a good reason for not wanting to have an explicit variable unified with the variable that is deeply buried inside some structure. This means paying the price of dismantling that structure to go looking for it, but this can save a greater price elsewhere. This section gives an example.

One of the major deficiencies of the standard Prologs, from a programmer's point of view, is that there is no easy way to store terms in some known place, say by index or key value, and later access them or update what is stored at that index or key value. Constructs such as arrays or hash tables serve this purpose in other languages. From the purist's point of view, this might be seen as a strength of Prolog, because it means that there is no way to irrevocably break the connection between a term and its origins in the execution of the program; which means that programs can be written to analyse and perhaps control the behaviour of other programs.

This deficiency is easily avoided in the many current Prologs that offer good interfaces to routines written in other languages such as C or Pascal. Some systems offer built-in predicates for handling hash tables or balanced trees very efficiently, but most do not. Many Prolog textbooks also offer implementations of some flavours of balanced tree for 'efficient' term storage, such as 2-3 trees or AVL-trees. O'Keefe [1983] has suggested an ingenious idea for providing 'updatable arrays' in Prolog. These can be more efficient than balanced trees, whose insertion performance is normally $O(\log(N))$. However, in practice none of these methods is particularly wonderful when implemented in Prolog, and if you need excellent performance you should try calling out to routines written in a lower-level language.

The question to be tackled is how to store a number of terms, say N, such that any can be accessed rapidly and it is cheap in space and time to replace any of them by another. Lists are bad for this purpose; replacing an element calls for recursing down the list, building a new one on the way, like this:

```
% replace/4: replace Nth element of a list by another,
% instantiating last argument to the resulting list.
replace(1, [_|T], Element, [Element|T]).
replace(N, [H|T], Element, [H|NewT]) :-
    N > 0,
    N1 is N-1,
    replace(N1, T, Element, NewT).
```

However, the typical cost of replacing an arbitrary element is going to be $O(N)$ in time, and perhaps in space too. This remains true even if you try storing the N terms as the arguments of a term of arity N; you still have to construct a new term, and the normal built-in predicates such as `functor/3` and `arg/3` are going to require that arguments be installed in the new term one by one, even the unchanged ones. Because of this, some have proposed a `rplacarg/3` predicate modelled on the 'rplaca' LISP function, which will do destructive surgery on the internal form of terms. You can already achieve this with a few Prologs whose foreign language interface gives direct access to the internal structures, rather than copying terms and handing the copy across the interface. The dangers should be apparent.

Richard O'Keefe's idea is to use a term of the form, say,

```
array( [VeryOldValueA, OldValueA, CurrentValueA | VarA],
       [OldValueB, CurrentValueB | VarB],
       [CurrentValueC | VarC],
       [CurrentValueD | VarD],
       [CurrentValueE | VarE]
    )
```

where the first has been updated twice, the second once and the others not at all. You can pick out any desired argument of this term by using `arg/3`, and then recurse down the list so grasped to get to the variable at the end. This variable can then be instantiated to a term of the form `[NewValue|NewVariable]`, so that `NewValue` is now in there and there is still a variable at the end to be used for later updates. Accessing the current value of a particular array entry is done in essentially the same way, merely locating the last element before the tail variable. The main cost of this is one call of **arg/3** and a recursion of the length of the selected argument, which initially will be small but could in the worst case be big.

If you do the updating 10,000 times on the five-element 'array' shown above, obviously the cost of recursing down one of these lists is likely to get really nasty. So why not, every N updates, restart the whole process by constructing a brand new term

> array([ValA| VA], ... , [ValE | VE])

in which every argument is a list with one element followed by a variable for its tail? To build this involves recursing down all N lists of the old 'array', but since there have been only N updates the total recursion cost is still only $O(N)$. Since this $O(N)$ cost is only paid once per N updates, the average update cost still remains $O(1)$ plus the cost of a single update. If those N updates are uniformly spread around, this means the average update cost will be $O(1)$ overall, since none of the lists will grow to significant length before the new array term gets constructed. What if the updates are not uniformly spread across the array? The answer must be, what are those statistically static entries doing in this array at all? They should be in another such array, or be handled by other means. The whole idea is neat, although it is rendered rather impractical by the inability of many Prologs to handle terms with more than a few (say 256 or 1024) arguments.

Figure 5.11 shows a simple implementation of this. Arrays are represented by terms of the form **array(...)/(K,N)**, where K is the number of updates done so far and N is the length of the array. The length could be easily found by using **functor/3**, but it is cheaper to preserve this information from the time of the array's creation. The top-level predicates are **new_array/3** and **update_array/4**. It should be obvious how to define a predicate to access current values.

```
new_array(N, NewArray/(0,N)) :-
    N > 0,
    functor(NewArray, array, N).

update_array(J, Array/(K,N), NewValue, Array/(K1,N)) :-
    K < N,                          % The 'usual update'
    !,
    K1 is K+1,
    arg(J, Array, ListJ),
    further_instantiate(ListJ, NewValue).
update_array(J, Array/(N,N), NewValue, Result) :-
    functor(Newterm, array, N), % Update after N of them
```

```
            install_array_arguments(N, Array, NewTerm),
            update_array(J, NewTerm/(0,N), NewValue, Result).

further_instantiate(Term, NewValue) :-
    ( var(Term) ->
        Term = [NewValue|NewTailVar]
    ;   Term = [_|Tail],
        further_instantiate(Tail, NewValue)
    ).

% install_array_arguments/3 recurses N times. At each
% step it 'initialises' another argument of the new
% array.

install_array_arguments(0, _, _) :-
    !.
install_array_arguments(J, Array, NewTerm) :-
    J > 0,
    arg(J, Array, ListJ),
    get_current_value(ListJ, CurrentValue),
    arg(J, NewTerm, [CurrentValue|_]),
    J1 is J-1,
    install_array_arguments(J1, Array, NewTerm).

get_current_value([H|T], Val) :-
    ( var(T) ->
        Val = H
    ;   get_current_value(T, Val)
    ).
```

Figure 5.11   A version of O'Keefe's updatable arrays.

Exercise 5.2   Define the necessary predicate for accessing values.

Remember that the updating causes a side-effect in the **array/N** term. The second clause of **update_array/4** might seem to you to be suboptimal, since the updating of array entry J could be done during the creation of the new **array/N** term. After all, why copy over the old value just to supersede it immediately? However, an extra test would be needed to see whether any argument being copied over was the argument to be updated; this would probably cost more than the way shown above.

Use of difference lists instead of ordinary lists in the `array/N` term might appear to save the cost of recursing down a list in search of the tail variable. However, the new tail variable would have to appear explicitly in the resultant array term – and this is just the problem that the 'updatable arrays' idea is trying to solve, namely updating part of a structure at low cost.

Other approaches to incorporating arrays and hash tables into Prolog are described in Barklund and Millroth [1987] and Eriksson and Rayner [1984].

5.3.3   Structural transformation of data

Variables can be used to great effect when trying to transform one data structure into another in some elaborate way. In particular they can be used as 'placeholders' in the new data structure, to be filled out when the analysis of the old structure reaches a point where that part of the data becomes known. The following example was suggested by Michael Donat.

Suppose that you have a set of rules, such as the following (using a non-Prolog notation):

> *rule1: room(X) and public(X) → bookable(X)*
> *rule2: door(D) and openable(D) and accesses(D, R) → public(R)*
> *rule3: → room(a76)*
> *rule4: → door(d213)*
> *rule5: → accesses(d213, a76)*
> *rule6: → openable(d213)*

A simple theorem prover might establish *bookable(a76)* like so:

Goal Stack	**Next Operation**
bookable(a76)	
	expand stack item 1 by rule1
room(a76), public(a76)	
	expand stack item 2 by rule2
room(a76), door(D), openable(D), accesses(D, a76)	
	delete stack item 1 by rule3
door(D), openable(D), accesses(D, a76)	
	delete stack item 2 by rule6
door(d213), accesses(d213, a76)	
	delete stack item 1 by rule4
accesses(d213, a76)	
	delete stack item 1 by rule5 – DONE

Do not worry about how this theorem prover actually works in general, just observe that it seems to behave differently from Prolog. In particular, it is not restricted to a depth-first search, since it does not always concentrate on the topmost (right-hand, in the above printout) item on the goal stack.

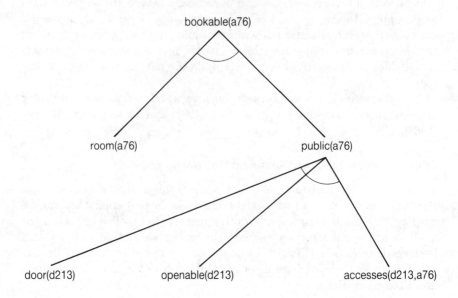

Figure 5.12   The proof tree for *bookable(a76)*.

All that matters for the sake of this example is that the theorem prover picks a goal on the stack somehow, and expands it according to the rule set. Any new goals are added to the top of the stack, in the order of their appearance in the premise of the rule used. Facts are represented by rules with empty premises; expanding them is equivalent to deleting the goal from the stack.

The problem to be tackled is this. The proof sequence can easily be represented as a series of stack operations, like this:

```
[[rule1, 1], [rule2, 2], [rule3, 1],
 [rule6, 2], [rule4, 1], [rule5, 1]]
```

but for the purposes of some beautiful user interface to the theorem prover, perhaps for some explanation mechanism that needs an overall picture of what happened during the proof, a proof tree (see Figure 5.12) is needed. The sequence of operations hides the reasons why particular rules were invoked, the proof tree displays those dependencies but hides the sequencing of rule use. In Prolog this might be represented by a term such as

```
ptree(rule1,            % bookable(a76)
     [ ptree(rule3,[]),    % room(a76)
       ptree(rule2,        % public(a76)
            [ ptree(rule4, []), % door(d213)
```

```
                    ptree(rule6, []), % openable(d213)
                    ptree(rule5, [])  % accesses(d213,a76)
              ]
    ])
```

or you might want to adorn this with lots of extra information. The problem
is how to resurrect a proof tree from the sequence of stack operations.

The starting point is to observe that the information about the stack
operations only makes sense if you know the rules, and if you know the
state of the stack at that moment. The rules can be easily represented,
perhaps like this:

```
rule(rule1, [room(X), public(X)], [bookable(X)]).
rule(rule2, [door(D), openable(D), accesses(D,R)],
                                        [public(R)]).
rule(rule3, [], [room(a76)]).
rule(rule4, [], [door(d213)]).
rule(rule5, [], [accesses(d213,a76)]).
rule(rule6, [], [openable(d213)]).
```

In order that the program can make sense of the stack operation data, it
will need to simulate the stack. A difference list can be used for this, but
it need not contain the actual goals since that information can be easily
recovered from the rule information itself. A difference list is better than
an ordinary list here, since the stack operations are relative to the front of
the list but new goals are added to the other end.

The essence of the job lies in deciding what rules were used to tackle
the premise goals in any rule. The key idea is to simulate the stack by a list
of variables, so that when a stack operation such as 'item 27 was expanded
by rule74' is encountered, the 27th variable on the list can be instantiated
to a proof subtree, containing variables where the proof subtrees for each
premise in `rule74` will eventually hang. Thereafter, a new state of the stack
is constructed, in which that 27th variable has vanished and those same
variables corresponding to the premise goals in `rule74` have been added
to the stack. Thus the variables keep track of the connections between the
stack and the proof tree, as it were. A program to accomplish the job is
given in Figure 5.13.

Observe the subterm `ptree(Name,PtreeList)` in the head of the first
clause for `adjust_stack/4`. This will be matched with some variable on
the simulated stack, in any goal that matches the head of this clause. The
`PtreeList` remains a variable until the `add_to_stack/4` sub-goal is done,
whereupon it is instantiated to a list containing as many variables as there
are terms in the premise of the rule used. These variables are also attached
to the end (alias top) of the simulated stack, and are later instantiated to
proof trees themselves by later `adjust_stack/4` goals.

```
% convert_stack_to_tree/2: given a list of 'stack
% operations', build the proof tree

convert_stack_to_tree(StackOps, ProofTree) :-
    stack_to_tree(StackOps, [ProofTree|TVar]-TVar).

stack_to_tree(StackOps, Var-Var) :-
    var(Var),
    !,
    ( StackOps = [] ->
        true             % Got here? Correct termination.
    ;   write('bad news: empty stack, still got ops'),
        nl,
        fail
    ).
stack_to_tree([], _) :-
    write('bad news: no more ops, but nonempty stack'),
    nl,
    fail.
stack_to_tree([[Name,Number]|MoreOps], StackPair) :-
    adjust_stack(Name, Number, StackPair, NewStackPair),
    stack_to_tree(MoreOps, NewStackPair).

% adjust_stack/4 instantiates one variable on the
% simulated stack to be a ptree/2 structure, the proof
% tree for the goal that stood here on the real goal
% stack. Then a new stack is constructed, without that
% term and with variables added to the end (top) of the
% simulated stack to stand for the proof subtrees for in
% that ptree/2

adjust_stack(Name, 1, [ptree(Name,PTreeList)|T]-V,
                                          T-NewV) :-
    rule(Name, PremiseList, _),
    add_to_stack(PremiseList, PTreeList, V, NewV).
adjust_stack(Name, N, [H|T]-V, [H|NewT]-NewV) :-
    N > 1,
    N1 is N-1,
    adjust_stack(Name, N1, T-V, NewT-NewV).

% add-to-stack/4 is given a list of the parts of a
% rule's premise and adds variables to the end of the
```

```
% simulated stack, one per part of the premise. These
% same variables are also collected into a list (the
% second argument) which is to be the second argument
% of the skeletal ptree/2 in the head of adjust-stack/4

add_to_stack([], [], NewTailVar, NewTailVar).
add_to_stack([_|MorePs], [Var|More], [Var|MoreVars],
                                            NewV) :-
        add_to_stack(MorePs, More, MoreVars, NewV).
```

Figure 5.13   Transforming stack data to a proof tree.

An example might help to make this all clearer. Let us use the set of rules given above, to prove the goal

    public(a76)

Suppose that the set of stack operations used to prove this is as follows:

(1) expand the goal by `rule1`

(2) handle the second subgoal by using `rule6`

(3) handle the second of the remaining subgoals, `accesses(d213,a76)`, by using `rule5`

(4) handle the one remaining subgoal by `rule4`

Consider the arguments of `stack_to_tree/2`. Initially they are

    Operations: [[rule1,1], [rule6,2], [rule5,2], [rule4,1]]
    Stack pair: [ProofTree|Var] - Var

First, `adjust_stack/4` instantiates `ProofTree` to

    ptree(rule1,[P1,P2,P3])

and removes `ProofTree` from the stack pair and adds P1, P2 and P3 to it. At the recursive step, `stack_to_tree/2` is called with

    Operations: [[rule6,2], [rule5,2], [rule4,1]]
    Stack pair: [P1,P2,P3|NewVar] - NewVar

This time, `adjust_stack/4` instantiates P2, the second item on the stack, to

    ptree(rule6, [])

so that `ProofTree` has become further instantiated. The stack pair merely shrinks, since `rule6` has no premise. At the next step in the recursion, `stack_to_tree/2` is called with

```
Operations:  [[rule5,2], [rule4,1]]
Stack pair:  [P1,P3|NewVar] - NewVar
```

Once again, `adjust_stack/4` instantiates the second item on the stack, this time to

```
ptree(rule5,[])
```

and now we have

```
Operations:  [[rule4,1]]
Stack pair:  [P1|NewVar] - NewVar
```

Finally, `adjust_stack/4` instantiates the first item on the stack appropriately, leaving an empty stack and an empty operations list, so the process terminates. By this time, `ProofTree` has been fully instantiated to

```
ptree(rule1,
      [ ptree(rule4, []),
        ptree(rule5, []),
        ptree(rule6, [])
      ])
```

Exercise 5.3   The stack operation information in this example was given in terms of unique rule tags. Imagine instead that there were no rule tags, as is the case in a Prolog program. Could this example be easily modified so as to be able to resurrect the proof tree purely from information about which goal on the stack had been expanded at each step? Try to implement such a variation.

5.4 'Simple' is not always 'best'

Many Prolog programs, like the one just given, have a pleasing simplicity and elegance. This is not always a valuable hallmark. Sometimes, a program that is only a little more sophisticated than the 'obvious' approach can be dramatically better. This can be a matter of taking a more sophisticated view of the problem or it can be one of taking a more sophisticated view of the way to express it in Prolog.

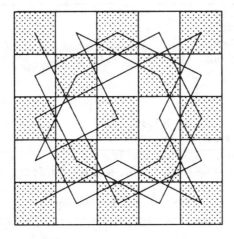

Figure 5.14   A knight's tour of a 5 × 5 board.

5.4.1   The knight's tour

The search for a knight's tour of a chess board N squares on a side, in which the knight has to visit every square just once, is a widely used exercise in searching. Figure 5.14 shows one possible tour on a 5 × 5 board. There are no tours possible on boards smaller than this, as a few moments' thought should convince you. To write a Prolog program to search for a tour, you must first consider the representation of the squares and of the tour so far. In order to make a point, let's just use the term (X,Y) to represent a square. The tour so far can be represented by a simple list, since although you will need to be able to check whether some given square has already been visited, for small values of N the list will not grow so long that this check will waste vast amounts of time. A check for the completion of the tour can be that the tour so far is N^2 in length. Naturally, it pays just a little to compute this number once and then pass it as an argument of the search predicate rather than recalculating it at each step of the recursion. Since the search depth is bounded and not very large, some kind of depth-first search seems feasible and indeed best. A breadth-first search might involve horribly large data structures: since there are between two and eight next squares that a knight can jump to from any given square on the board (ignoring the issue of whether it has visited them already), this suggests that there might be $O(2^{N^2})$ tours to worry about.

Figure 5.15 shows a simple program to achieve the task. It makes use of Prolog's control flow to do the searching, contrary to the advice given earlier, for the sake of speed. Prolog programmers with instinctive reactions about efficiency might automatically replace that **member/2** goal with **memberchk/2** instead – that is, the version of **member/2** with a cut

```
tour(N, Tour) :-
    N2 is N*N,
    tour(N, N2, (1,1), [(1,1)], Tour).

tour(_, N2, _, Tour, Tour) :-
    length(Tour, N2).
tour(N, N2, (A,B), SoFar, Tour) :-
    jump(N, (A,B), (C,D)),
    \+ member((C,D), SoFar),
    tour(N, N2, (C,D), [(C,D)|SoFar], Tour).

% jump(+Size, +From, -PossibleNextSquare) enumerates
% potential next squares, on succesive backtrackings
% to it.

jump(N, (A,B), (C,D)) :-
    ( ( C is A+1, C =< N
      ; A > 1, C is A-1
      ),
      ( D is B+2, D =< N
      ; B > 2, D is B-2
      )
    ; ( C is A+2, C =< N
      ; A > 2, C is A-2
      ),
      ( D is B+1, D =< N
      ; B > 1, D is B-1
      )
    ).
```

Figure 5.15   A simple-minded knight's tour.

in it. However, it makes no difference whatsoever here because the \+/1 goal will fail as soon as the first solution to the member/2 is found, and will only succeed if none is found, so there is no question of ever backtracking through alternate solutions to the member/2.

Try this program. In tests using a local Prolog system on a SUN-3/75, it took 1103.0 CPU seconds to find the first solution on a 5×5 board. Using the popular C-Prolog, or running it on a VAX-11/750, took a *lot* longer – around 6000 CPU seconds on the VAX. If you thought it might run faster if the terms (X,Y) were replaced by two adjacent elements, ..,X,Y,.., in the tour and by two adjacent arguments in jump/3 (so it becomes jump/5), then congratulations on thinking about what's really going on internally, but bad luck – this makes no measurable difference.

One of the reasons that the knight's tour is such a popular exercise is that there appear to be no useful and simple shortcuts. Nevertheless, Figure 5.14 does suggest that one strategy might be to emulate the path of a bouncing billiard ball as often as possible, so that the tour tends to orbit the centre. This presupposes that any departure from this basic strategy that is needed in order to claim the centre can happen fairly late, so that not too much backtracking is needed to find it. You are strongly encouraged to do some experiments with different strategies at this point!

When this problem was set as a class exercise, Alex Thame discovered a simple heuristic (that is, a 'rule of thumb') that makes a dramatic difference to the speed and very little difference to the space requirements. In the version given below (Figure 5.16), the running time for the 5×5 board, again on a SUN-3/75 using the same Prolog system as before, was a mere 0.48 seconds of CPU time – an improvement by a factor bigger than 2200! The simple heuristic is:

- Cost the choices of square to jump to, giving each a cost of the form (min. dist. from horizontal edge) * (min. dist. from vertical edge). Go for minimum cost. This makes the tour tackle the more inaccessible squares early on.

- Where two choices have the same cost, the tie-breaker depends on the quadrant of the square it is jumping from. The choices are shown in Table 5.1.

In the program, the quadrants are referred to by atoms such as topleft and bottomright. You might have a computing instinct that the program would run faster if you used 0,1,2,3 instead, since numeric comparison ought to be faster than string comparison. However, the overhead of using atoms is indistinguishably small and the benefit in readability is huge.

Table 5.1   Choosing between equal-cost squares.

Coming from?	Choose:
top left	point with larger X
top right	point with smaller X
bottom left	point with larger Y
bottom right	point with smaller Y

```
tour(N, _) :-
    N < 5,
    !, fail.
tour(N, Tour) :-
    HalfN is (N+1)//2,
    NSq is N*N,            % useful for termination check
    tour(N, NSq, HalfN, topleft, (1,1), [], 1, Tour).

% tour/8 does the work. The arguments are
%    N, N-squared, half-N (handy constants calculated
%    just once), the quadrant of the square the knight
%    is jumping from, the coordinates of the square it
%    is jumping from, the tour so far, most recent
%    square first, the length of the tour so far, and
%    a variable to be instantiated to the final tour

tour(_, NSq,      _, _, (X,Y), Tour,     NSq,
                                        [(X,Y)|Tour]).
tour(N, NSq, HalfN, PQ, (X,Y), SoFar, Length, Tour) :-
    jump_choices(N, (X,Y), Choices),
    include_costs(N, HalfN, PQ, Choices, CostedList),
    select_next((NewX,NewY), NewPQ, CostedList),
    (\+ member((NewX,NewY), SoFar)),
    Length1 is Length+1,
    tour(N, NSq, HalfN, NewPQ, (NewX,NewY),
                        [(X,Y)|SoFar], Length1, Tour).

jump_choices(N, (X,Y), List) :-
    Xp1 is X+1, Xp2 is X+2, Xm1 is X-1, Xm2 is X-2,
    Yp1 is Y+1, Yp2 is Y+2, Ym1 is Y-1, Ym2 is Y-2,
    remove_baddies(N, [(Xp2,Yp1), (Xp1,Yp2),
                       (Xm1,Yp2), (Xm2,Yp1),
                       (Xm2,Ym1), (Xm1,Ym2),
                       (Xp1,Ym2), (Xp2,Ym1)],
                                        List).

remove_baddies(_, [], []) :-
    !.
remove_baddies(N, [(X,Y)|More], Result) :-
    ( X < 1
    ; Y < 1
    ; X > N
```

```
    ; Y > N
    ),
    !,
    remove_baddies(N, More, Result).
remove_baddies(N, [(X,Y)|More], [(X,Y)|Rest]) :-
    remove_baddies(N, More, Rest).


include_costs(_, _, _, [], []) :-
    !.
include_costs(N, HalfN, PQ,
              [(X,Y)|More], [(C,V,Q)-(X,Y)|Rest]) :-
    ( X =< HalfN ->
        ( Y =< HalfN ->
            Q = topleft,
            C is X*Y
        ;   Q = bottomleft,
            C is X*(N+1-Y)
        )
    ;   ( Y =< HalfN ->
            Q = topright,
            C is (N+1-X)*Y
        ;   Q = bottomright,
            C is (N+1-X)*(N+1-Y)
        )
    ),
    ( PQ = topleft ->
        V is N-X
    ; PQ = topright ->
        V is X
    ; PQ = bottomleft ->
        V is N-Y
    ;   V is Y
    ),
    include_costs(N, HalfN, PQ, More, Rest).
```

```
% select_next/3 backtracks through the choices of square
% to jump to, from the given list of choices, returning
% the best choice first and so on. This is where the
% heuristics are encoded.
%
% You would think that select_next/3 is better than
% using keysort/2 and member/2, since at best it only
% needs to scan the choices once and hopefully no more
% than two or three times, whereas a keysort should do
% no better than L*log(L) in general, and 2L or 3L scans
```

```
% of the choices should be better than L*log(L) of them
% even for small L. In fact select_next/3 is not
% noticeably better, since L is at most 8 (at most 8
% choices of where to jump to) and if you're not careful
% it can be noticeably worse.

select_next((BestX,BestY), NewPQ, Choices) :-
    pick_best(Choices, Best, Rest),
    !,
    ( Best = (_,_,NewPQ)-(BestX,BestY)
    ; select_next((BestX,BestY), NewPQ, Rest)
    ).

pick_best([(C,V,Q)-(X,Y)|More], Best, Rest) :-
    pick_best((C,V,Q)-(X,Y), More, Best, [], Rest).

pick_best(This, [], This, Rest, Rest).
pick_best((C,V,Q)-(X,Y), [(C1,V1,Q1)-(X1,Y1)|Tail],
                                        Best, SoFar, Rest) :-
    ( C < C1 ->
        pick_best((C,V,Q)-(X,Y), Tail, Best,
                        [(C1,V1,Q1)-(X1,Y1)|SoFar], Rest)
    ; C > C1 ->
        pick_best((C1,V1,Q1)-(X1,Y1), Tail, Best,
                        [(C,V,Q)-(X,Y)|SoFar], Rest)
    ; V < V1 ->
        pick_best((C,V,Q)-(X,Y), Tail, Best,
                        [(C1,V1,Q1)-(X1,Y1)|SoFar], Rest)
    ;   pick_best((C1,V1,Q1)-(X1,Y1), Tail, Best,
                        [(C,V,Q)-(X,Y)|SoFar], Rest)
    )
```

Figure 5.16   A much improved knight's tour program.

The top-level predicate in this version is tour(N,Tour). To understand the essence of this program, look at the body of the recursive clause for tour/8. The first subgoal,

    jump_choices(N, (X,Y), Choices),

instantiates Choices to a list of the squares accessible from the current one, even though some might already have been visited on the tour that brought the knight to this point. If the current square were (1,2) the choices would be [(3,3), (2,4), (3,1)]. The next subgoal,

```
include_costs(N, HalfN, PQ, Choices, CostedList),
```

creates a similar list, but with a cost triplet attached to each. The first element of the triplet is the 'cost' of the square. The second is a number to be used in applying the tie-breaker heuristic; it depends on the quadrant of the square being jumped from. These numbers are such that the square with the smaller of these is the one to choose. The third element of the triplet is the quadrant of the proposed new square, and this information is only included for use when the square is actually chosen, not in the decision process of which square to choose. Pursuing the same example, assuming a 5 × 5 board, the list of costed squares will be (since HalfN is 3 for this board):

```
[(9,2,topleft)-(3,3),
 (8,3,bottomleft)-(2,4),
 (3,2,topleft)-(3,1)]
```

The next subgoal accepts this list and instantiates its first and second argument to the preferred choice of next square, and its quadrant:

```
select_next((NewX,NewY), NewPQ, CostedList),
```

You may recall the advice given earlier that the fully instantiated arguments in some goal ought to be the first ones, and yet this contradicts it. It does not matter, however – there is only one clause for select_next, so no efficiency issue arises. In the example, the chosen square will be (3,1) since this has the lowest cost of 3 and no other has the same cost. It remains to check that this square has not been visited already:

```
(\+ member((NewX,NewY), SoFar)),
```

and, assuming that it has not, the new tour so far will be 1 longer:

```
Length1 is Length+1,
```

The tour ends when this length reaches 25.

The timings are given in Table 5.2, all on a SUN-3/75 under the same conditions as before. As you can see, the saving over the brute force method is useful (time enough to write this program, in fact!). The run time is extraordinarily sensitive to the heuristics. For instance, changing

```
HalfN is (N+1)//2
```

in an apparently trivial way to be

```
HalfN is N//2
```

instead, changes the time for a board of size 7 from 2.37 seconds to over 70 seconds. The uneven rise of the times with board size is curious, and should suggest to you that the heuristics employed in this program are not

Table 5.2   Timings for the improved knight's tour.

Size of board	CPU seconds
5	0.48
6	69.72
7	2.37
8	2.47
9	191.45
10	11.95
11	16.77

perfect – if you assume that there is any regularity waiting to be discovered about solutions to the problem as the board size varies.

This is not the end of the story, however. There is a simpler heuristic that is worth trying: when choosing which square to jump to next, pick one that has the fewest successors itself. A program for this is shown in Figure 5.17. It is rather simpler than the previous one; for one thing, there are no costs to compute.

```
tour(N, Tour) :-
    tour(N, (1,1), [(3,2),(2,3)], [], 0, Tour).

tour(N, Place, Tour) :-
    bagof(X, jump(N,Place,X), Successors),
    tour(N, Place, Successors, [], 0, Tour).

% tour/6: the main recursive loop. The arguments are:
% 1) the size of the board
% 2) the square we are now at
% 3) a list of the possible next squares (generated
%    last time around, we chose the current square
%    because it had fewest 'next squares' of the
%    ones we have not yet considered).
% 4) a list giving the path by which we got to the
%    current square; excludes the current square
% 5) length of that path (0..N^2-1)
% 6) a variable to be instantiated to the path found.
```

```
tour(N,Place,SuccessorsOfPlace,PathToPlace,Length,Tour):-
    LengthOfPath < N*N - 2,    % At least two places left?
    !,
    pick_next_place(N, Place, SuccessorsOfPlace,
            PathToPlace, NewPlace, SuccessorsOfNewPlace),
    NewL is Length + 1,
    tour(N,NewPlace,SuccessorsOfNewPlace,
                        [Place|PathToPlace],NewL, Tour).
tour(N,Place,_,PathToPlace,_,[Last,Place|PathToPlace]) :-
    jump(N, Place, Last),
    \+(member(Last, PathToPlace)).

jump(N, (X,Y), (NewX,NewY)) :-
    delta(DX,DY),
    NewX is X+DX,
    valid_coordinate(N,NewX),
    NewY is Y+DY,
    valid_coordinate(N,NewY).

delta( 2, 1). delta( 1, 2). delta( 2,-1). delta(-1, 2).
delta(-2, 1). delta( 1,-2). delta(-2,-1). delta(-1,-2).

valid_coordinate(N,Value) :-
    Value > 0,
    Value =< N.

pick_next_place(N, Place, ItsSuccessors, PathToPlace,
                    NewPlace, SuccessorsOfNewPlace) :-
    find_most_limited(N, ItsSuccessors,
                    [Place|PathToPlace],
                    NewPlace, SuccessorsOfNewPlace).

remove_visited([], _, []).
remove_visited([H|T], Unwanted, Result) :-
    member(H, Unwanted),
    !,
    remove_visited(T, Unwanted, Result).
remove_visited([H|T], Unwanted, [H|Rest]) :-
    remove_visited(T, Unwanted, Rest).

find_most_limited(N,Choices,Path,Choice,NewChoices) :-
    form_choice_counts(N,Choices,Path,ChoiceCountList), ·
    keysort(ChoiceCountList, SortedList),
    member(_-(Choice,NewChoices), SortedList).
```

```
form_choice_counts(_, [], _, []).
form_choice_counts(N,[H|T],Path,
                              [Count-(H,Possibles)|Rest]) :-
    bagof(X, jump(N,H,X), List),
    remove_visited(List, Path, Possibles),
    length(Possibles, Count),
    form_choice_counts(N, T, Path, Rest).
```

Figure 5.17   A more interesting version of the knight's tour.

In this program, the next square is selected by first generating a list of valid successor squares. Then `form_choice_counts/4` works recursively down this list, to form a new list containing terms of the form

    Count - (Square, ListOfItsSuccessors)

where `Count` is merely the length of `ListOfItsSuccessors`. This new list is in a form suitable for the built-in predicate `keysort/2`, which will sort the terms in order of `Count`, smallest first. It is worth keeping the actual `ListOfItsSuccessors` explicitly, rather than just its length, because it will save recreating the list for the selected square. Each of the lists, even those for squares not selected, has to be created in order to determine the length; why throw them away when it costs so little to keep them?

The timings, in Table 5.3, are interesting. They are much more uniform than the timings for the earlier program, which had used two rather more elaborate heuristics; these just increase steadily with the board size, and are usually rather worse than those in Table 5.2.

Hiding in this information there is a very interesting fact. It is that, for all these board sizes and a few more at least, this program does no

Table 5.3   Timings for the improved knight's tour.

Size of board	CPU seconds
5	1.42
6	2.97
7	5.23
8	8.55
9	13.14
10	19.43
11	27.43

backtracking at all in order to find the first solution! The earlier version does involve backtracking, even in cases where that one is faster. Experiment has shown that it is possible to change the ordering of the delta/2 clauses in various ways, and still no backtracking is needed in order to find the first solution. This suggests two things:

- that there are many possible solutions for any board size of 5 or larger;

- that there is a simple algorithm for finding a solution (the algorithm represented by this program, in fact) that works on *any* board size of 5 or larger.

There is probably an interesting result in number theory lurking in all this, but that is outside the scope of this book. A four-hour, non-exhaustive search running on a SUN-3 found 136 tours on a board of size 5, each starting at (1,1) and moving first to (3,2) – this latter condition rules out searches that are purely reflections in the diagonal from (1,1). All 136 were found within the first hour.

Finally, the following exercises are left for the reader:

Exercise 5.4   How can you ever tell that a Prolog program like this did not backtrack – must you use the trace package?

Exercise 5.5   Devise some means of printing out a knight's tour as an $N \times N$ board (hint: use keysort/2).

Exercise 5.6   *Prove* that the algorithm given above does find a tour without backtracking.

SUMMARY

- Prolog itself uses a depth-first flow of control with chronological backtracking, but this is not a serious limitation. Programs written in Prolog can employ any search method.

- Explicit use of an agenda makes it easy to represent many search strategies.

- setof/3, bagof/3 and findall/3 are useful, powerful, frequently misused and misunderstood. It is often possible to avoid having to use them.

- The concept of 'difference structures' is an extremely useful one.

- The notion of a variable in Prolog is one of the great strengths of the language.

- Simple programs are not always the best or fastest.

- It is worth experimenting systematically with the heuristics you incorporate into a program.

- Studying the behaviour of a program carefully can often repay the effort needed.

ADDITIONAL EXERCISES _____

5.7 Various ways of searching a graph are described in this chapter. A Prolog program could be viewed as a special kind of graph, with nodes representing either heads or bodies of clauses. The arcs from a head node would go to body nodes, the arcs from body nodes would go to each of the head nodes of appropriate clauses for those goals or to some 'built-in predicate' node. Build a simple interpreter for a limited subset of Prolog that uses breadth-first rather than depth-first search.

5.8 Experiment with searches for a rook's tour of a chessboard that visits every square just once, makes a minimum number of turns and ends on the square it started from. The minimum number of turns required is 16.

5.9 A representational problem: the Danish mathematician Piet Hein devised a simple puzzle called 'the Soma cube'. It consists of seven pieces – the seven possible arrangements of either three or four unit cubes that you are left with if you rule out three-in-a-line, four-in-a-line and four-in-a-square. These seven can be arranged into a 3×3 cube in 240 ways (see, for example, Berlekamp *et al.* [1982]). Devise a way of representing these pieces and a program to find the ways of packing them into a cube.

6
CRESS: an expert system shell

This chapter is concerned with a project that is a lot larger in scope than the earlier programs, namely an expert system shell. Several small-scale examples of Prolog expert system shells have already appeared in print. The one described here is designed to be used in teaching about expert systems. It is called CRESS, an acronym for CRude Expert System Shell. As it stands it is not (quite) a toy, and yet it offers a great deal of scope for being extended in many directions. The original source consists of around 2000 lines of Prolog, including comments, together with a further 600 lines of user documentation. The aim of this chapter is to illustrate how a moderate-scale project such as this can be put together, and why certain design decisions were taken at various stages.

6.1 About simple rule-based expert systems

A considerable number of expert systems have been built already; a 1987 directory [CRI 1987] lists over 600 documented systems, and there are many others used but unpublicized by their creators. The large majority of these are rule-based. Very few are commercially available products, partly because it is rare for the knowledge captured in such a system to be both 'expert' and widely applicable without local modification. Another stumbling block is that it can be very hard to prove that such a system works – what, after all, are the test criteria to be? In the absence of such a proof the issue of legal liability for inexpert performance is still an interesting question. You may wonder how 'expert' a Prolog-based expert system can be, without being humanly incomprehensible. The answer is, very good indeed: a system that can construct squeezes in contract bridge, with an expert rating without being unreasonably complex, is described in Sterling and Nygate [1987]. There are also a large number of expert system 'shells' now on sale. These typically offer:

- A language for encoding 'knowledge' somehow. Because the shell is usually destined for use by people who do not want to take the time and trouble to work in some general-purpose language, its language is usually simpler and (you hope) more appropriate for its purpose than Prolog, LISP, C or whatever. This tends to mean that the 'shell' language is tailored to some kinds of knowledge representation and not others.

- An inference mechanism, which swallows the encoded 'knowledge' and produces consequences of some kind, usually to order. Some way of coping with uncertain data and uncertain links between data is also useful, although many of the shells on sale do not provide one.

- A user interface of some kind. The user typically wants to know 'Can the following be shown: ...?', 'Given this data, what is the best option for achieving ...?' and so on. Some mechanism that allows the user to check the sense of the results, by being given a comprehensible explanation, is also very desirable.

- A developer's interface of some kind. This should provide at least simple checks on the structural consistency of the 'knowledge' – that is, checks that the atomic, unanalysable ingredients of the 'knowledge' have not been fitted together in a few of the more commonly silly ways.

The majority of shells are also rule-based. Many acknowledge an intellectual debt to MYCIN, the best-publicized and one of the oldest expert systems, and the EMYCIN shell that evolved from it. However, few commercial shells are even yet as sophisticated as those. This chapter describes a MYCIN-like shell; for contrast, a different one is described in Littleford [1984].

In a rule-based system, the 'knowledge' is represented as a collection of *if ... then ...* rules. For the moment, let us use individual lower-case letters to stand for simple factual components, such as 'today is Friday' or 'the average giraffe is taller than the average elephant' or 'your preferred type of holiday is so-and-so'. Then, given even a tiny collection of rules such as

if m and n then b
if g and a then n
if a and b and g then d
if a then f
if e and f then d

it can nevertheless be hard to appreciate the structure of this at first glance. In fact, d is the only ingredient that can be concluded by a rule but which does not lend support to any other rule's conclusion – it is the sole top-level goal, so to speak. Figure 6.1 shows these same rules organized into a tree. There is no requirement that it should be a tree rather than any directed graph, it just happens to be a tree in this case. In some topics, loops occur naturally when trying to represent the 'vicious circles' of causality.

In a typical *backward-chaining* system, if the user enquires about the truth of *d* the system might be set up so as to search this tree left-to-right and depth-first. In this case, it might have to ask the user about the truth of *a* first, and then of *m* and then of *g* – assuming it was given satisfactory answers. This would be sufficient to answer the original question. An alternative derivation could be found if requested, by asking for the truth of *e* too. In a typical *forward-chaining* system, the user might start by volunteering that *a* and *g* were true, but then the system could only conclude that *n* and *f* were true, in the absence of other information.

The distinction between forward-chaining and backward-chaining is slim. Although the tree in Figure 6.1 expands outward as your eye moves down it, other trees can be wide at the top and shrink inward instead. Although backward-chaining might be construed as a process of looking backward from rule conclusions to see what rule premises must be established, by deduction or enquiry, a rule such as

> if *e* and *f* then *d*

can be recast without change of meaning as

> if we want to establish *d*,
> then try to establish *e* and *f*

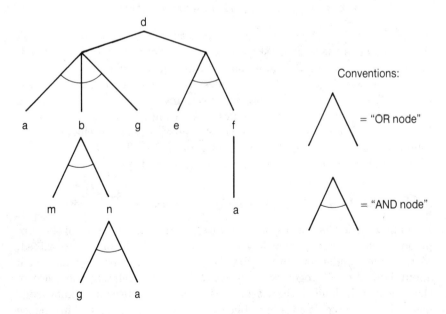

Figure 6.1   A very simple rule tree.

Forward-chaining on this form is the same as backward-chaining on the other. A distinction of sorts does emerge when you consider what those lower-case letters stand for. Consider the rule

> if nationality of father = british
> and nationality of mother = canadian
> then eligibility for citizenship = yes

In the typical backward-chainer, the first subgoal might be to find out all that could be known about 'nationality of father' rather than the specific requirement shown. Only when the system has finished that would it then consider the truth of the first part of the premise. In a typical forward-chainer, knowing that 'nationality of father = canadian' is useless as far as this rule is concerned, even though a man may have both British and Canadian nationality simultaneously. But clearly a forward-chainer can also be engineered to pursue the whole truth.

The typical backward-chainer also provides a rudimentary explanation mechanism. Using the example given earlier, the user might ask 'why (are you asking that)?' when the system enquires about the truth of g. An answer can be constructed from the goal stack and the rules:

```
I need to know g in order to conclude n by rule ...
I need to know n in order to conclude b by rule ...
I need to know b in order to conclude a by rule ...
which was what you originally asked about.
```

A question such as 'how did you conclude b?' – your first chance to ask this being when the system asks you about e, or perhaps when it first tells you that it concluded d – can be handled in a very similar way.

As a sweeping generalization, rules are most suited to capturing 'expertise' that consists of applying any of many short reasoning steps, in which the essence of the expertise lies in knowing which particular step is justifiable and appropriate at any stage, and in which the chains of reasoning are not very long. See Buchanan and Shortliffe [1984] for a much wider-ranging discussion of all aspects of rule-based systems.

6.1.1 The limits of simple rule-based systems

It should be said that such systems have severe limitations. One of the supposed virtues of rules is that any individual rule should be self-contained, so that the builder can just throw in rules without worrying too much about how they fit together. For instance, a rule relating the price of sharkmeat in Iceland to the season of the year can appear in a 'knowledge base' about fire regulations in public schools, without conflict. This means that the individual parts of a rule's premise tend to divide up into those parts that set a context, and those that are discriminatory within that context. For example, the connection between cloudiness and the likelihood of rain depends where you are and on the time of year, at least. The location and season set the context for the nature of the link. However, there is nothing in the syntax of a rule to say which parts relate to context and which to discrimination. In a simple system, there is no explicitly available information about the contexts and their arrangement, although it is sometimes possible to extract an approximation by statistical, and therefore subject-independent, processing of the rule set. However, context information rather than generalities about the rules can be very important for the generation of meaningful explanations. It also takes a fair degree of skill to create rules in such a way that they are genuinely independent, and so that the system then asks questions in an order and style that the user will find comprehensible and tolerable. There is a further point here, a somewhat abstract issue as far as such simple systems are concerned. Given a rule of the form

$$\text{if } p_1 \text{ and } p_2 \text{ and } \ldots \text{ and } p_N \text{ then } c_1 \text{ and } \ldots$$

if N is too large, it can always be rewritten in the form

if p_1 and p_2 then $reached(2)$
if $reached(2)$ and p_3 then $reached(3)$
. . .
if $reached(N-1)$ and p_N then c_1 and $\ldots$

This makes no difference to execution, but an enormous difference to explanations. Nor is it clear that an encoding of 'knowledge' into rules can always lead to acceptably short rules; in some domains the contexts may only be defined by a large set of conditions, and may not divide into a neat hierarchy. The best that can be said is that rules are not appropriate for an encoding of such a domain.

The standard method of providing explanations often proves inadequate in practice. If the tree or graph is too deep, the rule trace is likely to be incomprehensibly long.

The available methods of handling uncertainty all have serious theoretical flaws – they can just be made to work fairly well in practice. However, they can also go horribly wrong in practice, so be warned! The following section describes the method to be used in CRESS. The method is derived from the one developed for MYCIN – see Buchanan and Shortliffe [1984] if you want to know about its origins and shortcomings.

6.1.2   Handling uncertainty: certainty factors

There are really two kinds of uncertainties: of rules themselves and of data. In the shell to be described, they are handled in the same way. Any datum has an associated *certainty* or *confidence factor* (alias CF), a number lying between 0 and 100. 0 means 'no credibility at all', 100 means 'definitely'.

MYCIN used certainty factors in the range $-1 \cdots 1$, with negative numbers indicating a negative belief; thus, 'yes cf -1' meant 'no'. In CRESS the negative values are ruled out; you must have separate values 'yes' and 'no' and it will be up to you to ensure that the system cannot conclude both values simultaneously, or to modify the shell suitably to handle negative values.

When answering questions, the user can qualify his answer to indicate a degree of belief, in the range 0 to 100. Only CFs that are larger than 20 get propagated at all; anything with a lower certainty factor is deemed to have a CF of 0. The number 20 here was chosen arbitrarily. The idea of having such a threshold is to spare the system having to do much work on anything whose certainty is 'unreasonably' low. It turns out that the shell is relatively insensitive to this threshold provided that the chains of reasoning are never too long and that any CF that appears in the original knowledge base is one of a small well-spaced set of values (such as 20, 40, 60, 80, 100). This insensitivity is an experimental rather than a theoretical result.

Uncertainties are propagated through the rules by the following algorithm. In rules of the form

if A and B and C then ...

the CF of (A and B and C) is taken to be the minimum of the three CFs of A, B and C, and is then reset to 0 if that minimum is 20 or less. In

IF A or B or C THEN ...

the maximum is taken instead. By this means, a CF for the combined premise is derived. A CF for the conclusion is derived by scaling this down by the confidence factor attached to the conclusion, regarded as a percentage. So:

$$CF_{AandB} = \min(CF_A, CF_B)$$
$$CF_{AorB} = \max(CF_A, CF_B)$$
$$CF_{conclusion} = CF_{premise} \times CF_{rule}$$

Once a CF is available for the conclusion, the information about the conclusion is updated by combining this CF with any previous CF for the same conclusion as follows. Suppose the CF from some rule is cf_1, and the already recorded CF is cf_2. Then

$$NewCF = cf_1 + cf_2 - (cf_1)(cf_2)/100$$

Note that the new CF is definitely larger than the old value. This means that CFs never decrease; this is acceptable provided you are only using CFs to rank the possible answers, rather than using them to indicate some absolute degree of possibility. The equation given above is based upon some considerations of probability theory, as you can see if you rearrange the above expression in the form

$$NewCF = 100(1 - (1 - cf_1/100)(1 - cf_2/100))$$

but it makes the wholly unjustified assumption that the derivation of the new CF and the old CF are independent. Nevertheless, it works, mainly because the AND/OR tree in a typical consultation is so shallow that the errors between this simple method and what would be obtained by proper probabilistic calculations do not build up to something significant.

There are, however, subtle traps waiting for you even if you use a much more elaborate way of handling uncertainty. Consider this example. Suppose there are two medical treatments, each effective against two diseases. Suppose that, purely according to statistical evidence, treatment A is the more effective one for a patient who has either disease. It may nevertheless be the case that, for a patient who is suffering from both diseases, treatment B is much more effective than treatment A – again, purely on the statistical evidence. A reason might be that, whenever treatment A is effective against the first disease, it is because of certain biological factors within that patient. Whenever the treatment is effective against the second disease, it is because of certain *different* biological factors. However, it may be that it is rare for the two sets of factors to occur simultaneously in the one patient, so that treatment A is rarely effective for a patient with both diseases. The general form of this phenomenon is called Simpson's paradox in the statistical literature, although it is not a paradox and it was not originally discovered by the E. H. Simpson after whom it is named. He did, however, discuss it in a paper in 1951.

The phenomenon can easily occur within a rule-based system if the certainty factors used are derived purely from statistical incidence data. The problem stems from assuming that some conclusion holds with a *uniform* incidence in the domain in question. Clearly the problem can only be avoided by reasoning explicitly about causes. However, let us stick with the very simple certainty factor mechanism outlined above and return to the design of a simple shell.

6.2 A basic design and some consequences

There are various aspects of the design to be considered:

- The rule language that the user is to employ for representing the 'knowledge'.

- The functionality of the system – what it does, what utilities and options it provides.

- The main interpreter – how will it do its job?

- The loader – what happens when a collection of rules gets loaded? There is likely to be a lot of internal structure within the rules, so it is likely to need cross-indexing of some form.

- Handling a screen – how is the system going to look to the user?

- Asking the user – when the user provides input during a consultation, what forms might it be allowed to take?

6.2.1   The rule language

The ideas presented here have been influenced somewhat by the languages employed in various commercial systems such as Teknowledge's M.1 (at least, insofar as these are described in books such as Harmon and King [1985]).

Each rule should have a unique name, so that it can be referred to in some compact way. Therefore, let the general form be

NAME : if PREMISE then CONCLUSION .

The final full stop is a convenient marker to denote where a rule ends. There is an ulterior motive in requiring it, of course. The intention is that the rules should just be Prolog terms, although in a 'natural' form that can be used by someone who knows no Prolog. This can be achieved by defining suitable operators, as it turns out. The reason for making the rules be Prolog terms is that the built-in predicate **read/1** can be used to read them in as fast as possible. It would be hardly any extra trouble to provide a character-by-character input mechanism, akin to one of the many line-reading predicates exhibited in introductory texts. For some reason these line-reading predicates are designed with some care in order to avoid ever backtracking over a **get0/1** goal, which would result in the loss of that character. However, it requires much less ingenuity just to gather up a list of characters as far as a newline character, and then hand this list to a definite clause grammar which parses it and returns a suitable list of atoms such as a list of the words in the line. Backtracking during the parsing step is then not a problem to be avoided. However, the problem remains that such methods of input, when implemented in Prolog, are normally appreciably slower than the term reader and parser that form part of the system itself; this is likely to be a serious drawback if the user's rule set is of any size.

However, if a rule were to be made available on input as a list of words, it would be possible to use one of the matchers described earlier (see Section 4.2) to check its syntax. For example, you might do something like this:

```
. . . . . ,
match([Name,:,if,Premise,then,Conclusion], UsersRule),
. . . . . ,
```

and then go on to analyse the lists **Premise** and **Conclusion** looking for the appropriate keywords inside them, and so on. The disadvantage of this is that it is slow, since elements of the original list are li ely to be looked at many times. The advantages are that much more so, histicated error checking is possible, and that the rule language need only be concerned with keywords – arbitrary sequences of words can occur between the keywords. A definite clause grammar could also be used to achieve this latter bonus, but at the expense of requiring some ingenuity to provide decent error reporting.

Let us stick with the intention that rules will be represented by valid Prolog terms. Although the system's input will object noisily to syntactic flaws, there is no need to have the error diagnosis done by the shell itself. A separate program could be provided that reads a flawed rule base character by character rather than as terms, and takes one of the approaches outlined above to do a decent job of reporting the real problems. The expectation is that a user will rapidly learn how to write correct rules and how to diagnose faulty ones, and that after that he would be grateful if the shell did not carry the memory overhead of having a near-redundant syntax analysis tool built into it.

In the skeletal form of rule syntax suggested above, the NAME need not be limited much. The user can employ mere atoms, but there could be wonderful applications for compound terms too, such as being able to build in a way of filtering a rule set so that only certain rules, whose names match some general term, are used in certain circumstances. However, there is one limitation. Clearly, ':', 'if' and 'then' are to be names of operators. The ':' must be infix or postfix, the 'if' adjacent to it must be correspondingly prefix or infix. The 'then' must be infix. Their precedences should be less than 1000, of course, but need to be high because it would be nice to allow the possibility of having arithmetic expressions within the rule. So, let us just define them as follows:

```
:- op(999, yfx, :).
:- op(998,  fx, if).
:- op(997, xfx, then).
```

If you are using Quintus Prolog version 2.0 or later, you should beware of the fact that :/2 is predefined and is used as a way of overriding the Quintus module system. You might want to use another operator instead, such as ::/2.

In these operator definitions, the 'then' is deemed to be xfx because Prolog's term reader will then object if it finds two of them accidentally put in the same rule. The colon is deemed to be of associativity yfx because that will allow the rule name to include colons, and

```
electric:simple:
    if battery = connected then current = flowing.
```

will unify happily with

```
Name : if Premise then Conclusion
```

causing `Name` to be instantiated to the compound term `electric : simple`.

The allowable forms of the premise and conclusion must be broadly similar; after all, the conclusion of one rule is likely to be used as the premise of another. In MYCIN, the atomic ingredients were concerned with the possible values of various attributes of the entities involved. For example, an English rendering of one rule might be

```
if   1) the gramstain of the organism is negative
and  2) the morphology of the organism is rod
and  3) the aerobicity of the organism is anaerobic
then ....
```

Look at the second part here. It concerns an attribute, the morphology, of a particular entity in the drama, namely the organism, a possible value for that attribute (a 'rod') and a relational test – does the attribute have that particular value?

For our purposes we can generalize this slightly by allowing attributes to have attributes, to any depth, merely by defining an infix operator called 'of':

```
:- op(600, xfy, of).
```

This will mean that

```
colour of cover of book = red
```

is a valid Prolog term, which can unify with a term of the form

```
Thing = Value
```

You could argue that 'of' should have associativity `yfx` instead, so that 'book' could be extracted from the term above by a single unification; in what follows, the actual choice does not matter that much.

It would be possible to allow other relations, such as inequalities, but this leads to awkward problems of interpretation. What, for instance, should follow from these two rules?

```
rule1: if   type = retired
       then age > 65.

rule2: if   age < 70
       then eligibility = low.
```

For simplicity, such inequality relations will be accepted by this shell but it will be up to the user to ensure they are used sensibly. There are various ways in which a clean semantics might be enforced; the necessary research and implementation is left as an exercise for the reader. One easy way forward might be to try to trap and object to such overlapping ranges in a rule set. However, it's not as easy as it looks: what if that number 65 is only available as the result of some run-time calculation?

It will, on the other hand, be very useful to allow certain metalogical tests, such as whether an attribute has any known value at all, and to allow the user to include arbitrary Prolog goals in the premise of a rule. It is also useful to allow the use of variables wherever values are allowed:

```
rule93: if   colour of front of house = X
        then colour of back of house = X cf 70.
```

This example also illustrates how confidence factors might be given. Just define an infix operator 'cf', of a precedence higher than any allowable relation – say 725, since the built-in relational operators have precedences of 700 or less.

A distinction should be made as to whether an attribute is to be single-valued or not. There could be several possible diagnoses of what is wrong with a radio. What day of the week it is today is, on the other hand, single-valued: if it is Tuesday it cannot be Wednesday too and there is no point in having the system trying to show that it could be. Of course, the concept of 'possible day of the week' might be multi-valued. If the shops are shut, it might well be Sunday but it could be a public holiday on a weekday. An attribute could be marked as being single-valued like so:

```
day of week is single_valued.
```

The need for an underscore here is rather awkward; fixing this is a further exercise left for the reader. Anything that is not specifically single-valued is assumed to be multi-valued.

Figure 6.2 is a formal description of the proposed grammar for rules. A knowledge base will consist of a collection of QUESTIONs, STATE-MENTs and RULEs in any order, possibly split across several files. Note that 'or' is not allowed in conclusions, for the reasons explained earlier in Section 1.2.7. Also, although the grammar lists the most basic ingredients as being 'Atomic', this need not be rigidly enforced. The grammar merely tries to ensure that the user's rules are valid Prolog terms according to the various operator definitions in force. There may be as yet unforeseen benefits in using various kinds of compound term in places where the description 'Atomic' appears.

The QUESTION entry provides a way for the system to ask the user about the value of certain THINGs; this is how the system acquires its basic data. Thus a rule base might include a term of the form

```
'What is the colour of the cover of the book'
        finds colour of cover of book.
```

The system should supply the necessary question mark automatically.

QUESTION	::=	Atom finds THING .
STATEMENT	::=	THING is single-valued .
RULE	::=	TAG : if PREMISE then CONCLUSION .
TAG	::=	Atomic | TAG : Atomic
PREMISE	::=	CHUNK
		| CHUNK and PREMISE
		| CHUNK or PREMISE
CHUNK	::=	RELATION | STATUS | PROLOG
RELATION	::=	THING = VALUE
		| THING < VALUE
		| THING > VALUE
STATUS	::=	THING is known
		| THING is unknown
		| THING is askable
PROLOG	::=	prolog(AnyPrologGoal)
THING	::=	Atomic
		| Atom of THING
VALUE	::=	Atomic | PrologVariable
CONCLUSION	::=	BASIC
		| BASIC and CONCLUSION
BASIC	::=	RELATION
		| RELATION cf Number
		| PROLOG

Figure 6.2   The rule grammar.

It is useful to allow arbitrary Prolog goals in rules, even if this feature is only used to write out messages from time to time. Such a goal will be deemed to have a CF of 100 if it succeeds and 0 if it fails; this ensures that such a goal does not affect the combined CF in the rule in which it appears.

6.2.2   The functionality of the system

Given a set of rule and questions in the above language, what should the shell let you do with it? The following is a minimal set of options:

- *Load a file of rules and questions.* You may want to split the knowledge base into several files: therefore loading one file should not erase anything previously loaded.

- *Reload a file.* You might, on the other hand, want to edit a set of rules and questions and reload them; this operation should erase anything previously loaded from that file. Rather than keeping track of what was loaded from each file, it is easiest just to cause this option to erase everything previously loaded.

- *Save the current knowledge base.* If you have loaded many files, it can be convenient to save the complete state of Prolog. Many implementations provide the predicates `save/1` and `restore/1` for this purpose. Normally the effect of the latter is to make execution continue from a point just after the `save/1` goal that created the saved state in the first place. It is handy if the 'save' option is available in the middle of a consultation too, so that the consultation can be continued at some later time.

- *See various aspects of what has been loaded.* For example, there should be options to:

  - see what THINGs the rules are composed of
  - see which rules mention a specific THING
  - see what has been concluded about a specific THING
  - see a specific rule
  - make simple checks on the complete knowledge base

- *Run an arbitrary operating system command.* For example, you might want to edit a file of rules without leaving the shell.

- *Get some help.*

- *Start a consultation.*

In the middle of a consultation, whenever the system asks a question, most of these options still make sense and should be available. The user should also be able to ask why the system is asking that question. Two further options are useful:

- *See a history of the consultation so far.*

- *See a history of the attempt to find out about a specified THING.*

For this purpose, the interpreter needs to keep a 'history list' of the story so far. In the program that follows, this list contains elements of the following form. For this purpose, `=>/2` merely needs to be declared as some kind of infix operator, but the details are not critical.

- `THING => user` indicates the point at which the user was asked to supply value(s) for THING.

- THING => RULE indicates the point at which the named RULE was invoked in order to conclude some value for THING.

- THING => lookup indicates the point in a rule premise where the system discovered the need to check on the value of THING, and found that THING had already been or was being investigated, so that it only tried to look up values already recorded for it.

- THING => s/RULE indicates the point where that part of the named rule's premise concerned with THING was found to have a CF greater than 20.

- THING => f/RULE indicates the point where that part of the named rule's premise concerned with THING was found to have a CF less than 20. At this point, the system would abandon the rule since the premise could not have a combined CF larger than 20.

- RULE => s indicates the point where the named rule succeeded.

- RULE => f indicates that the named rule failed.

Whenever the system asks a question, it is a good idea to tell the users the answers that would seem to be expected by any of the rules. Nevertheless they should be allowed to give another answer; they may, for instance, be building a set of rules incrementally and so wish to give an answer that will be handled by some as yet non-existent rule.

At the end of the consultation, the value(s) of the THING that the user originally asked about, so starting the consultation, should be displayed in order of CF.

6.2.3   What happens in a consultation: the rule interpreter

The user starts a consultation by asking the system to find out the value(s) of some chosen THING. To find the value(s) of this or any other THING, the system checks first to see if it has tried to investigate possible values for it earlier in the consultation. If so, it merely looks up the values (if any) that were concluded earlier. If not, it next checks to see if there is some question that the user can be asked about it. If so, the user is asked and that is the end of the matter: the system does not then go on to try to deduce any value(s). If there is no available question, and no record of any earlier attempt to find values, it then uses the rules to try to deduce any values by backward chaining, as explained at the beginning of Section 6.1.

It makes sense to use Prolog's recording database to store values. The values of a THING need to be efficiently accessible at run time, so they cannot be held in a list. They could be stored in some sort of balanced tree that is grown at run time; however, it could also be useful to have access to them after a consultation has finished, and this suggests that they should not be kept solely in some dynamically produced structure.

6.2.4   Run-time efficiency: how the rule loader can help

At the time the rules are loaded, various useful sets can be constructed:

- The set of all THINGs used in any rule, either in premises or in conclusions.

- Three important subsets: the set of all THINGs used in any rule premise, the set of all THINGs used in the rule conclusions and the set of all THINGs for that there is a question available. These are useful when the knowledge base needs to be checked for 'loose ends'. The user may also wish to know this kind of information.

- For each THING, the set of rules that can conclude it. This will spare the system from having to dismantle every rule at run time in order to find out which rules to invoke to try to conclude some value for the THING.

- For each THING, the set of rules that use it in their premise part.

- For each THING, the set of values it might have, according to the rules. This is slightly harder to construct than you might at first realize. Consider this rule, which might be used to make the system pay some small attention to the user's preferences in the absence of other information:

```
rule49: if   colour of wall is unknown
        and  preferred_colour of wall = X
        then colour of wall = X cf 25.
```

The possible values of `colour of wall` must therefore include all the possible values of `preferred_colour of wall` too.

These sets can be used to cut out a lot of searching at run time. Further improvements are possible.

6.2.5   Using the screen

Teletypes should by now be just a part of history. Almost every computer system provides some screen control functions. For generality, let us suppose that the minimal set of Prolog predicates below is available. It is usually very easy to define such a set.

```
go_to_xy(Col,Row)  – sends the cursor there – top left is (0,0)
clear_to_eol       – clears from the cursor to end of line
clear_screen       – clears the whole screen
back_space(N)      – moves the cursor N places left
home               – moves the cursor to (0,0)
screen_limits(MaxCols,MaxRows)
                   – gives size of the screen
```

The original version of CRESS was developed on a UNIX system, in which the type of terminal in use was available as a UNIX environment variable. The Prolog program read this variable and asserted the appropriate clauses for these predicates. If the terminal type was not one of those known to the program, it presented the user with a list of known types and the default option 'unknown'. If the response was 'unknown' the program asserted a set of clauses that would lead to comprehensible (if not beautiful) behaviour, even on an old-fashioned teletype. However, all this is left as yet another exercise for the reader. In what follows, it will only be assumed that the necessary initialization and screen control functions are done by a predicate `screen_ctl/0`.

6.2.6   Asking the user questions

The screen is cleared before each question. The question is then presented, along with the set of possible answers that occur in the set of rules; a certain amount of calculation is necessary to be able to put all this in the middle of the screen. The users' input should not be restricted to valid Prolog terms, and they should not be expected to have to remember to put a full-stop at the end of every input. Instead, the input is collected as a list of words, and parsed by a simple definite-clause grammar, which returns an appropriate term. If this term corresponds to a question or a command, it is dealt with and then the original question is asked again. This continues until the user finally provides a value or values. The form of the ultimate reply can be quite complicated. For example, in response to the question 'What are the main ingredients?' the user should be able to reply with something like

```
eye of newt cf 50
and toe of frog cf 60
and wool of bat cf 70
```

– in this case, the corresponding Prolog term will look just the same as this.

6.3   The program

The actual program is large enough to be worth splitting into several files. The `lib/1` utility defined in Chapter 3 can be used to make sure that every file is consulted once and only once. For example, if the part of the program in `fileA` makes use of predicates defined in `fileB` and `fileC`, then you need only put

```
:- lib([fileB, fileC]).
```

in `fileA`. It will not matter if, for example, the Prolog command

```
:- op(975, xfy, :).       % separates rule tag from rule
:- op(950, fx,  if).
:- op(949, xfy, then).
:- op(800, xfy, and).
:- op(750, xfy, or).
:- op(725, xfy, cf).      % cf => certainty factor
:- op(710, xfx, finds).   % as in Question finds THING
:- op(599, xfy, of).
:- op(599, xfx, =>).      % used in the 'history list'
```

Figure 6.3   The operator definitions.

```
:- lib([fileC, fileD]).
```

occurs in `fileB`. The `lib/1` predicate will ensure that `fileC` is consulted only once.

6.3.1   The operator definitions

Figure 6.3 shows the full set of operator definitions needed.

6.3.2   The top level of the shell

Figure 6.4 shows the top level of the system. There is a failure-driven loop that handles the user's top-level commands, such as loading a file or running an entire consultation. Some of the predicates involved are defined later in this chapter.

```
% cress_version/1: this atom is printed
%      at the top of the main screen

cress_version('Version 1.2, of 13 Jan 1986').

% run_cress/0: the top-level goal.

run_cress :-
      screen_ctl,    % set up the screen control stuff
      command_loop.  % enter the failure-driven loop
```

```
command_loop :-
    repeat,
    single_command_cycle,
    fail.

single_command_cycle :-
    clear_screen,
    tab(4),
    write('CRESS expert system shell   '),
    ( cress_version(Version) ->
    write(Version)
    ;   write('(test version only)')
    ),
    go_to_xy(0,4),
    showlist(4, ['Choose:',
      '- reload filename  to flush, then load',
      '- load filename    to load a knowledge base',
      '- save filename    to save loaded knowledge base',
      '- things           to see what THINGs there are',
      '- apropos THING    to see where THING is used',
      '- show THING       to see what is known about it',
      '- show RULE        to see the rule',
      '- find THING       to start a consultation',
      '- vet              to check the rule base',
      '- !unix command    to run any UNIX command',
      '- help             to get some help',
      '- quit             to return to UNIX']),
    tab(4), write('Choice: '), ttyflush,
    get_valid_answer(Ans, [history, history of X, why]),
          % The second argument of get_valid_answers/2 is
          % a list of those commands in the total set
          % that are UNacceptable at this point
    do_command(Ans),
    !.

do_command(A) :-
    ( A = load(Filename) ->
    try_to_load(Filename, load)
    ; A = reload(Filename) ->
    try_to_load(Filename, reload)
    ; A = things ->
        things
    ; A = apropos(THING) ->
    apropos(THING)
    ; A = show(ITEM) ->
```

```
    show(ITEM,[])
    ; A = find(THING) ->
    find(THING)
    ; A = save(Filename) ->
    clear_screen,
    write('Saving the compiled knowledge base in '),
    write(Filename), nl,
    write('The file will be executable.'), nl,
    save(Filename),
    screen_ctl     % Just in case the user restores later
                   % using some other kind of terminal!
    ; A = vet ->
    clear_screen,
    vet,
    await_return
    ; A = unix_command(List) ->
    clear_screen,
    do_without_fail(sys_command(List)),
    await_return
    ; A = help ->
    command_help
    ; A = quit ->
    halt
    ;          screen_limits(_, Ymax),
    Y is Ymax-1,
    go_to_xy(0,Y),
    write('That didn''t make sense.'), nl,
    await_return
    ).

command_help :-
    clear_screen,
    write('Your choices are:'), nl,
    showlist(8,
      ['- reload file    first flushes any old knowledge',
       '                 base, then loads the knowledge',
       '                 base from the file',
       '- load filename  loads a knowledge base',
       '- save filename  saves the compiled knowledge',
       '                 base. If you do this after a',
       '                 find command, then the results',
       '                 will be saved too for later',
       '                 inspection by the show, apropos',
       '                 and things commands',
       '- things         lists what THINGs can be',
```

```
            '                         mentioned in the apropos, show',
            '                         and find commands',
            '- apropos THING          shows which rules mention it',
            '- show THING             shows known values so far',
            '- show RULE              displays the rule',
            '- find THING             actually starts a consultation',
            '- vet                    does simple checks on your',
            '                         knowledge base, and tries to',
            '                         guess what the top-level THINGs',
            '                         seem to be. However, any THING',
            '                         can be a top-level one',
            '- !unix command          runs the command',
            '- help         .         prints this screenful',
            '- quit         ·         exits. All is lost']),
        await_return.


% try_to_load/2 tries to load or reload a named file
try_to_load(Filename, Reload) :-
    exists(Filename),
    !,
    tab(4),
    write('Please wait. This may take a while...'),
    ttyflush,
    ( Reload = reload ->
    reload(Filename)
    ;    load(Filename)
    ),
    write(' loaded'), nl,
    await_return.
try_to_load(Filename) :-
    screen_limits(_, Ymax),
    Y is Ymax-1,
    go_to_xy(0,Y),
    write('Couldn''t find '), write(Filename),
    write(' - better luck next time'), nl,
    await_return.


% showlist/2: a utility to print a list of terms,
%    one per line, each indented by a given amount
showlist(_, []).
showlist(N, [Term|MoreTerms]) :-
    N > 0,
    tab(N),
    write(Term), nl,
    showlist(N, MoreTerms).
```

```
% await_return/0: succeeds when the user
% presses <return>
await_return :-
    screen_limits(_,Ymax),
    go_to_xy(0,Ymax),
    write('--- Press <return> to continue ---'),
    ttyflush,
    skip(10).

% do_without_fail/1: calls its argument, but always
%    succeeds even if the call failed
do_without_fail(Goal) :-
    call(Goal),
    !.
do_without_fail(_).
```

Figure 6.4   The top level of the shell.

6.3.3   The rule loader

As explained earlier, a great deal of useful work can be done at load time. In order to see what happens, it is simplest to look at some examples. First, consider a question item such as

'What day of the week is it' finds day of week.

This is asserted. However, the user might supply a very long question, with several embedded newline characters, in which case it is useful to know how many lines the question will need if the program is going to centre the question vertically. The loader will assert unit clauses of the form

    question_lines(day of week,1).
    askable_things([...,day of week,...]).

as well. A term of the form

    day of week is single_valued.

is asserted as

    single_valued(day of week).

A rule such as

```
rule103: if    day of week = tuesday
         and   weather = sunny
         then  place = paris cf 60.
```

is asserted directly, but also gives rise to several further assertions:

- `rulebit(premise,rule103,day of week,equals,tuesday)` and two similar assertions record the other parts of the rule, but not the CF attached to the conclusion.

- `rules_to_find(place,[...,rule103,...])` records the fact that this rule can be used when trying to find the values for `place`.

- `rules_that_use(day of week,[...,rule103,...])` records the fact that the `rule103` is one of those that have `day of week` in the premise. There will be a similar assertion for `weather`.

- `expected_values(day of week,[...,tuesday,...])` says that `tuesday` is one of the possible values for `day of week`. There will be a similar assertion for `weather` but not for `place` if it does not occur in the premise of any rule. Strictly speaking, such an assertion is only needed for those THINGs that occur in a premise and for which there is an available question. However, the excess information could well be useful for debugging.

- `premise_things([...,day of week,...,weather,...])` records all THINGs that appear in any premise. There is just one such assertion, no matter how many rules there are.

- `conclude_things([...,place,...])` records all THINGs that appear in any conclusion. There is just one such assertion, no matter how many rules there are.

- `list_of_things([...])` records the union of the previous two lists.

When a file is to be loaded, `read/1` is used to read in each term and `loadprocess/1` dismantles it. When the entire file has been read, `massage_data/0` is called to create the remainder of the above assertions. In the program as given below, there is an implicit assumption that the rules will not be split into several files; for example, `massage_data/0` gets to work at the end of the file-reading. The necessary extensions are left as a very lightweight exercise. Figure 6.5 shows the top levels of the loader.

```
load(File) :-
    ( exists(File) -> true
    ; write('File does not exist'), nl, fail
    ),
    seeing(Old),
    see(File),
    repeat,
        read(Item),
        ( Item == end_of_file
        ; loadprocess(Item),
          fail
        ),
    seen,
    see(Old),
    massage_data.

reload(File) :-
    abolish(rulebit, 5),   % clobber any old assertions
    abolish((finds), 2),
    abolish(single_valued, 1),
    abolish(question_lines, 2),
    abolish(rules_to_find, 2),
    abolish(rules_that_use, 2),
    abolish(expected_values, 2),
    abolish(premise_things, 1),
    abolish(conclude_things, 1),
    abolish(askable_things, 1),
    abolish(list_of_things, 1),
    abolish((:), 2),
    load(File).

loadprocess(Question finds Thing) :-
    ( already_questioned(Thing) ->
        nl,
        write('You already have a question about '),
        write(Thing), nl,
        write('Duplicate question scrapped.'), nl
    ;   assertz(Question finds Thing),
        question_line_count(Question, N),
        assertz(question_lines(Thing, N))
    ),
    !.
loadprocess(Thing is single_valued) :-
```

```
            assertz(single_valued(Thing)),
            !.
    loadprocess(RuleTag: if Premise then Conclusion) :-
        ( already_used(RuleTag) ->
            nl,
            write('The rule tag '), write(RuleTag),
            write(' is already in use. '),
            write('Duplicate rule scrapped.'), nl
        ;   dismantle(premise, RuleTag, Premise,
                        [], PremiseList),
            dismantle(conclusion, RuleTag, Conclusion,
                        PremiseList, CombinedList),
            assert_clauses(CombinedList),
            find_expected_value_links(CombinedList,
                                        LinkList),
                % given a list of rulebit/5 terms from this
                % rule, look for values that are variables;
                % these 'link together' sets of expected
                % values for different THINGs. The
                % information will be needed by
                % massage_data/0 when it tries to find out
                % what the complete set of expected values
                % of any THING is.
            assert_expected_value_links(LinkList),
                % Just assert that information for the moment.
            assertz(RuleTag: if Premise then Conclusion)
        ),
        !.
    loadprocess(Random) :-              % If we have not dealt
        nl,                             % with it by now, it
        write('Ignoring this item: '), % must be junk! But
        writeq(Random), nl.             % we'd better say so

    question_line_count(Q, N) :-        % Given a Question
        name(Q, QL),                    % atom, count the
        count_up_nls(QL, N).            % newlines in it

count_up_nls([], 1).
count_up_nls([10|More], Nplus1) :- % 10 is ASCII newline
    count_up_nls(More, N),
    Nplus1 is N+1,
    !.
count_up_nls([_|More], N) :-
    count_up_nls(More, N).
```

```
already_questioned(Thing) :-
    _ finds Thing.

already_used(Tag) :-
    rulebit(_, Tag, _, _, _).
```

Figure 6.5 The basics of the rule loader.

When a single rule is dismantled, a list of `rulebit/5` terms is built up for use by `find_expected_value_links/2`. The various terms could also be asserted at the same time; but it looks slightly neater to pass the list to another predicate, `assert_clauses/1`, to do the assertions, even though this is somewhat less efficient because it means that the list is traversed an unnecessary extra time. Figure 6.6 shows how this is done. At this stage, it is also necessary to gather some information about which THINGs have a variable as value, for use in deciding what the possible values for any named THING are. Here is the example mentioned earlier:

```
rule49: if   colour of wall is unknown
        and  preferred_colour of wall = X
        then colour of wall = X cf 25.
```

At the stage of processing this rule, the best that can be done is to assert a unit clause of the form

```
link_list([link(premise, preferred_colour of wall),
          link(conclusion, colour of wall)]).
```

Remember, users can, if they wish, put the question data after all the rules, and so it is impossible to tell reliably whether any such THINGs are to be askable of the user until the end of the whole loading. However, because CRESS is a backward-chaining system, only those THINGs that appear in some rule's premise are even potentially askable; therefore it is useful to make the distinction at this stage. The entire set of `link_list/1` clauses will be processed after the actual loading has been completed.

```
% dismantle/5: the first argument is 'premise' or
%   'conclusion'. Second is the rule tag. Third is
%   the premise or conclusion to be dismantled.
%   The last two are an accumulator/result pair
%   used to build a list of the rulebit/5 terms
```

```
dismantle(Part, Tag, A and B, SoFar, Ans) :-
    !,
    dismantle(Part, Tag, A, SoFar, Further),
    dismantle(Part, Tag, B, Further, Ans).
dismantle(Part, Tag, A or B, SoFar, Ans) :-
    !,
    dismantle(Part, Tag, A, SoFar, Further),
    dismantle(Part, Tag, B, Further, Ans).
dismantle(Part, Tag, A cf CF, SoFar, Ans) :-
    !,
    dismantle(Part, Tag, A, SoFar, Ans).
dismantle(Part, Tag, not(A), SoFar, Ans) :-
    !,
    dismantle(Part, Tag, A, SoFar, Ans).
dismantle(Part, Tag, Thing = Value, SoFar,
    [rulebit(Part, Tag, Thing, equals, Value)|SoFar]).
dismantle(Part, Tag, Thing is Something, SoFar,
    [rulebit(Part, Tag, Thing, is, Something)|SoFar]).
dismantle(Part, Tag, Thing > Value, SoFar,
    [rulebit(Part, Tag, Thing, greater, Value)|SoFar]).
dismantle(Part, Tag, Thing < Value, SoFar,
    [rulebit(Part, Tag, Thing, less, Value)|SoFar]).
dismantle(Part, Tag, prolog(Goal), SoFar, SoFar).

% assert_clauses/1 asserts a list of unit clauses
assert_clauses([]).
assert_clauses([H|T]) :-
    assert(H),
    assert_clauses(T).

% find_expected_value_links/2: given a list of rulebit/5
%    terms from the current rule, find those values that
%    are variables. For each such variable, build a list
%    of terms of the form
%        link(Part, Thing)
%    (where Part is 'premise' or 'conclusion') so we know
%    which THINGs are going to share 'expected values'.
%    As usual, use an accumulator when recursing through
%    the list of rulebit/5 terms
find_expected_value_links(List, LinkList) :-
    find_expected_value_links(List, [], LinkList).

find_expected_value_links([], A, A).
find_expected_value_links(
        [rulebit(Part,_,Thing,_,Value)|Rest], SoFar, A):-
```

```
     ( nonvar(Value)             % If Value is not a variable,
     ; val_member(Value, SoFar)  % or if we've seen
     ),                          % it already, then we do not
     !,                          % care about it. Do the Rest.
     find_expected_value_links(Rest, SoFar, A).
get_expected_value_links(
        [rulebit(Part,_,Thing,_,Value)|Rest], SoFar, A):-
     var(Value),                 % Otherwise this is the first
     !,                          % appearance. Handle it now!
     gather_var_occurrences(Value, Rest, List),
     get_expected_value_links(Rest,
        [val(Value, [link(Part,Thing)|List])|SoFar], A).

% val_member/2 is somewhat like member/2; used when
%    checking whether we have seen a particular variable
%    as a value in the current rule already.
val_member(Var, [val(Var2, _)|_]) :-
     Var == Var2.
val_member(Var, [_|T]) :-
     val_member(Var, T).

% gather_var_occurrences/3: called when we first use a
%    certain variable as a value, in the current rule,
%    for the first time. Collect up data about all
%    occurrences in the rule.
gather_var_occurrences(Var, [rulebit(P,_,T,_,Var2)|More],
                            [link(P,T)|Rest]) :-
     Var == Var2,
     !,
     gather_var_occurrences(Var, More, Rest).
gather_var_occurrences(Var, [_|More], List) :-
     gather_var_occurrences(Var, More, List).
gather_var_occurrences(_, [], []).

% assert_expected_value_links/1 is regrettably similar to
%    assert_clauses/1 above, but why struggle for too
%    much parsimony?
assert_expected_value_links([]).
assert_expected_value_links([val(_,List)|Rest]) :-
     assert(link_list(List)),
     assert_expected_value_links(Rest).
```

Figure 6.6   Dismantling a single rule and processing the parts.

When the actual loading has been completed, it is possible to collect up some global data. The predicate `massage_data/0` in Figure 6.7 does this job. It makes extensive use of `setof/3` to do so.

```prolog
massage_data :-
    ( setof(T1,A^B^C^D^rulebit(A,B,T1,C,D),AllThings) ->
        true
    ;   AllThings = []
    ),
    analyse_usage_of_things(AllThings, PremiseThings,
                                      ConcludeThings),
    ( setof(T2, E^ (E finds T2), AskableThings) ->
        true
    ;   AskableThings = []
    ),
    assert(premise_things(PremiseThings)),
    assert(conclude_things(ConcludeThings)),
    assert(askable_things(AskableThings)),
    assert(list_of_things(AllThings)),
    build_rules_to_find_clauses(ConcludeThings),
    build_rules_that_use_clauses(PremiseThings),
    build_linkage_clauses,
    build_expected_values_clauses(PremiseThings).

% analyse_usage_of_things/3: given a list of all the
%    known THINGs, find out which occur in premises
%    and which in conclusions. Some appear in both,
%    of course.
analyse_usage_of_things([Thing|More], Ps, Cs) :-
    ( rulebit(premise,_,Thing,_,_) ->
        Ps = [Thing|OtherPs]
    ;   Ps = OtherPs
    ),
    ( rulebit(conclusion,_,Thing,_,_) ->
        Cs = [Thing|OtherCs]
    ;   Cs = OtherCs
    ),
    analyse_usage_of_things(More, OtherPs, OtherCs).
analyse_usage_of_things([], [], []).

% build_rules_to_find_clauses/1: given a list of THINGs
%    that appear in some conclusion, for each one
```

```
%    construct and assert a rules_to_find/2 unit clause.
build_rules_to_find_clauses([]).
build_rules_to_find_clauses([Thing|Things]) :-
    rules_to_find_thing(Thing),
    build_rules_to_find_clauses(Things).

rules_to_find_thing(Thing) :-
    % use bagof, not setof - we do not want a sorted
    %    list, we want the rule tags in order of
    %    appearance:
    bagof(Tag, A^B^rulebit(conclusion,Tag,Thing,A,B),
                                                    List),
    remove_duplicates(List, CleanList),
    assert(rules_to_find(Thing, CleanList)).

% build_rules_that_use_clauses/1: given a list of THINGS
%    that appear in some premise, for each one construct
%    and assert a rules_that_use/2 unit clause.
build_rules_that_use_clauses([]).
build_rules_that_use_clauses([Thing|Things]) :-
    rules_that_use_thing(Thing),
    build_rules_that_use_clauses(Things).

rules_that_use_thing(Thing) :-
    % use bagof, not setof - we do not want a sorted
    %    list, we want the rule tags in order of
    %    appearance:
    bagof(Tag, A^B^rulebit(premise,Tag,Thing,A,B), List),
    remove_duplicates(List, CleanList),
    assert(rules_that_use(Thing, CleanList)).

% remove_duplicates/2: given any list, remove duplicates,
%    but otherwise preserve the original ordering
remove_duplicates([], []).
remove_duplicates([H|T], Answer) :-
    remove_duplicates(T, L),
    ( member(H, L) ->
        Answer = L
    ;    Answer = [H|L]
    ).

% build_expected_values_clauses/1: given the list of
%    THINGS that appear in some premise, for each one
%    construct and assert a unit clause of the form
%        expected_values(THING, ListOfValues).
```

```
%    These values are just those suggested by the rules,
%    nothing mandatory about it.
build_expected_values_clauses([]).
build_expected_values_clauses([Thing|Things]) :-
    assert_expected_values_for_thing(Thing),
    build_expected_values_clauses(Things).

assert_expected_values_for_thing(Thing) :-
    get_expected_values_for_thing([Thing], [], [],
                                          UnSortedList),
    sort(UnSortedList, List),
    assert(expected_values(Thing, List)).

% build_linkage_clauses/0: for every THING related to a
%    variable value in some premise, find those THINGs in
%    the corresponding conclusion. Collect up the set of
%    all THINGs in such a conclusion. Assert a link/2
%    unit clause for each such premise THING.
build_linkage_clauses :-
    setof(T,
          L^( link_list(L),
              member(link(premise,T),L)
            ),
          TList),
    setof(link(T,CL),
          ( member(T,TList),
            setof(C,
                  M^(`link_list(M),
                     member(link(premise,T),M),
                     member(link(conclusion, C),M)
                    ),
                  CL)
          ),
          ListOfLinkStructures),
    assert_clauses(ListOfLinkStructures),
    !.
build_linkage_clauses.

% get_expected_values_for_thing/4: when FIRST called,
%    the first argument is a list of one element, the
%    original THING whose expected values we are
%    pursuing. It may turn out that we have - because
%    of variables as values - to consider the expected
%    values of many other THINGs. In that case, those
%    THINGs get added to the list. The second argument
```

```
%    records which THINGs were dealt with by some parent
%    call: we do not want to get into an infinite loop.
%    The third and fourth arguments are a conventional
%    accumulator-result pair.
get_expected_values_for_thing([Thing|More],
                              AlreadyChased,
                              SoFar,
                              FinalList) :-
    not(member(Thing, AlreadyChased)),
    !,                          % Not yet processed it?
    ( setof(possible(B,C),      % First, find possibles...
            A^(rulebit(premise,A,Thing,B,C),
               nonvar(C)
              ),
            L) ->
       append(L, SoFar, Further) % add to result so far.
    ; Further = SoFar,          % Maybe setof/3 failed
    ),
    ( link(Thing, OtherThings) -> % Maybe other things?
       append(More, OtherThings, YetMore)
    ;   YetMore = More          % Or maybe not?
    ),
    get_expected_values_for_thing(YetMore,
                                  [Thing|AlreadyChased],
                                  Further,
                                  FinalList).
get_expected_values_for_thing([_|More],
                              Chased, SoFar, Result) :-
    % Use this clause if we've already chased values of
    % the first THING in the list.
    get_expected_values_for_thing(More,
                                  Chased, SoFar, Result).
get_expected_values_for_thing([],
                              _, FinalList, FinalList).
```

Figure 6.7   Preparing global data after loading.

The results can be used to make rudimentary checks on the knowledge base. The user can choose to ask for such checks to be made. Figure 6.8 shows a very simple form of this. You may wish to enlarge this to include some further checks, as suggested by the following exercises.

```
vet :-
  premise_things(PremiseThings),
  conclude_things(ConcludeThings),
  askable_things(AskableThings),
  setdiff(AskableThings, PremiseThings, AskedButNotUsed),
  setdiff(PremiseThings, ConcludeThings, ShouldBeAsked),
  setdiff(ShouldBeAsked, AskableThings,ShouldAskButDont),
  setdiff(ConcludeThings, PremiseThings, TopLevelThings),
  ( TopLevelThings = [] ->
        write('There seems to be no top-level THING'), nl
  ;    write('These seem to be top-level THINGs:'),
        nl,
        showlist(8, TopLevelThings)
  ),
  ( AskedButNotUsed = [] ->
        true
  ;    write('These THINGs are askable but not used:'),
        nl,
        showlist(8, AskedButNotUsed)
  ),
  ( ShouldAskButDont = [] ->
        true
  ;    write('These things should be askable '),
        write('but are not:'), nl,
        showlist(8, ShouldAskButDont)
  ).

% setdiff/3:given two lists, build a list of those in
%   the first but not the second
setdiff([], _, []).
setdiff([H|Rest], L, Tail) :-
    member(H,L),
    !,
    setdiff(Rest,L,Tail).
setdiff([H|Rest], L, [H|Tail]) :-
    setdiff(Rest, L, Tail).
```

Figure 6.8   A simple check of the knowledge base.

Exercise 6.1   Add a test of whether the premise of one rule is wholly subsumed by another, for example:

```
rule60: if today = tuesday
        then action = teaching.
 . . . .
rule81: if today = monday
        or today = tuesday
        then action = teaching.
```

Exercise 6.2   Add a test of whether a rule can be folded into another because its conclusion is used only once, in the premise of a single other rule.

Exercise 6.3   Add a test of whether two rules directly conflict, because the premise of one subsumes the premise of the other but the conclusions conflict. This is a difficult case to detect: there are times when you might want to regard this as a feature rather than a flaw of a knowledge base.

Many other improvements should occur to you.

6.3.4   Handling the user's input

Suppose that a knowledge base has been loaded and some consultation is in progress. CRESS must sometimes ask the user for the value(s) of a given THING. The predicate that does this must decide exactly where to put the question and the set of expected answers on the screen, and return the user's reply. It must also be capable of returning a term that corresponds to a user's command rather than to any legitimate answer to the question. A convenient way to do this is to employ the definite-clause grammar mechanism.

6.3.5   About definite-clause grammars

A definite-clause grammar (DCG) is used to parse the list of words input by the user and to build a suitable Prolog term describing the essence of the input. For example, if the input is

```
show price of apples
```

then the DCG returns the term

```
show(price of apples)
```

This subsection provides a brief account of DCGs, and can be skipped if you are already familiar with them. Definite-clause grammars were first introduced into Prolog by Pereira and Warren [1980] building on a simplification of an earlier grammatical formalism, metamorphosis grammars, due to Colmerauer [1975]. They are so useful for parsing tasks that the appropriate support for them is provided as standard in any reasonable Prolog, and many people use Prolog solely for the sake of using the DCG features.

The DCG mechanism in Prolog is just a syntactic convenience, a way to write certain kinds of Prolog clauses without having to specify all the details. It concerns unit clauses whose principal functor is -->/2. When such a clause is read in by the system, it applies some standard transformations to it in order to get the actual form of clause to assert. This is done as part of a much more general mechanism, in fact: the term expansion process when clauses are being loaded. All terms read into Prolog as part of loading are first passed to a built-in predicate `expand_term/2`, which tries to call a user-defined predicate `term_expansion/2` to make any necessary changes before asserting the clause. If there is such a predicate and it succeeds, that is the end of the matter. Otherwise it checks to see if the term has principal functor -->/2, in which case it applies the DCG transformations. All other terms are returned unmodified, to be asserted. Thus `expand_term/2` might look like this:

```
expand_term(UserClause, ModifiedClause) :-
    term_expansion(UserClause, ModifiedClause),
    !.
expand_term((LHS --> RHS), ModifiedClause) :-
    !,
    .... do DCG transformations ....
expand_term(UserClause, UserClause).
```

The main job of the DCG transformations is as follows. A term such as

```
alpha(X) --> beta, gamma(X), delta
```

is transformed to

```
alpha(X, Input, Remains) :-
    beta(Input, RemainsFromBeta),
    gamma(X, RemainsFromBeta, RemainsFromGamma),
    delta(RemainsFromGamma, Remains).
```

that is, an extra two arguments are added to each term on each side of the -->. As the naming of variables suggests here, the first of these extra arguments is meant to be an input of some kind, usually a list, and the second is meant to be instantiated in due course to whatever remains of the input after some initial part of the input has been 'recognized' by the predicate concerned. The disjunct operator ;/2 and the cut can appear on the right-hand side of the --> and are unaffected by the transformation. Indeed, any sequence of goals enclosed by curly brackets is passed through unmodified. A list can appear on the right-hand side too; it does get modified. For example, the list

    [why,not]

is translated to

    'C'(X,why,Y), 'C'(Y,not,Z)

where 'C'/3 is defined as though by the single unit clause

    'C'([Word|Rest], Word, Rest).

Its job is to 'recognize' a single atom of input; the input list is the first argument here, merely for historical reasons.

Thus the definite-clause grammar

```
command(X) -->
    single_word_question(X).
. . . .
single_word(user_is_perplexed) -->
    ([what] ; [eh] ; [pardon]),
    optional_question_mark.
. . . .
optional_question_mark -->
    [?].
optional_question_mark -->
    [].
```

can be used as follows. Remember, the first grammar rule here is really a clause for command/3 rather than some command/1, so if you have clauses for command/3 expressed in full rather than in DCG form, you are likely to obtain interesting effects. The question

    ?- command(Analysis, [pardon,?,i,am,puzzled], Rest).

will succeed with Analysis instantiated to user_is_perplexed and Rest instantiated to

    [i,am,puzzled]

Very often, the third argument is constrained in the call to be an empty list, thus forcing the grammar to try to recognize the whole of the input.

There are several other useful features of DCG notation but these will not be covered in this book. The reference manual for your system should describe them. An excellent account of the use of DCGs for language analysis, together with many examples, can be found in Pereira and Sheiber

[1987]. An example of the use of DCGs in the analysis of gene sequences in DNA can be found in Searls [1988].

Figure 6.9, below, shows how the user's input can be handled by making use of a DCG. The predicate `enquire_about/2` is the entry point, although `get_valid_answer/2` was also used in CRESS's top-level loop, in Figure 6.4. The only missing ingredient is the predicate `sentence/2`, which will depend heavily on your own Prolog and the operating system. The job of `sentence/2` is to return a list of words typed in by the user, and also the original list of ASCII codes. The ASCII codes are needed only if the very first character happens to be a question mark, in which case the rest of the line is presumed to be an arbitrary operating system command, to be called by `system_command/1`. It is assumed that this built-in predicate expects a list of ASCII codes. Multiple spaces in the original input might be significant if it is an operating system command, and so `sentence/2` must provide that original input as well as the transformed version.

Many operating systems provide some kind of input-line processing, so that the Prolog program does not have to handle any kind of character deletion, for example. Some small systems, such as MS-DOS, do not do this – for such a system, `get0/1` might just return the ASCII code 8 when the 'rubout' key is pressed. The appropriate definition of `sentence/2` is therefore left as an exercise.

```
% enquire_about/2: Thing is a thing to be asked of
%     the user, Value gets instantiated to the value(s)
%     given by the user (e.g. red cf 30 and blue cf 45).
%     This causes the screen to be cleared, the question
%     plus a list of 'expected' values to be displayed,
%     approx centred vertically on the screen. All
%     temporizing replies such as 'help', 'show ...' etc.
%     are also acceptable replies. The caller of
%     enquire_about/2 will be responsible for handling
%     such replies and calling it again to get the
%     value(s) needed for Thing. NOTE: The user is not
%     confined to the 'expected' values.

enquire_about(Thing, Value) :-
        Question finds Thing,
        question_lines(Thing, N),
        expected_values(Thing, List),
        choose(List, yes, Question, N, Value).

% choose/5:
```

```
%     +List gives a list of 'expected' values to display
%     +MentionRuleBase is 'yes' or 'no'; if 'yes' then the
%         display makes reference to these values being
%         in the rules
%     +Question: an atom giving the question to ask
%     +N: the number of lines the question takes to print
%         (could be calculated here, but why bother wasting
%         run time?)
%     -Value: the user's answer, perhaps after various
%         other inputs such as 'help'

choose(List, MentionRuleBase, Question, N, Value) :-
    clear_screen,
        length(List, Length),
    Needed is N+Length+2,
        ( Needed > 20 ->
        true         .
    ; Gap is (23 - Needed)//2,
      nls(Gap)
    ),
    tab(4), write(Question), write('?'), nl,
    ( MentionRuleBase = yes ->
        tab(4),
        write('The rule base suggests these answers:'),
        nl
    ;   true     .
    ),
    ( Needed > 20 ->
        N1 is N+1,
        show_two_col_values(List,8,79,N1,20,8,N1),
        ( watching ->
            true
        ;    go_to_xy(4, 21)
        )
    ;   show_values(8, List),
        tab(4)
    ),
    ( MentionRuleBase = yes ->
        write('Choice (help, or any answer): ')
    ;   write('Choice: ')
    ),
    ttyflush,
    get_choice(Value).

% nls/1: print the given number of <nl> characters
```

```
nls(0).
nls(N) :-
    N > 0,
    nl,
    NMinusOne is N-1,
    nls(NMinusOne).


% get_choice/1: get the Answer from the user. Exclude
%    from the set of acceptable replies those commands
%    that only apply at the top level.
get_choice(Answer) :-
    get_valid_answer(Answer,
                [save(_),reload(_),load(_),find(_),vet]).


% show_two_col_values/7: given a list, and min/max X and
%    Y, print out the list in two columns in that region,
%    maybe breaking into pages if the list is too long
show_two_col_values([], _, _, _, _, _, _) :-
    !.
show_two_col_values(L, Xmin, Xmax, Ymin, Ymax, X, Y) :-
    Y > Ymax,
    X > Xmin,
    !,
    await_return,
    clear_screen,
    write('Display continued:'), nl,
    show_two_col_values(L,Xmin,Xmax,Ymin,Ymax,Xmin,Ymin).
show_two_col_values(L,Xmin,Xmax,Ymin,Ymax,X,Y) :-
    Y > Ymax,
    !,
    Xmid is (Xmin + Xmax + 1)//2,
    show_two_col_values(L,Xmin,Xmax,Ymin,Ymax,Xmid,Ymin).
show_two_col_values([H|T],Xmin,Xmax,Ymin,Ymax,X,Y) :-
    ( watching ->
        true
    ;   go_to_xy(X,Y)
    ),
    show_relation_and_value(0, H),
    Ynext is Y + 1,
    show_two_col_values(T,Xmin,Xmax,Ymin,Ymax,X,Ynext).


show_values(_, []).
show_values(N, [H|More]) :-
    show_relation_and_value(N, H),
```

```
    show_values(N, More).

show_relation_and_value(N, possible(Relation, Value)) :-
    !,
    ( Relation = equals ->
        tab(N), write('= '), write(Value), nl
    ; Relation = greater ->
        tab(N), write('> '), write(Value), nl
    ; Relation = less ->
        tab(N), write('< '), write(Value), nl
    ; true
    ).
show_relation_and_value(N, Value) :-
    tab(N), write(Value), nl.


% get_valid_answer/2:
%    -Answer: to be instantiated to the user's answer
%    +Exceptions: exclude any of the elements of this
%        list, an irrelevant subset of the 'special'
%        temporizing answers
% YOU MUST SUPPLY sentence/2, WHICH ACTUALLY READS IN
% A LIST OF WORDS - see, for example, Chapter 4
get_valid_answer(Answer, Exceptions) :-
    sentence(Input, CharList),     % YOU SUPPLY THIS
    ( CharList = [33|Tail] ->      % 33 = ASCII for '!'
        Answer = system_command(Tail)
    ; (parse_input(PossAnswer, Input, []),
      not(member(PossAnswer, Exceptions))) ->
        Answer = PossAnswer
    ; tab(4),
      write('Didn''t understand that.'),
      write(' Try again (e.g. help): '),
      ttyflush,
      get_valid_answer(Answer, Exceptions)
    ).


% The following DCG parses the list of words input by
%    the user and returns a corresponding Prolog term.
parse_input(A) -->
    es_command(A).          % Was it a CRESS command?
parse_input(A) -->
    values(A).
values(A) -->
    single_item_input(A).   % Was it a value? with CF?
values(A and B) -->
```

```
        single_item_input(A),    % A conjunction of values,
        [and],                   % maybe each with a CF?
        parse_input(B).

    single_item_input(A) -->     % A single value can be
        get_of_struct(A).        % X of Y of Z of ...
    single_item_input(A cf B) -->
        get_of_struct(A),        % or maybe there's a CF too.
        [cf],
        get_number(B).


    get_of_struct(A) -->
        one_word(A).             % Could be just a single word
    get_of_struct(A of B) -->
        one_word(A),             % or of the form '..of..of..'
        [of],
        get_of_struct(B).


    get_number(N) -->            % When getting the attached CF,
        [M],                     % check it's in range.
        { number(M),
          ( M > 100 ->
            write(M),
            write(' is too big a cf. I''ll assume 100.'), nl,
            N = 100
          ;      N = M
          )
        }.


    one_word(A) -->
        [A].


    es_command(why) -->          % All the valid commands:
        [why] ; [why, '?'] ; ['?'].
    es_command(help) -->
        [help].
    es_command(show(X)) -->
        [show],
        get_of_struct(X).
    es_command(apropos(X)) -->
        [apropos],
        get_of_struct(X).
    es_command(things) -->
        [things].
    es_command(reload(X)) -->
```

```
    [reload],
    one_word(X).
es_command(load(X)) -->
    [load],
    one_word(X).
es_command(save(X)) -->
    [save],
    one_word(X).
es_command(find(X)) -->
    [find],
    get_of_struct(X).
```

Figure 6.9   Asking a question.

6.3.6   The consultation mechanism

A consultation is started by a command to find the value(s) for a given
THING. The backward-chaining process finds those values; as they are
found, they are noted by using the built-in predicate `recorda/3`. This
brings the useful bonus, for teaching purposes at least, that the conclusions
persist after the end of the consultation. Thus it is possible to build a
post-processor along the lines of TEIRESIAS (see Buchanan and Shortliffe
[1984] for the details) that takes an unsuccessful consultation to pieces,
backwards, in order to make appropriate changes to the rule set so as to
produce an acceptable result. One such post-processor for CRESS has
been constructed as part of a master's degree project; the source code was
roughly three times as large as that of CRESS.

Recorded values are stored under the uninformative key `datum`. Since
a recording key has to be atomic, and since there is no one-to-one mapping
from THINGs to atoms, there is no easy way to exploit the recording keys
for the sake of efficiency in this simple system. Your own Prolog may
provide more elaborate facilities for term storage.

A call of `investigate/6` starts the backward chaining. The data
needed during backward chaining are:

- The THING whose values are currently being sought.

- An 'agenda' of those other THINGs that are also in course of being
  sought, and that led to the need to find values for the current THING.
  This 'agenda' takes the form of a list of terms of the form

```
SomeTHING => ListOfRuleTagsOfRulesThatConcludeIt
```

- A 'trail' of all the THINGs that are being sought or that CRESS has already finished seeking values for. This takes the form of a list of THINGs.

- A 'history list' of all that has happened so far. The user can examine its current state either during or at the end of a consultation.

In fact, the 'trail' could be resurrected from the 'history list', but it makes the program somewhat clearer and faster to have both available explicitly.

Figure 6.10 shows the top level of the consultation mechanism. The essence of it is that `find/1` calls `investigate/6` to find the values of a THING. If backward chaining is needed, the predicate `investigate/6` calls `process_set/6` to try all the rules that can conclude a value for the THING. In turn, `process_set/6` calls `consider_rule/6` for each rule. This uses `establish/8` to try to establish the truth of the premise of the rule; this may involve backward chaining by calling `investigate/6` to find values for any THING in the premise.

```
% find/1: find the values of a given Thing,
%     report them to the user at the end of the
%     consultation, finally give him or her a chance
%     to see the complete history list beautifully
%     laid out and paginated.
find(Thing) :-
    clobber_any_old_recordings(datum),
    investigate(Thing, [], [], _, [], FinalHistory),
        % At this point, the consultation is complete;
        % now show the user the results
    show(Thing, FinalHistory),
    choose([possible(equals,no), possible(equals,yes)],
            no,
            'Do you want to see the final history list',
            1,
            YesNo),
    ( YesNo = yes ->
        show_history(FinalHistory)
    ;   true
    ).


% clobber_any_old_recordings/1: eliminates old data
clobber_any_old_recordings(Key) :-
    recorded(Key, _, Ref),
    erase(Ref),
```

```
        fail.
clobber_any_old_recordings(_).

% investigate/6: the arguments are
%     +Thing: try to find all values for this Thing,
%         by asking or by backward chaining (not both)
%     +Agenda: a record of all the other THINGs that
%         are CURRENTLY being investigated, and the
%         rules that are as yet untried for each of them
%     +Trail: a list of all those THINGs currently
%         being investigated or that had been so earlier
%         in the consultation
%     -FinalTrail: a variable to be instantiated to a
%         list of things investigated when this call
%         finally succeeds
%     +History: the 'history list' so far
%     -FinalHistory: the updated 'history list'
% Note the last (unit) clause, in case the user provides
% neither rules nor questions about some Thing. In this
% case investigate/6 just succeeds; a parent goal will
% handle the fact that nothing is known about Thing.

investigate(Thing, Agenda, Trail, Trail, History,
                           [Thing=>lookup|History]) :-
    member(Thing, Trail), % if known, it can be looked up
    !.
investigate(Thing, Agenda,
        Trail, [Thing|Trail],
        History, [Thing=>user|History]) :-
    get_data_from_user(Thing, Agenda, History, Answer),
    stash(Thing = Answer, 100, 'you told me'),
    !.
investigate(Thing, Agenda, Trail, FinalTrail, History,
                                   FinalHistory) :-
    rules_to_find(Thing, ThingRules),
    process_set(ThingRules, [Thing=>ThingRules|Agenda],
            [Thing|Trail], FinalTrail,
            History, FinalHistory),
    !.
investigate(_, _, Trail, Trail, History, History).

% get_data_from_user/4: handles the question-asking
%     process completely. The agenda and history record
%     are passed as arguments in case the user gives
%     various commands before finally answering the
```

```
%       question
get_data_from_user(Thing,Agenda,History,FinalAnswer) :-
    enquire_about(Thing, Answer),
    ( Answer = why ->
        why(Agenda),
        get_data_from_user(Thing, Agenda, History,
                                           FinalAnswer)
    ; Answer = help ->
        help,
        get_data_from_user(Thing, Agenda, History,
                                           FinalAnswer)
    ; Answer = show(Something) ->
        show(Something, History),
        get_data_from_user(Thing, Agenda, History,
                                           FinalAnswer)
    ; Answer = history of Something ->
        show_history(Something, History),
        get_data_from_user(Thing, Agenda, History,
                                           FinalAnswer)
    ; Answer = history ->
        show_history(History),
        get_data_from_user(Thing, Agenda, History,
                                           FinalAnswer)
    ; Answer = things ->
        things,
        get_data_from_user(Thing, Agenda, History,
                                           FinalAnswer)
    ; Answer = apropos(Something) ->
        apropos(Something),
        get_data_from_user(Thing, Agenda, History,
                                           FinalAnswer)
    ; Answer = system_command(CharList) ->
        clear_screen,
        do_without_fail(system_command(CharList)),
        await_return,
        get_data_from_user(Thing, Agenda, History,
                                           FinalAnswer)
    ; Answer = quit ->
        halt
    ;       FinalAnswer = Answer
    ).


% process_set/6: works through the given list of rules,
%    adding to the trail and history lists on the way
%    and returning the updated versions of these lists.
```

```
%      This is where we check whether a Thing is single-
%      valued; if it is, and a value has been concluded
%      for it (we test by looking for 'Rule => s' at the
%      front of the history list, which is a cheaper test
%      than looking for any recorded data about Thing),
%      then abandon the other rules  that could conclude
%      a value for it.
process_set([],_,T,T,H,H).
process_set([Rule|More], [T=>[Rule|More]|Rest],
               Trail, FinalTrail,
               History, FinalHistory) :-
     consider_rule(Rule, [T=>[Rule|More]|Rest],
                   Trail, MidTrail,
                   [T=>Rule|History], MoreH),
     ( (single_valued(T), MoreH = [Rule=>s|_]) ->
          FinalTrail = MidTrail,
          FinalHistory = MoreH
     ;    process_set(More, [T=>More|Rest],
                      MidTrail, FinalTrail,
                      MoreH, FinalHistory)
     ).


% consider_rule/6: this is responsible for trying to
%      'execute' one backward-chaining step, by 'proving'
%      that a given rule's preconditions actually hold.
%      This may involve calling investigate/6 for any
%      THING in the premise.
consider_rule(Rule, Agenda,
                 Trail, NewTrail, History, Final) :-
     Rule : if Premise then Conclusion,
     establish(Rule, Premise, CF, Agenda,
               Trail, NewTrail, History, MidH),
     ( CF =< 20,
       Final = [Rule=>f|MidH]
     ; stash(Conclusion, CF, Rule),
       Final = [Rule=>s|MidH]
     ).
```

Figure 6.10   The rule interpreter, part 1.

The predicate establish/8 in Figure 6.11 below tries to establish that a rule's premise holds with a CF greater than 20. The first three arguments are:

- +RuleTag: the rule's tag, needed when information is added to the history list, such as RuleTag => s, to show it succeeded.

- +Premise: the rule's premise. This is clearly not essential – if the tag is known, then the premise can be found by matching rather than being passed as an argument. However, the predicate that called establish/8 needs to get hold of the conclusion, and so the premise will also be available at that level. It is therefore cheaper to pass it as an argument rather than to get hold of it again by matching.

- -CF: a variable to be instantiated to the final, combined CF of the whole premise.

The other five arguments are the current agenda, the current trail and a variable to be instantiated to the updated trail, the current history list and a variable to be instantiated to the updated history list. These are needed each time establish/8 calls investigate/6.

```
establish(R, This or That, CF, Agenda,
        Trail, NewTrail, History, Final) :-
    establish(R, This, CF1, Agenda,
            Trail, MidTrail, History, MoreH),
    ( CF1 = 100 ->
        CF = 100,
        NewTrail = MidTrail,
        Final = MoreH
    ;   establish(R, That, CF2, Agenda,
                MidTrail, NewTrail, MoreH, Final),
        max(CF1, CF2, CF)
    ).
establish(R, This and That, CF, Agenda,
        Trail, NewTrail, History, Final) :-
    establish(R, This, CF1, Agenda,
            Trail, MidTrail, History, MoreH),
    ( CF1 =< 20 ->
        CF = CF1,
        NewTrail = MidTrail,
        Final = MoreH
    ;   establish(R, That, CF2, Agenda,
                MidTrail, NewTrail, MoreH, Final),
        min(CF1, CF2, CF)
    ).
establish(R, Something = Value, CF, Agenda,
        Trail, NewTrail, History, Final) :-
```

```
        investigate(Something, Agenda,
                    Trail, NewTrail, History, MidH),
        ( recorded(datum,
                    datum(Something,Something=Value,CF,_),
                    _),
          Final = [Something => s/R|MidH]
        ; CF = 0,
          Final = [Something => f/R|MidH]
        ).
    establish(R, Something < Value, CF, Agenda,
              Trail, NewTrail, History, Final) :-
        investigate(Something, Agenda,
                    Trail, NewTrail, History, MidH),
        ( recorded(datum,
                    datum(Something,Something=OtherV,CF,_),
                    _),
          number(OtherV),
          OtherV < Value,
          Final = [Something => s/R|MidH]
        ; recorded(datum,
                    datum(Something,Something < OtherV,CF,_),
                    _),
          OtherV =< Value,
          Final = [Something => s/R|MidH]
        ; CF = 0,
          Final = [Something => f/R|MidH]
        ).
    establish(R, Something > Value, CF, Agenda,
              Trail, NewTrail, History, Final) :-
        investigate(Something, Agenda,
                    Trail, NewTrail, History, MidH),
        ( recorded(datum,
                    datum(Something,Something=OtherV,CF,_),
                    _),
          number(OtherV),
          OtherV > Value,
          Final = [Something => s/R|MidH]
        ; recorded(datum,
                    datum(Something,Something > OtherV,CF,_),
                    _),
          OtherV >= Value,
          Final = [Something => s/R|MidH]
        ; CF = 0,
          Final = [Something => f/R|MidH]
        ).
```

```
establish(R, Something is State, CF, Agenda,
        Trail, NewTrail, History, Final) :-
  ( State = investigated ->
      ( member(Something, Trail) ->
          CF = 100, S = s
      ;   CF = 0,   S = f
      ),
      NewTrail = Trail,
      Final = [Something => S/R|History]
  ;   investigate(Something, Agenda,
                  Trail, NewTrail, History, MidH),
      ( State = askable ->
          ( _ finds Something ->
              CF = 100, S = s
          ;   CF = 0,   S = f
          )
      ; discovered(Something) ->
          ( State = known ->
              CF = 100, S = s
          ;   CF = 0,   S = f
          )
      ;   ( State = unknown ->
              CF = 100, S = s
          ;   CF = 0,   S = f
          )
      ),
      Final = [Something => S/R|MidH]
  ).
establish(R, prolog(Goal), CF, Agenda,
        Trail, Trail, History,
        [prolog(Goal)/R|History]) :-
  ( call(Goal) ->
      CF = 100
  ;   CF = 0
  ).


% discovered/1: tests whether anything at all has been
%     concluded about a THING. This could be a cheaper
%     test than looking for a 'RuleTag => s' entry on the
%     history list, if THING is not single-valued, because
%     there could be many 'RuleTag => f' entries to wade
%     through first.
discovered(Thing) :-
    recorded(datum, datum(Thing, _, _, _), _).
```

```
% max/3 and min/3 find the max and min of two numbers.
%     Would be cheaper but more obscure to have a single
%     predicate maxmin/4 instead, of course
max(A, B, A) :- A >= B.
max(A, B, B) :- A < B.

min(A, B, A) :- A =< B.
min(A, B, B) :- A > B.
```

Figure 6.11   The rule interpreter, part 2: establishing a premise.

Once a rule's premise has been established by `establish/6`, then its caller, `consider_rule/6`, can go on to record the conclusion of the rule using `stash/3` as defined in Figure 6.12 below. The predicate `stash/3` takes as its arguments the conclusion to be recorded – there may be a qualifying CF buried within it, and it may be a composite conclusion – and the combined CF of the premise, and the rule's tag. The tag is needed so that it can be added to the list of rules that contributed to the recorded conclusions. Such a list is needed in case the user wants to know how any given conclusion was derived.

```
% stash/3: record the conclusion(s) of a rule, as some
%     kind of persistent data. The code below uses
%     recorda/3 for that purpose.
stash((P1 and P2), CF, Reason) :-
    !,
    stash(P1, CF, Reason),
    stash(P2, CF, Reason).
stash(Thing = (Val1 and Val2), CF, Reason) :-
    !,  % ..because (Val1 and Val2) was a user input
    stash(Thing = Val1, CF, Reason),
    stash(Thing = Val2, CF, Reason).
stash(Thing = (Value cf CF1), CF2, Reason) :-
    !,
    merge_cfs(CF1, CF2, CF3),
    stash(Thing = Value, CF3, Reason).
stash((Item cf CF1), CF2, Reason) :-
    !,
    merge_cfs(CF1, CF2, CF3),
    stash(Item, CF3, Reason).
```

```
stash(_ is unknown, _, _) :-
    !.
stash(Item, CF1, Reason) :-
    arg(1, Item, Thing),
    ( recorded(datum,
                datum(Thing, Item, CF2, ListOfReasons),
                Ref) ->
        erase(Ref),
        combine_cfs(CF1, CF2, CF3),
    ;   ListOfReasons = [],
        CF3 = CF1
    ),
    ( CF3 > 20 ->
        recorda(datum,
                datum(Thing, Item, CF3,
                        [Reason|ListOfReasons]),
                _),
    ;   true
    ).


% merge_cfs/3: computes the combined CF of a
%    rule's premise and the CF attached to the
%    whole rule, in order to obtain a CF for the
%    conclusion of the rule.
merge_cfs(CF1, CF2, CF3) :-
    CF3 is (CF1 * CF2)/100.


% combine_cfs/3: computes the updated CF given a
%    newly-acquired CF (as the conclusion of some
%    rule) and an already known CF for some Thing.
combine_cfs(CF1, CF2, CF3) :-
    CF3 is CF1 + CF2 - (CF1 * CF2)/100.
```

Figure 6.12   The rule interpreter, part 3: recording conclusions.

There are some easy improvements to CRESS that can be incorpo-
rated at this point. The following two exercises suggest some possibilities.

Exercise 6.4   You may wish to allow some kinds of 'action'
in a rule's conclusion, such as writing out some
text on the screen or indeed calling an arbitrary

Prolog goal: `stash/3` could do that for you. Implement this.

Exercise 6.5 You may want to introduce forward-chaining rules, either as a separate set of rules or by using the same rule set in a different manner. It would be easy to make `stash/3` call such rules. Implement this.

6.3.7 The remaining user commands

The 'help' command is shown in Figure 6.13.

The commands `quit` and `system_command` were implemented within `get_data_from_user/4` in Figure 6.10. Three of the commands (why,

```
help :-
    clear_screen,
    write('You can answer any question as follows:'), nl,
    showlist(4, ['- a  direct answer to the question.']),
    showlist(6,
        ['This can take any of the following forms:',
         '   - any word or positive number',
         '   - any expression of the following forms',
         '         This of That',
         '         A of B of C of ... of That',
         '   - or any expression qualified by a cf:',
         '         Expression cf Number',
         '     where the Number is in the range 0..100']),
    showlist(4,
        ['- why                get a justification',
         '- things             see what THINGs there are',
         '- apropos THING      get analysis of its use',
         '- show RULE          have that rule printed',
         '- show THING         see current values of it',
         '- history            see the history of',
         '                     consultation so far',
         '- history of THING   see a selected history',
         '- !system command    get any OS command run',
         '- quit               leave CRESS.']),
    await_return.
```

Figure 6.13   The `help` commmand.

things and apropos) will involve the output of a list of atoms or THINGs.
Such a list could be quite long, and so it would be inappropriate to print
them one per line. It makes more sense to print them suitably spaced across
the screen, provided that any single atom or THING is not split across the
end of a line. To ensure this it will be important to know how long such
a term is when printed. Some Prologs provide a built-in predicate for this
purpose, but if yours does not then Figure 6.14 shows a simple way to find
out the length.

The predicate spaced_list/4, also in Figure 6.14, uses this to output
a list of terms or THINGs, with a given space between each, starting in a
given column on each line, going no further right than a given column on
each line.

```
% length_of_thing/2: the arguments are
%     +Thing, a Thing whose printing length is wanted
%     ?N, usually a variable to be instantiated to length
length_of_thing(A of B, N) :-
    !,
    length_of_thing(A, Na),
    length_of_thing(B, Nb),
    N is Na + Nb + 4.
length_of_thing(A, N) :-
    atomic(A),
    name(A, L),
    length(L, N).


% spaced_list/4: the arguments are
%     +List, a list of atoms or THINGs to output
%     +(RightCol - CurrentCol), a compound term showing
%         the rightmost column boundary and what the
%         current screen column (X coordinate) is. There
%         is no very good reason for this being a single
%         argument rather than two separate ones!
%     +BaseColumn, which column to start in, on a new line
%     +Gap, the number of spaces between each item
spaced_list([],_,_,_) :-
    nl.
spaced_list([H|T], R-L, Base, Gap) :-
    length_of_thing(H,N),
    ( NewL is L+N+Gap,
      NewL < R,
      write(H), tab(Gap),
```

```
      spaced_list(T, R-NewL, Base, Gap)
    ; nl,
      tab(Base),
      spaced_list([H|T], R-Base, Base, Gap)
    ).
```

Figure 6.14   Finding the length of an atom or THING and printing it.

The `spaced_list/4` predicate is used in several places to print out some of the information requested by the user. The **why** command shows the current rule and which of its premises, if any, have already been established. It also shows various useful items of information extractable from the agenda. Thus the relevant predicate must take the current agenda as its argument; a suitable version is shown in Figure 6.15.

```
why([T=>[Rule|More]|Rest]) :-
    clear_screen,
    write('I am investigating '), write(T), nl, nl,
    write('Your answer to this question '),
    write('will help me determine'),
    nl,
    write('whether the following rule is applicable:'),
    nl,
    print_rule(Rule),
    ( More = []
    ; nl,
      write('I have yet to consider: '),
      spaced_list(More, 80-24, 24, 1),
      nl
    ),
    ( Rest = [] ->
        true
    ;   write('The current state of the agenda is: '),
        nl,
        report_agenda(Rest)
    ),
    await_return.

report_agenda(Agenda) :-
    tab(2),
```

```
            write('Thing                Rules yet to be tried'),
            nl,
            report_agenda_items(Agenda).

    report_agenda_items([]).
    report_agenda_items([T=>List|More]) :-
        tab(2),
        write(T),
        length_of_thing(T, N),
        N1 is 22 - N,
        tab(N1),
        spaced_list(List, 80-24, 24, 1),
        nl,
        report_agenda_items(More).
```

Figure 6.15   The why command.

The apropos, things and the two forms of history commands are straightforward and are shown in Figure 6.16.

```
apropos(Thing) :-
    clear_screen,
    write('Here is the available information about '),
    write(Thing), write(':'), nl, nl,
    ( _ finds Thing ->
        write(Thing), write(' is askable'), nl
    ;   true
    ),
    ( rules_to_find(Thing, L1) ->
        write('These rules conclude it:  '),
        spaced_list(L1, 80-26, 26, 1), nl
    ;   write('No rules conclude it'), nl
    ),
    ( rules_that_use(Thing, L2) ->
        write('These rules invoke it:    '),
        spaced_list(L2, 80-26, 26, 1), nl
    ;   write('No rules use it in their premise'), nl
    ),
    await_return.
```

```
things :-
    clear_screen,
    ( list_of_things(L) ->
        write('These THINGs are used in the rules:'),
        nl,
        tab(4),
        spaced_list(L,77-4,4,3)
    ;   write('You need to load a file first.'), nl
    ),
    await_return.

show_history(Thing, L) :-
    ( L=[]
    ; not(member(Thing=>_, L))
    ),
    !,
    clear_screen,
    write(Thing),
    write(' has not yet been investigated'), nl,
    await_return.
show_history(Thing, History) :-
    clear_screen,
    write('This is the current history trace for '),
    write(Thing),
    write(':'), nl,
    select_things(Thing, History, Selected),
    show_history_list(Selected),
    await_return.

select_things(_, [], []).
select_things(T, [T=>R|More], [T=>R|Rest]) :-
    !,
    select_things(T, More, Rest).
select_things(T, [X=>_|More], Rest) :-
    select_things(T, More, Rest).

show_history([]) :-
    clear_screen,
    write('No history to show yet'), nl,
    await_return.
show_history([H|T]) :-
    clear_screen,
    write('This is the current history trace:'), nl,
    show_history_list([H|T]),
    await_return.
```

```
show_history_list(L) :-
   ( watching ->
       showlist(8, L)
   ;    screen_limits(Xmax, Ymax),
       Ylast is Ymax-1,
       show_two_col_values(L, 0, Xmax, 1, Ylast, 0, 1)
   ).
```

Figure 6.16   The `apropos`, `things` and `history` commands.

The commands that show a selected rule or the currently known values for a selected THING are also fairly simple, although there is one subtlety to worry about in the showing of a rule. What if the rule contains variables? In most Prologs, variables are printed out in a standard but inscrutable form rather than by employing the user's originally chosen name. However, a user of CRESS who knows little Prolog might find it rather mysterious to see a variable printed out as, say:

    _3076

and might well prefer to see something like this instead:

    (variable) X

This can be done by instantiating each variable in a rule to an appropriately constructed atom, as in Figure 6.17. The predicate `variables_of/2` generates a list of all the variables in a given, arbitrary term. The list might contain two variables that had been unified. Although it would be easy to weed out such terms, merely by testing whether any newly encountered variable was unified with an already found one (using `==/2` for this), this would slow the predicate down somewhat. As given, it merely has to look at each leaf of the tree that represents the term in question; if it also guaranteed that no two variables in the resulting list had been unified, then there would be an extra cost of order V^2 where V was the number of variables in the term. This cost is likely to be small for CRESS's purposes, but it does not matter anyway; CRESS just needs to work through the list of variables obtained, instantiating each *un*instantiated variable to a suitable new atom.

```
% variables_of/2: given a Term, return a list of the
%    variables within it. Note that two variables in
%    the list might be already unified; that is,
%    uniqueness is NOT guaranteed here.

variables_of(Term, Vars) :-
    variables_of(Term, [], Vars).

variables_of(Term, Sofar, [Term|Sofar]) :-
    var(Term),
    !.
variables_of(Term, Sofar, Vars) :-
    functor(Term, _, N),
    variables_of(N, Term, Sofar, Vars).

variables_of(0, _, Vars, Vars) :-
    !.
variables_of(N, Term, Sofar, Vars) :-
    arg(N, Term, Arg),
    variables_of(Arg, Sofar, Mid),
    M is N-1, !,
    variables_of(M, Term, Mid, Vars).

% instvars/2: given a list of terms, instantiate any
%    variable appearing as an element of the list to
%    a unique atom of the form '(variable) X' for
%    suitable atom X made of upper-case letters: A-Z,
%    then AA-AZ, then AAA-AAZ, ... Thus some term
%    containing those variables can be printed
%    beautifully, then Prolog should be forced to fail
%    back over all this stuff to dispose of those
%    instantiations immediately after printing that term.
instvars([],N).
instvars([H|T],N) :-
    nonvar(H), !,
    instvars(T,N).
instvars([H|T],N) :-
    varmem(H,T), !,
    makename(H,N),
    N1 is N+1,
    instvars(T,N1).
instvars([H|T],N) :-
    H = 'DONT CARE', !,
```

```
      instvars(T,N).

  varmem(H,[H1|_]) :-
      H == H1.
  varmem(H,[_|T]) :-
      varmem(H,T).

  makename(Var,N) :-
      makelist(L,N),
      %          '(  v  a  r  i  a  b  l  e  ) sp'
      name(Var,[40,118,97,114,105,97,98,108,101,41,32|L]),
      !.

  makelist([N],N) :-
      N < 91.
  makelist([65|L1],N) :-
      N1 is N-26, makelist(L1,N1).
```

Figure 6.17   Instantiating variables in a term, for printing.

The show commands are given in Figure 6.18, and make use of the above predicates. The call of setof/2 in the second clause of show/2 illustrates a useful trick. This setof/2 collects up terms of the form

        [CF, datum(Thing, Item, CF, ListOfRuleTags)]

The CF is placed first in such a term so that when the list of such terms is sorted, they will be put into ascending order of CF. Then write_data/2 outputs the sorted list backwards, so that what appears on the screen is a list of conclusions about the THING in descending order of CF.

```
% show/2: show what is known about a given rule or THING
%    by showing the rule or THING and extracting what is
%    known about its use in the current run from
%    the given history list
show(Rule, History) :-
    Rule : _,
    !,
    clear_screen,
    print_rule(Rule), nl,
```

```
        report_rule_use(Rule, History),
        await_return.
show(Thing, History) :-
    Datum = recorded(datum,
                        datum(Thing, Item, CF, Reasons),
                        _),
        setof([CF, Datum],
            Datum,
            ListOfData),
        !,
        sort(ListOfData, SortedListOfData),
        clear_screen,
        write('This is what is known about '),
        write(Thing), write(':'), nl,
        write_data(SortedListOfData),
        await_return.
show(Thing, History) :-
        clear_screen,
        tab(8), write(Thing), write(' is unknown.'), nl,
        await_return.


print_rule(Rule) :-
        Rule: if Premise then Conclusion,
        variables_of(Rule: if Premise then Conclusion,
                    VarList),
        instvars(VarList, 65),
        tab(12), write(Rule), write(':'), nl,
        tab(16), write('if    '),
        write_rule_bit(Premise, 16), nl,
        tab(16), write('then  '),
        write_rule_bit(Conclusion, 16), nl.


% report_rule_use/2: tell user about current use of
%    given rule. Note that it may take some while to
%    search the history list, and so the message
%        (please wait)
%    is printed. In due course this is erased by
%    backspacing over it and printing spaces there
%    instead. So the terminal must be able to backspace.
report_rule_use(R, []) :-
        tab(4), write('Details: none now available'), nl,
        !.
report_rule_use(R, L) :-
        tab(4), write('Details (please wait)'),
        ttyflush,
```

```
        ( bagof(Thing/Outcome,
                member(Thing=>Outcome/R,L),
                PremiseUse)
        ; member(_ => R, L),
          PremiseUse = []
        ),
        !,
        back_space(14), write(':                '),
        nls(2),
        report_premise_thing_use(PremiseUse),
        nl, tab(4), write('The rule '),
        ( member(R=>Fired, L) ->
            ( Fired=s ->
                write('has succeeded')
            ;   write('has been tried but failed')
            )
        ;   write('is now being tried')
        ),
        nl.
report_rule_use(R, L) :-
        back_space(14), write(':                '),
        nls(2), tab(4),
        write('The rule has not yet been tried'), nl.

report_premise_thing_use([]).
report_premise_thing_use([T/O|More]) :-
        report_premise_thing_use(More),
        tab(4),
        ( O=s ->
            write('success: ')
        ;   write('failure: ')
        ),
        write(T), nl.

write_rule_bit(P1 and P2, Indent) :-
        !,
        write_rule_bit(P1, Indent), nl,
        tab(Indent), write('and    '),
        write_rule_bit(P2, Indent).
write_rule_bit(P1 or P2, Indent) :-
        !,
        write_rule_bit(P1, Indent), nl,
        tab(Indent), write('  or '),
        write_rule_bit(P2, Indent).
write_rule_bit(P, _) :-
```

```
        write(P).

write_data([]).
write_data([[CF, recorded(datum,
                          datum(_, Item, _, Reasons),
                          _)]|Rest]) :-
        write_data(Rest),
        tab(16), write(Item cf CF), nl,
        tab(20),
        spaced_list(['Reasons: '|Reasons], 80-29, 29, 1).
```

Figure 6.18   The show commands.

That concludes the basic version of CRESS. At the very start of this chapter, it was mentioned that this system was designed for use in teaching about expert systems; various exercises were suggested along the way. If you have been paying attention, however, you may have noticed a couple of worrying points about how CRESS behaves.

First, consider a rule such as this:

```
ouch: if   day = sunday
      and  place = scotland
      then shops = open
      and  bars = shut.
```

Suppose CRESS is trying to find values for **shops**, but has not yet tried looking for values for **bars**. Then if this rule fires, something will be concluded about **bars** and that will stop CRESS from trying any other rules for it in future. That is, the success of this rule would make **bars** behave as though it had been declared to be single-valued.

Exercise 6.6   You might not view this as a limitation, of course, but if you do it is worth fixing. The job is simple.

Second, consider a rule which involves variables:

```
oops: if   parent of father of user = X
      then grandparent of user = X.
```

Suppose that the system has been able to conclude that

```
parent of father of user = brunnhilde
parent of father of user = mustapha
```

CRESS will only use the first of these in asserting a conclusion. It will not conclude

```
grandparent of user = mustapha
```

but it should do so. The problem is considerably worse if there are several variables used in the premise of a rule; CRESS will only pick up the first available value for each, and produce a single conclusion rather than a whole set of them.

The flaw is to be found in the definition of `consider_rule/6` in Figure 6.10 above. It is not quite so easy as the first problem, but a little careful thought should show you how to do it.

> **Exercise 6.7** Fix this problem with variables. This exercise is compulsory if you want to make 'serious' use of CRESS.

SUMMARY

- Prolog is very suitable for constructing rule-based expert systems.

- It is possible and often relatively easy to implement new languages in Prolog.

- Load-time transformations of input can improve run-time efficiency dramatically.

- The DCG mechanism provides a convenient and simple way to write special-purpose parsers and analysers.

- Building enormous lists at run-time need not significantly slow your program. Searching them is likely to do so!

ADDITIONAL EXERCISES _____

6.8 In Section 6.2.1 it was suggested that a separate program could be used to find and comment on syntactic flaws in a set of rules, before they were ever loaded. Create such a program.

6.9 In Section 6.3.3 it was mentioned that the rule loader as it stands does not handle a set of rules correctly if the set is split across several files. Modify it so that it does.

6.10 In Section 6.3.6 it was mentioned that it is possible to build a program that would help you to debug and maintain a large set of rules, along the lines of Randall Davis' TEIRESIAS. The main idea in TEIRESIAS is to run a consultation first. At the end, the user identifies spurious, wrong or missing conclusions and the debugger then takes the whole consultation to pieces backwards in the attempt to find out why the wrong things happened and the correct things did not. Implement such a debugger. Nearly all the necessary run-time information can be found through the history list, although you may find that you will need to cause some extra information to be added to the history list at various points.

7

A simple disjunctive-concept learner

This chapter describes an unsophisticated 'concept learning' program that is capable of learning a single description that will cover a set of examples and non-examples. The description takes the general form of a disjunct of conjuncts:

(A and B and ...) or (F and G and ...) or ...

The main aim is to show how such a program is constructed from the abstract algorithm. Although it is a very simplistic kind of learner, the program can be used as a starting point for more interesting ones.

7.1 Machine learning

One of the major topics in current AI research is called 'machine learning'. The main thrust of this is to develop techniques that would enable a computer program to learn new information for itself, somehow. Various such techniques exist already; none even remotely approaches a human's abilities. One of the principal obstacles is that successful learning seems to depend on having a very great deal of prior knowledge; indeed, research in educational and cognitive psychology strongly suggests that a person cannot learn something unless he *almost* knows it already. For instance, if you are learning for the first time how to make an omelette, you presumably already know that a cooker is needed. You know how to turn it on and how to regulate the heat. You know how to crack open eggs, how to beat them, how to season them sensibly. You know how to read the cookery book, and what the cooking terms mean. You also have a large body of common sense to call upon if things go wrong: you know that a kilo of butter is too much to put into the pan at the start, even if you do overestimate, and you know that a likely cause of a dry or black-flecked omelette is having the pan too hot. When stated like this, it does not seem that much knowledge is involved. In computing terms, however, the quantity is vast; if you were to try to program a robot equipped with suitable sensors to be able to make a reasonable omelette in any typical modern kitchen, then you might have to work at it for some years. It would also be a lot of extra work to add fried and poached eggs to its repertoire. So if you want to undertake research in machine learning, you will be able to spend your whole life on it if you wish.

The current research is loosely grouped into several types of learning, which have not yet properly come together:

- *Learning by being told.* This is what a lot of teaching and lecturing is really about. It is not the kind of passive occurrence that the phrase suggests. When you are told something new, you have to be able to understand what has been said, and how it fits in with what you already know. However, typically you can suppose that what you are told has been appropriately structured for you to learn from – for example, the important factors have been made explicit. A form of this style of learning that is currently very popular in AI is called *explanation-based learning.* The typical scenario is:

  - the learning program starts with a considerable amount of domain knowledge, at least when compared with other flavours of machine learning;

  - the program is given a single example of some concept that is to be learned, and an explanation of some kind (perhaps a trace of a proof) showing why it is an instance of the concept;

  - the program has to generalize from this example to find some appreciably more efficient way of recognizing any further instances of the concept.

For example, in number theory a 'perfect number' is defined to be a number that is equal to the sum of all of its divisors other than the number itself. Thus 28 is such a number; its divisors are 1, 2, 4, 7 and 14 and these five numbers sum to 28. However, the computational cost of finding all the divisors of a number is typically very high. It is more useful to know that any number of the form

$$2^{n-1}(2^n - 1) \text{ where } (2^n - 1) \text{ is prime}$$

is a perfect number, and all even perfect numbers are of this form (it is not known whether there are any odd perfect numbers). Knowing this considerably reduces the cost of either generating or recognizing perfect numbers. It would, however, require a large amount of arithmetical knowledge to be able to deduce the general form from a single example. A mathematician would be much more likely to try to find several examples of perfect numbers and then to look for some kind of pattern, or to start by reasoning about the requirements that any general form must satisfy.

- *Learning from examples.* In the typical scenario here, there is a special-purpose description language in which the objects in the logical universe being considered can be described. The language is concerned with a set of attributes and, for each attribute, a set of values that the attribute might have. Thus an arbitrary object might be described by its colour and its size, where the colour is restricted to being one of 'red', 'green' or 'blue' and the size is restricted to being either 'small' or 'large'. The learning program is presented with a set of positive and negative examples described in the special language, and it has to generate a decision procedure that will correctly classify all past and future examples as being either positive or negative. Existing techniques tend to depend upon the answers to a number of questions:

  - Is the whole collection of positive and negative examples available before learning starts, or is the learning meant to be done incrementally?

  - Is the order of the examples significant or not?

  - Is it possible that some of the examples have been wrongly classified as being positive or negative?

  - Is it known that all the attributes are definitely relevant, or could it be that some are irrelevant?

  - Is anything known about the relations of the various values of any attribute to each other? For example, given the possible nationalities 'Scottish', 'English' and 'British', it helps to know that either of the first two implies the third.

  - Is there any significance to correlations between values of different attributes?

  - Can the program exercise any control over the choice of examples? For example, a robot might go exploring and so would have to decide where to go. A concept-learning program might· benefit by being able to generate examples and ask the user (or another program, or another part of the same program) whether it was a positive or negative example.

All learning is searching of some kind. The above factors influence what kind of space is being searched, and what kind of techniques can be used to search the space. In the machine-learning literature, there are many subclassifications such as *learning from failures*. The names of such classifications are usually just a shorthand for taking a certain set of answers to the above questions. A good introduction to the whole area can be found in Michalski *et al.* [1983, 1986].

7.2   A simple learning program

This chapter describes an implementation of a simple system that learns
to classify examples as positive or negative. Examples are described by a
set of attributes; the values of any attribute are hierarchically structured,
and the tree of possible values of each attribute is available to the program.
The design of the program assumes that:

- Learning is to be incremental. As each new example is presented,
  the program must modify the general description it has built to accommodate the new example.

- All examples are correctly classified, and the program is told the
  classification.

- The description being sought has the following form:

  $$C_1 \text{ or } C_2 \text{ or } \cdots \text{ or } C_n$$

  where each component C_i of this disjunct is an ordered conjunct of
  m items, one per attribute:

  $$A_{i1} \text{ and } A_{i2} \text{ and } \cdots \text{ and } A_{im}$$

  and each single item has the general form

  $$attribute\text{-}name = value$$

  meaning that the attribute can take that value or any other subsumed
  by that value in the tree for that attribute.

- Each example is presented as a set of values ordered by attribute,
  and this ordering is the same for all values. This assumption is a
  trivial one, very easily removed, but it makes the input and output
  a little simpler.

Consider, for instance, the classification of a set of geometrically
shaped objects. Suppose that each object is described by its colour and
its shape, according to the two trees shown in Figure 7.1. In these simple
trees, it is assumed that a 'rectangle' is not square and that an 'ellipse'
is not circular. To digress for a moment: suppose that these trees are
described by suitable Prolog terms, perhaps a single elaborate compound
term per tree or perhaps a collection of unit clauses each of which describes
a single link in a tree. How can the tree be printed out as shown? Each
vertical line in a tree starts and ends with a plus sign. This is a nice exercise
in recursion, which is left to the reader. Note that the width of the screen
matters: some of the subtrees may need to be placed carefully if they are
to fit. For some ideas, see Pique [1984].

To return to the main issue: if every possible example is a positive
example, then the most succinct description will be

```
any_colour -+-  primary_colour --+- red
            |                     |- blue
            |                     +- green
            |
            +- non_primary_colour -+- black
                                   |- violet
                                   |- grey
                                   |- yellow
                                   |- orange
                                   |- pink
                                   +- white


any_shape -+-  polygon -+- quadrilateral
           |            |   |
           |            |   +-+- rectangle
           |            |     +- square
           |            |
           |            |- hexagon
           |            |- pentagon
           |            +- triangle
           |
           +- smooth_shape -+- symmetric_smooth_shape
                            |   |
                            |   +-+- circle
                            |     +- ellipse
                            |
                            +- irregular_curve
```

Figure 7.1   Two attribute trees, displayable on a text screen.


```
any_colour any_shape
```

There are many other equivalent descriptions, such as

```
primary_colour any_shape
or
non_primary_colour any_shape
```

Consider, on the other hand, what must happen if not every example is a positive example. For instance, suppose that the first three examples are as shown in Figure 7.2. If the system is now told that a blue ellipse is a negative example, it will have to backtrack and it will be forced to resort to a disjunctive description, such as

Example	Positive?	Description so far
red square	yes	red square
blue circle	yes	primary_colour any_shape
green rectangle	yes	primary_colour any_shape

Figure 7.2   Examples of examples.

```
primary_colour quadrilateral
or
blue circle
```

If a further negative example also invalidated this, it would have to resort to the only other possibility remaining, namely a disjunct of the three positive examples so far. Because of this, there is no one 'correct answer' for the system to learn.

7.2.1   The basic algorithm

The basic idea of disjunctive-concept learning as implemented below is hinted at in a short paper by Bradshaw [1986]. A more elaborate system that tries to update every component of a disjunct when it receives a positive example, tries to index all components (including currently untenable ones) by example, and so on, is sketched in Murray [1987].

It is necessary to introduce a little terminology. Let us say that, in any tree, node A is an *ancestor* of node B if node A lies on the path from the single root node to node B. Write this as

$$A \prec B$$

Thus, in Figure 7.1, `smooth_shape` is an ancestor of `circle` but not of `square`. In accordance with the terminology used in lattice theory, define the *meet* of two nodes X and Y to be the node furthest away from the root node that is an ancestor of them both. Traditionally it is written as

$$X \wedge Y$$

(despite the natural confusion this may cause to logicians). In any tree, the meet of two nodes must exist and is unique. Also,

$$(X \wedge Y) \prec X$$
$$(X \wedge Y) \prec Y$$

In accordance with what was said earlier, a *concept* is represented as an *atomic concept* – an ordered set of nodes, each being a node in the corresponding tree of an ordered set of value trees – or as a disjunct of atomic concepts.

The algorithm is:

- The first positive example is taken to be the initial version of the concept to be learned.

- Whenever a new positive example is input, try to merge it with one of the concepts in the current disjunct, by replacing that concept by the meet of the concept and the new example. All negative examples known are then checked to see whether this new concept is currently valid. If it is not, try merging it with one of the other concepts instead. If none works out, as a last resort add the new example as a new element of the disjunct.

- Whenever a negative example is added, check to see whether it invalidates any component of the disjunct. If it does, then eliminate that component, and reprocess all the positive examples that supported it. The existence of the destroying negative example will prevent a destroyed component from being reformed, although that is unlikely in any case since the reprocessed examples will be spread about among the other components. Note that a negative example can invalidate at most one component, since the components cannot overlap.

This supposes that all the examples make sense, individually and collectively. On pragmatic grounds, therefore, any example must first be checked to see whether it conflicts with any of the examples previously given; if so, it should be discarded and the user should be told.

You will notice (perhaps) that the algorithm does not require a check, whenever a component is modified by the addition of a positive example, to see whether the new component subsumes any of the other existing components. This is because the components do not overlap, that is, there is no atomic concept that is subsumed by both components. Consider the following informal proof to support this claim. First, we can suppose we are dealing with a single tree; the same argument applies in each value tree that exists. Suppose we look at two non-overlapping concept components in the disjunct: these will just be nodes in the tree – say, C_i and C_j. Suppose now we add a new example, e, to C_i without subsuming any negative example; will the new component now overlap C_j? If not, then we have the basis of an inductive argument. So what we have to show is that there is no node x such that

$$(e \wedge C_i) \prec x$$
$$C_j \prec x$$

The crux of the argument is as follows; C_j (if $i > j$) exists only because the positive examples that support it could not be merged into C_i without forming a component that subsumed some negative example. That is, if positive examples $E_1 \cdots E_n$ formed C_j, then for each k there is some negative example n_k such that

$$(E_k \wedge C_i) \prec n_k$$

Now $e \wedge C_i$ subsumes no negative example, by the hypothesis that it is possible to add e to C_i at all. However, it is clear that, for any nodes a, b and c,

$$a \prec b \Rightarrow (a \wedge c) \prec (b \wedge c)$$

Now suppose that for some k,

$$(e \wedge C_i) \prec E_k$$

Since it is true that

$$(e \wedge E_k) \prec E_k$$

it would follow that

$$(e \wedge C_i \wedge E_k) \prec (C_i \wedge E_k) \prec n_k$$

This implies that $e \wedge C_i$ cannot be combined with any of the E_k. Therefore $e \wedge C_i$ and C_j still do not overlap. Initially there is only a single component in the disjunct, and so no overlaps; therefore the result remains true by induction. This argument also implies that one cannot ever safely retract a negative example, and that the algorithm as it stands cannot be easily adapted to cater for noise in the data.

It was also implied, in the statement of the algorithm, that a new negative example can invalidate at most one component of the disjunct. This is a further consequence of the fact that the components do not overlap. To see this, suppose that a new negative example N invalidates a component C_m and that this component is the meet of the positive examples $P_1 \cdots P_s$. The negative example N cannot be an ancestor of any of the P_i if the two are to be mutually consistent examples, since $N \prec P_i$ implies that P_i is a special case of N, therefore both must be positive or both must be negative. It follows that

$$C_m \prec N$$

Therefore, if N invalidated another component as well, it would follow that the two components would overlap, both subsuming N.

It pays to do even an elementary analysis such as this before starting the design or the programming. The analysis suggests that the algorithm as given will work. If you were to play safe and design the program so that, for example, it checked every component of the current disjunctive concept whenever a new negative example was input, then the program would still work. It would just run slower and take up more memory.

7.2.2   The form of the data

The program is to accept examples from the user. Although there are only two trees shown in Figure 7.1, the program should be designed to cope with any number of them. This suggests that an example should be represented as some kind of list. For simplicity, it will be assumed that the user enters an example as a sequence of values, always in the same order, so that it is not necessary to say to which tree each value belongs. Therefore an example can be represented as a simple list of values, such as

```
[white,quadrilateral]
```

The trees could be expressed in various ways, for example as a single term:

```
tree(any_colour, [
                tree(primary_colour, [...]),
                tree(non_primary_colour, [...])
                ])
```

This would be a bad choice for the present purposes, since it is necessary to be able to check whether a value such as white occurs within the tree when an example is first entered. That would mean dismantling the term, at a potentially large cost. Also, the program does not need to be concerned with any property of a tree or subtree as a whole, and so there is no great benefit in representing a tree as a single term.

A tree could be represented as a collection of unit clauses such as

```
tree_branch(colour, red, primary_colour).
```

where the first argument names the tree, and the second and third are the names of a pair of directly connected nodes with the child node first. Naming the tree makes it possible to check that the user has entered a proper sequence of values in the correct order. Let us take an even simpler course, trusting the user to be able to enter a correctly formed example, and suppose that a tree is represented as a collection of unit clauses of the form

```
cat(red, primary_colour).
```

Here, 'cat' is meant to be short for 'category of'. It is more usual to employ a functor name such as 'is_a', although that sometimes makes some of the unit clauses read rather strangely. Using any functor of arity 2, without a tree name, does have the drawback that nodes in different trees cannot have the same name.

The internal data needed is:

- A record of all the negative examples and a record of all the positive examples so far. This will be needed in order to check that a newly entered example neither subsumes nor is subsumed by any previous example. There is also a need to distinguish between the sets of positive and negative examples. The latter is needed whenever a component of the current disjunct is merged with a new example, according to the basic algorithm.

- The current disjunct of concepts, and a record of which positive examples gave rise to each.

Since the set of positive examples that support a component concept merely expands, or is trashed when a negative example finally destroys that component, it is simple and efficient to represent a component as a term of the form

```
component(Concept, ListOfPositiveExamples)
```

where `Concept` is a list of nodes, one per tree from the set of trees, just like an example. The disjunct can then be represented as a list of such terms, since the number of components is unknown in advance. The sets of known positive and negative examples also just grow in size, so they may as well be represented by a list, rather than anything more complicated such as difference lists.

There is no need to use asserts and retracts or the recording database. Indeed to do so would just complicate and slow down the program. For example, the need to delete just those examples that support a given component would force you to record an example along with the concept it supports somehow. But the concept that an example supports is changed as new examples are merged with it; thus the recorded (or asserted) data would need to be changed, or else you would need to 'gensym' some kind of unchanging tag for that set of examples.

7.2.3   The main low-level operations

There will be some fundamental tests and operations needed by the program, which can be defined immediately. First, does an atomic concept or a known example subsume a new example? Figure 7.3 shows how to do it. It will also be useful to have analogous tests for checking whether a newly entered example either subsumes or is subsumed by any of the known positive or negative examples. It will also be necessary to distinguish between these cases, since it will affect what the user is told about a bad example. Figure 7.4 shows the code. Given an atomic concept and a new example, a predicate is needed that will construct their meet. Only when it has been constructed can it be checked to ensure that no negative example invalidates it. The subsidiary predicate `subsumes_in_relevant_tree/2` from Figure 7.3 can be reused here; see Figure 7.5. The newly constructed meet can then be tested for validity by a goal of the form

```
\+(subsumes_any(NewConcept, NegativeExamples))
```

when necessary.

```
% subsumes/2: takes an atomic concept or example
%    (a list of entries, one per tree), and a new
%    example (same form) and succeeds if the former
%    subsumes the latter.

subsumes([],[]).
subsumes([C|MoreCs], [E|MoreEs]) :-
    subsumes_in_relevant_tree(C, E),
    subsumes(MoreCs, MoreEs).

subsumes_in_relevant_tree(C, C) :-
    !.
subsumes_in_relevant_tree(C, E) :-
    cat(E, ParentOfE),
    subsumes_in_relevant_tree(C, ParentOfE).
```

Figure 7.3   The subsumption test.

```
% subsumed_by_any/2: given example and list of examples,
%    see if the example is subsumed by any in the list

subsumed_by_any(Example, [H|T]) :-
    ( subsumes(H, Example)
    ; subsumed_by_any(Example, T)
    ).

% subsumes_any/2: given example and list of examples,
%    see if the example subsumes any in the list

subsumes_any(Example, [H|T]) :-
    ( subsumes(Example, H)
    ; subsumes_any(Example, T)
    ).
```

Figure 7.4   The test of lists of examples.

```
% merge_c_with_e/3: given an atomic concept, a positive
%    example, get a new concept by forming joins in each
%    tree. This routine does NOT do the validity checks,
%    that is, the checks that the result does not
%    subsume any negative example.

merge_c_with_e([], [], []).
merge_c_with_e([C|MoreCs], [E|MoreEs], [NewC|Rest]) :-
    form_meet(C, E, NewC),
    merge_c_with_e(MoreCs, MoreEs, Rest).

form_meet(C, E, C) :-
    subsumes_in_relevant_tree(C, E),
    !.
form_meet(C, E, NewC) :-
    cat(C, ParentOfC),
    form_meet(ParentOfC, E, NewC).
```

Figure 7.5   Forming the meet of a concept and an example.

7.2.4   The top level

The learning system needs to read in an example, find out whether it is
supposed to be a positive or negative example, check that it is consistent
with all previous examples, and only then try to modify the current disjunctive concept to accommodate it. This cycle is repeated until the user
decides otherwise. This suggests the need for a tail-recursive loop, with
four arguments: the current disjunctive concept, the lists of positive and
negative examples and a variable to be instantiated to the final version of
the concept. Figure 7.6 shows the form of this. The 'halting test' done by
test_for_halt/2 can be changed as desired; here, it merely checks to see
if the latest example entered by the user is empty. Not too much should
be done explicitly within such a loop. For example, the task of gathering
a satisfactory example is relegated to the predicate get_example/6, which
can also be given the job of updating the lists of positive and negative examples. These two lists are unaffected by the work of modifying the current
concept; that task is relegated to the predicate process/5.

7.2.5   Reading in an example

When the user types in an example, the first task is to check whether all the
words in it can be found in any of the value trees. If some word is unknown,

```
% learn/1 is the top level goal:

learn(Disjunct) :-
    learn([], [], [], Disjunct).

% learn/4: given a disjunct so far, and sets of positive
%    and negative examples so far, get another example
%    from the user and process it, then loop. Stop when
%    test_for_halt/2 says so, return the final disjunctive
%    concept.
learn(Disjunct, Positives, Negatives, Result) :-
    get_example(Example, YesNo,
                Positives, NewPositives,
                Negatives, NewNegatives),
    ( test_for_halt(Example, YesNo) ->
        Result = Disjunct
    ; process(Example, YesNo,
            Disjunct, NewDisjunct,
            NewNegatives),
      report_progress(NewDisjunct),
      learn(NewDisjunct, NewPositives,
          NewNegatives, Result)
    ).

% test_for_halt/2: given the example, and the user's
%    classification of it, decide whether to stop
%    learning. Succeeds if so.

test_for_halt([], _).
```

Figure 7.6   The top-level tail-recursive loop.

possibly because of a mistyping, the user should be told and asked to enter the example again. This means that another tail-recursive loop is needed. Moreover, if the variable to be instantiated to the kosher example is called (say) **Example**, then it ought not to be instantiated to what the user typed in until that input has passed all the necessary tests. It would be possible to write a failure-driven loop for this purpose, something like:

```
get_example(Example, YesNo, ...) :-
   repeat,
     write('Give an example: '),
     sentence(Example),  % as in Chapter 4?
     vet(Example),
     write('Is it a positive example? '),
     sentence([YesNo]),
     test_yes_or_no(YesNo),
     ....
   !.
```

but it is easy to get wrong. For instance, suppose the user answers 'mo'
rather than 'no' to the question about whether it is a positive example.
Presumably, this will cause backtracking to the **repeat** goal, which means
that the user will be asked to supply an example all over again.

Rather than having to take great care about which subsidiary predicates should be resatisfiable, it is much easier to have a tail-recursive loop
such as the one shown in Figure 7.7.

```
% get_example/6: returns a new example supplied by
%    the user, and also a yes (for positive example)
%    or no (for negative example). Given the current
%    sets of positive and negative examples, adds
%    the new example to the appropriate one.
%    This predicate checks that the example input
%    is a sensible one, and does not succeed until
%    the user has supplied one.

get_example(Example, Type,
            Positives, NewPositives,
            Negatives, NewNegatives) :-
   get_plausible_example(List),
   !,
   ( List = [] ->
         YesNo = end_of_examples
   ; pos_neg(YesNo),
     ( YesNo = yes,
       check_positive(List,
                      Positives, Negatives),
       Example = List,
       Type = yes,
       NewPositives = [Example|Positives],
       NewNegatives = Negatives
```

```
      ; YesNo = no,
        check_negative(List,
                       Positives, Negatives),
        Example = List,
        Type = no,
        NewPositives = Positives,
        NewNegatives = [Example|Negatives]
      ; get_example(Example, Type,
                    Positives, NewPositives,
                    Negatives, NewNegatives)
    )
  ).


% get_plausible_example/1: tries to read in something
%    that resembles an example. Keeps trying.
get_plausible_example(Input) :-
    write('Give a positive or negative example: '),
    sentence(List),
    ( vet(List) ->
          Input = List
    ;     get_plausible_example(Input)
    ).


% vet/1: checks to see if a list looks OK, words known
vet([]).
vet([H|T]) :-
    ( cat(H, _)
    ; cat(_, H)
    ),
    !,
    vet(T).
vet([H|_]) :-
    write('The word '), write(H),
    write(' is not in any of the value trees'),
    nl,
    fail.


% pos_neg/1: gets a 'yes' or 'no' from the user
pos_neg(YesNo) :-
    write('Is it a positive example (yes/no)? '),
    sentence([Reply]),
    ( yesno(Reply) ->
          YesNo = Reply
    ;     write('You must reply either yes or no. '),
          pos_neg(YesNo)
```

```
    ).

yesno(yes).
yesno(no).
```

Figure 7.7   Reading in an example.

The predicates

```
    check_positive(List, Positives, Negatives)
```

and

```
    check_negative(List, Positives, Negatives)
```

need to check whether the input List either subsumes or is subsumed by any of the previous positive or negative examples. If so they should output an appropriate message and fail. They should only succeed if the input List is not inconsistent with any of the previous examples. So, for instance, check_positive/3 needs to test whether the possible positive example is subsumed by any earlier positive example (this makes the new example redundant) and whether it subsumes or is subsumed by any of the earlier negative examples (this would make the new example inconsistent). The definition of these two predicates is left as a trivial exercise; Figure 7.4 contains the necessary tools.

Exercise 7.1   Define these two predicates.

7.2.6   Modifying the current concept

In Figure 7.6, the predicate process/5 does the actual work of modifying the current concept in the light of the new example. An appropriate definition is given in Figure 7.8.

```
% process/5: given the example, a yes/no indication
%    of whether it is a positive example, the current
%    disjunct and set of negative examples, update
%    the disjunct.
%
% Case 1: positive example, disjunct empty. Just
%    make it the concept, unless it conflicts
%    directly with any negative examples, in
```

```
%     which case the call should fail.
process(Example, yes,
        [], [component(Example,[Example])],
        Negatives) :-
    \+(subsumes_any(Example, Negatives)).
% Case 2: positive example, but it does not add
%    anything new, because some existing component
%    of the disjunct covers it. Just add it as
%    an example supporting that component, in case
%    that component is split up some time later.
process(Example, yes,
        Disjunct, NewDisjunct,
        _) :-
    subsumed_by_one(Example, Disjunct, NewDisjunct),
    !.
% Case 3: positive example, which we can safely merge
%    with the first component to form a new first
%    component. Do it.
process(Example, yes,
        [component(C,List)|More],
             [component(NewC,[Example|List])|More],
        Negatives) :-
    merge_c_with_e(C, Example, NewC),
    \+(subsumes_any(NewC, Negatives)).
% Case 4: positive example. Look for another component
%    to try merging it into.
process(Example, yes,
        [Component|More], [Component|Rest],
        Negatives) :-
    process(Example, yes, More, Rest, Negatives).
% Case 5: negative example. Find a component, if
%    any, which it invalidates. Break it up. Add the
%    example to the list of known negative examples.
%    Then reprocess all the orphaned positive examples.
%    Note, a negative example cannot invalidate more
%    than one component at once; the components do not
%    overlap.
process(Example, no,
        Disjunct, NewDisjunct,
        Negatives) :-
    destroy_if_necessary(Example, Disjunct,
                         Negatives, NewDisjunct).

% subsumed_by_one/3: checks to see if a given (positive)
%    example is already covered. If so, just add the
```

```
%   example to the set that supports the atomic concept
%   in question, lest the set be split up later.

subsumed_by_one(Example,
                [component(C,List)|More],
                [component(C,[Example|List])|More]) :-
    subsumes(C,Example).
subsumed_by_one(Example,
                [Component|More],
                [Component|Rest]) :-
    subsumed_by_one(Example, More, Rest).
```

Figure 7.8   Updating the current concept.

The predicate subsumed_by_one/3 is very similar to the predicate
subsumed_by_any/2 in Figure 7.4 in Section 7.2.3. However, the list that
it is given as second argument is not just a list of examples; it is a list
of component/2 structures. Thus it is necessary to have both of these
predicates, rather than having just one used in two different ways.

The crucial ingredient is the predicate destroy_if_necessary/4,
which does the job of locating the component, if any, that is invalidated by
a negative example and then recycling all the positive examples that had
given rise to that component. Figure 7.9 defines it.

```
% destroy_if_necessary/4: given negative example and
%    current disjunct, and current set of negative
%    examples (in case we need to destroy any concept
%    and so form new ones to cover the orphaned
%    examples), recurse down the disjunct to see if
%    any is invalidated. If so, remove it and
%    reprocess each of the positive examples that
%    supported it to form a new disjunct.

destroy_if_necessary(Example, Disjunct,
                     Negatives, NewDisjunct) :-
    find_invalid(Example, Disjunct,
                 AllButInvalid, ListOfOrphans),
    !,
    process_orphans(ListOfOrphans, AllButInvalid,
                    Negatives, NewDisjunct).
```

```
destroy_if_necessary(_, Disjunct, _, Disjunct).

% find_invalid/4: given the negative example and the
%     current disjunct, recurse down it looking for
%     a single component that the example will clobber.
%     Return the disjunct with that component removed
%     and return the list of positive examples from
%     that component.

find_invalid(Example, [component(C,List)|More],
              More, List) :-
    subsumes(C, Example),
    !.
find_invalid(Example, [Component|More],
                [Component|MoreValidOnes], ListOfOrphans) :-
    find_invalid(Example, More,
                  MoreValidOnes, ListOfOrphans).

% process_orphans/4: given a list of newly unattached
%     positive examples, the current disjunct and the
%     current list of negative examples, modify the
%     disjunct to include those positive examples

process_orphans([], Disjunct, _, Disjunct).
process_orphans([PosEx|More], InitialDisjunct,
                  Negatives, FinalDisjunct) :-
    process(PosEx, yes,
              InitialDisjunct, NewerDisjunct,
              Negatives),
    process_orphans(More, NewerDisjunct,
                      Negatives, FinalDisjunct).
```

Figure 7.9   Making changes to accommodate a negative example.

Suppose, just for a moment, that you had not done the simple analysis in Section 7.2.1. Then you would probably decide to write a version of the predicate destroy_if_necessary/4 that would recurse through the entire list of components to find all those that were invalidated, and it would also have to build a list containing all the sets of orphaned positive examples. This suggests a new version of find_invalid/4:

```
find_invalid(_, [], [], []).
find_invalid(Example,
```

```
                    [component(C,List)|More],
                    Rest, Orphans) :-
          subsumes(C, Example),
          !,
          find_invalid(Example, More, Rest, SomeOrphans),
          append(List, SomeOrphans, Orphans).
     find_invalid(Example,
                    [Component|More],
                    [Component|Rest],
                    Orphans) :-
          find_invalid(Example, More, Rest, Orphans).
```

However, all that list appending is unnecessary. Nor do you have to resort
to difference pairs, which would be even less efficient because you would
have to recurse down each list of positive examples to build a similar list
with a variable for its tail. The more efficient way to handle a situation
like this is to build a list of lists of orphans. No appending is involved, and
all that is needed is one extra intermediate predicate to handle such a list
of lists:

```
     process_orphan_lists([], Disjunct, _, Disjunct).
     process_orphan_lists([H|T], InitialDisjunct,
                             Negatives, FinalDisjunct) :-
          process_orphans(H, InitialDisjunct, Negatives, D),
          process_orphan_lists(T, D, Negatives, FinalDisjunct).
```

7.2.7   Output to the user

Finally, Figure 7.10 contains the predicate that tells the user what the
current concept is.

Figure 7.11 shows the output when the trees in Figure 7.1 were used,
and the system was being taught the concept

```
     primary_colour quadrilateral
     or
     grey smooth_shape
```

It over-generalizes initially to the universal concept

```
     any_colour any_shape
```

and is then forced to break up that concept when the next negative example
invalidates it. Try to work out what happens, in the general case rather
than in this specific example, if the top-level goal learn/1 finally succeeds
(because the user finished his run of examples with an empty one) and then
control later backtracks to it.

```
% report_progress/1: given a disjunct, tell the user
%    what it is. Print it nicely

report_progress(List) :-
       write('Concept so far: '),
       report_concepts(List).

report_concepts([component(C,_)]) :-
       !,
       write_concept(C), nl.
report_concepts([component(C,_)|More]) :-
       write_concept(C), nl, tab(13), write('or '),
       report_concepts(More).

write_concept([]).
write_concept([Item|More]) :-
       write(Item),
       tab(1),
       write_concept(More).
```

Figure 7.10   Telling the user about a concept.

SUMMARY

- Learning programs need not be complicated.

- At the design stage, it pays to analyse the algorithms thoroughly, both for their efficiency and for their correctness.

- It is often possible to do without asserts and retracts when managing reasonable quantities of data.

- Tail recursion can be more flexible than failure-driven loops.

ADDITIONAL EXERCISES

7.2   The simple system described in this chapter is able to learn disjuncts of conjuncts. A user-defined Prolog predicate is just such an object; could this program be modified to learn new predicates?

```
| ?- learn(L).
Give a positive or negative example: red square
Is it a positive example (yes/no)? yes
Concept so far: red square
Give a positive or negative example: grey circle
Is it a positive example (yes/no)? yes
Concept so far: any_colour any_shape
Give a positive or negative example: pink hexagon
Is it a positive example (yes/no)? no
Concept so far: grey circle
              or red square
Give a positive or negative example: green rectangle
Is it a positive example (yes/no)? yes
Concept so far: grey circle
              or primary_colour quadrilateral
Give a positive or negative example: grey irregular_curve
Is it a positive example (yes/no)? yes
Concept so far: grey smooth_shape
              or primary_colour quadrilateral
Give a positive or negative example:
 . . . .
```

Figure 7.11   A sample run of the disjunctive-concept learner.

7.3 Suppose that the learning of the disjunctive concept is not to be done incrementally. Instead, a full set of positive and negative examples is available as raw data at the start. Modify the program to learn a suitable description from this data efficiently.

7.4 The program described in this chapter backtracks when the current form of a concept is invalidated by a new negative example. The method hinted at in Bradshaw [1986] is to keep track of all the possible forms of the disjunctive concept simultaneously. Implement such a learning program.

7.5 Learning by analogy is yet another subclassification within the topic of machine learning. One of the problems there is to test how similar two structures are, according to some application-specific measure of similarity. This kind of problem is very important in mathematics, for example, where the fact that you can solve an equation such as

$$\sin(x) + \sin(2x) + \sin(3x) = 0$$

means that you can apply analogous methods to solve equations such as

$$\cos(x) + \cos(2x) + \cos(3x) = 0$$

and

$$\cos(7x) + \cos(11x) + \cos(15x) = 2$$

Devise a predicate that tests for such analogies between two mathematical expressions. You could look on it as a sort of 'fuzzy unification' algorithm, so you might find it useful to try to construct a useful precise unification algorithm explicitly in Prolog first.

7.6 Devise a program that learns to translate whole numbers as spoken in French (or some other foreign language with which you are familiar) into standard decimal notation. Your program should not have any knowledge of the foreign language built into it, it should be capable of learning how numbers are expressed in a wide variety of foreign languages. For example, it should be able to learn from (a lot of) examples that 'quatre-vingt douze' means 92 and 'mille neuf cent cinquante' means 1950. First, consider how the translation could be represented in the form of a definite-clause grammar in a way that would be roughly the same in a wide variety of languages, and then consider how such a grammar could be learned from examples.

8
An active chart parser

This chapter describes the implementation of an active chart parser. This is a type of non-deterministic parser in which the main data structure is an elaborate representation of the syntactic structure of the input, called a *chart*. The parser requires a user-specified grammar. The grammar symbols are not limited to being atoms, they can be arbitrary Prolog terms. The parser can build the syntactic structure representation either top-down or bottom-up, and in either case it can do so in a breadth-first or in a depth-first manner. These choices are represented as explicit parameters.

The design poses some interesting problems. For instance, for the sake of generality, it turns out to be necessary to avoid unifying two arbitrary Prolog terms at certain points, and instead it is necessary to construct a term that is equivalent to the one that would have been the result of unifying them. The design also highlights some of Prolog's limitations when it comes to handling elaborate data efficiently.

8.1 About chart parsing

To say that a parser is *non-deterministic* does not mean that there is some random element within it. It means merely that at any step, the choice of what to add to the growing representation of the syntactic structure of the input is not fully and finally determined by the current state of the parser and the current input symbol, as is the case in many of the simple parsers used in programming language compilers. A non-deterministic parser can (and in the case of a chart parser, does) generate alternative representations of the structure of the input.

Within AI, parsing technology is mainly encountered within the area of natural-language processing. In that context, the input to a parser is a sequence of words, possibly complete and possibly incomplete. For example, there is an ambiguity about the sentence

He sent the letter to the ambassador to the Pope.

– did the ambassador to the Pope receive the letter, or did the Pope receive a letter addressed to some ambassador? The ambiguity cannot be resolved without knowing the context of the sentence. Such ambiguity rarely troubles humans, partly because they have typically made decisions about the context early in the processing of such a sentence, and partly because they do not wait for the end of the sentence before starting to work on it. Indeed, how can a human recognize where a sentence ends in the first place? But then, what has a human done with a partial input such as

>*He sent the letter to the ...*

which helps so much? Clearly it is not just a matter of syntactic analysis; the knowledge that the sentence concerns sending something, that the action happened in the past, and that it was a letter that was sent, arouses considerable expectations about the nature of the forthcoming input. Such expectations are derived from a huge body of 'common knowledge'.

Although parsing is not the whole story, it is as obviously a small but important part. Parsing technology has therefore been a 'hot topic' within the area of natural-language processing. But the technology is useful in many other areas too. The input to a parser need not be a sequence of words, it can be any linear sequence such as a sequence of arm and finger movements or a sequence of operating system commands. In such contexts parsing can form a useful early part of what is called *plan recognition*, although it might be better referred to as *intention recognition* since both introspection and experiment confirm that people frequently do not work to a fully detailed plan.

Chart parsing grew out of work in the early 1970s on language processing, such as the work of Earley [1970] and Kay [1973]. A chart is a graph of directed labelled edges in which each edge spans some part of the input sequence. The starting place is the input sequence; for simplicity let us suppose that it is a sequence of words, such as

```
The saw bit
```

Imagine that there are four vertices, numbered from 0 to 3, interspersed in this sequence so that vertex 0 is just to the left of the first word, and vertex n is just to the right of the nth word. These will be the only vertices in the final graph too; all the edges that are added to the graph will start at one of these vertices and finish at one of them (possibly the same one but never – in this implementation – an earlier one). The label attached to any edge will say something about the portion of the input sequence that the edge spans. For instance, an edge might say something like 'that chunk of the input sequence looks like the start of a noun phrase but is lacking the noun itself' in which case, if there were a noun immediately after the chunk in question, a new edge could be added with a label saying 'this chunk is a complete noun phrase, lacking nothing at all'. In due course the completed

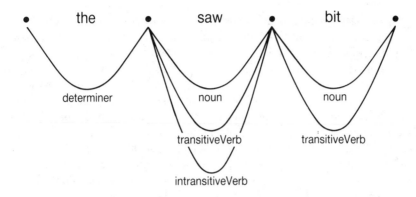

Figure 8.1   An example of the initial state of a chart.

chart will contain edges identifying all the parsable subsequences of the original input.

In this implementation, the initial steps in the parsing process are, first, to set up the vertices at either end of the input sequence and between each consecutive pair of input elements. This means that if the input sequence has length N there will be $N + 1$ vertices. Second, edges are added that describe the possible lexical categories of each element of the input. There is one edge per possible category of an input element, and each edge spans from one vertex to the next one. Thus, in the short example given above, the word **bit** might be spanned by various edges labelling it as a noun (perhaps a drill bit, or a horse's bit, or a hardware bit, or $12\frac{1}{2}$ US cents) and one edge labelling it as a past tense form of 'to bite' and another labelling it as a past participle also derived from 'to bite'. These edges are constructed by consulting a lexicon of some kind. In the simplified diagram of the initial state of a chart shown in Figure 8.1, the word **bit** is only spanned by a single 'noun' edge and by a single 'transitiveVerb' edge, rather than by several edges for each possible meaning it might have as a noun. After this initialization, active chart parsing need make no further use of lexical information. The algorithm is driven only by the set of edges created so far and by the grammar rules. It has been shown that the algorithm, described below, can find all parses of all subsequences of the input in no more than $O(N^3 R^2)$ steps, where N is the length of the input sequence and R is the number of grammar rules; for a proof see, for example, Aho and Ullman [1972]. It has also been shown that in some cases this bound cannot be improved upon.

In order to describe the algorithm it will be necessary to introduce some specialized terminology.

8.1.1 Some terminology

A grammar rule has a left-hand side that describes some kind of *syntactic category*, perhaps qualified by a variety of parameters if the grammar is not a context-free one. A rule's right-hand side consists of a sequence of syntactic categories and/or *terminal symbols*, representing one possible expansion of the category named by the left-hand side of the rule. A *terminal symbol* is merely something that cannot be expanded further by rules; the bottom line, so to speak. A *left-recursive* rule is one in which the first, that is the leftmost, category on the right-hand side can be expanded further by using the same rule. A grammar that includes left-recursive rules can usually be conveniently recast as an equivalent grammar without such rules. However, the implementation to be described here will handle left-recursive rules directly, by preventing the infinite loops that might result.

An *edge* is a data structure that describes a subsequence in terms of the grammar and that contains at least the following information:

- The *start vertex* (the left-hand end of the edge).

- The *end vertex* (the right-hand end).

- The *category* in question, which the subsequence spanned by the edge forms the beginning of, and is perhaps all of it.

- The *'found' list*, the initial part of the right-hand side of some rule for the given category. The subsequence spanned by the edge can be viewed as consisting of the sequence of categories given by this list.

- The *'needs' list*, consisting of the remainder of that rule or the given category. It represents the sequence of categories that need to be located after the spanned subsequence, if the ultimate recognition of an instance of the given category is to be successful.

For example, if there is a grammar rule specifying that a sentence can consist of a noun phrase followed by a verb phrase, then in the sample sentence 'The `saw bit`' the first two words might in due course be spanned by an edge representing an instance of the category 'sentence', showing that the first two words represent a noun phrase, and that if a verb phrase can be identified after them then a complete instance of a sentence will have been found. In the implementation to be described, an edge will be represented by a Prolog term of the form

```
edge(Category,
     FoundList, NeedsList,
     StartVertex, EndVertex)
```

Table 8.1   A trivial grammar and lexicon.

S	→	NP, VP
NP	→	Determiner, Noun
VP	→	IntransitiveVerb
VP	→	TransitiveVerb, NP
Determiner	:	*the*
Noun	:	*saw* or *bit*
IntransitiveVerb	:	*saw*
TransitiveVerb	:	*saw* or *bit*

An edge with an empty 'needs' list is called an *inactive edge*, because it carries no expectations about what follows the edge. An edge with a non-empty 'needs' list is called an *active edge* – it does carry expectations about what might follow. An edge whose start vertex and end vertex are the same is called an *empty active edge*; its 'found' list is empty and its 'needs' list is the complete right-hand side of some grammar rule for the named category. By tradition a chart is depicted as being built upon a horizontal line consisting of the original input sequence, with inactive edges shown below that line and active edges shown above it. Consider the trivial context-free grammar and lexicon shown in Table 8.1. A possible state of the chart, part of the way through the parsing process, is shown in Figure 8.2. This particular state might never be reached; it depends on the decisions about top-down versus bottom-up and so on.

New edges are created by applying what is called the *fundamental rule* of chart parsing. Suppose that a certain active edge A ends at vertex V, and that an inactive edge I starts at that same vertex. These two edges are said to *meet* at V. If the category of I matches the first category of the 'needs' list of A, then a new edge can be constructed that spans from the left-hand end of A to the right-hand end of I, has the same category as A, has a 'found' list that now begins with I (so the 'found' list is ordered so that the most recently found category is first), and has a 'needs' list that is the tail of the old 'needs' list of A. There is a wide range of possible variants of this fundamental rule. For instance, the two edges that will give birth to a new one need not meet at a vertex, for certain applications.

A pair comprising an active and an inactive edge to which the fundamental rule might apply is called a '*config*', and is typically put on an agenda to be considered at some later point than when the pair was put there. In this implementation, there is an agenda but checks are made before a config is ever put onto it to ensure that the fundamental rule will definitely be applicable to that pair. This complicates the program slightly but prevents the agenda from growing to terrifying lengths.

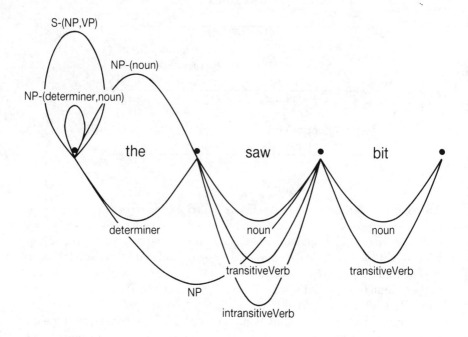

Figure 8.2   An intermediate state in building a chart.

8.1.2   The algorithm

The algorithm as implemented in this chapter is:

- Initialize the chart by looking up the possible lexical categories of each word in the input.

- Add empty active edges. How this is done in general depends on whether parsing is to be top-down or bottom-up:

  - *top-down*: add an empty active edge for the topmost category of the grammar (in Table 8.1 it would be S). Just one such edge can be added at vertex 0, or such an edge can be added at every vertex.

  - *bottom-up*: add empty active edges at the left-hand end of each inactive edge. Add all the possible empty active edges whose 'needs' list starts with a category that matches that of the inactive edge – that is, add those empty edges that can immediately be used to create new edges by marrying with one of the existing inactive edges.

- Form an agenda of configs.

- Now repeat the following loop:

  - Test whether to stop parsing. Typically this will just be a test of whether the agenda is empty. If it is not time to stop:

  - Take the front config off the agenda. Apply the fundamental rule to it to create a new edge. Add this edge to the chart.

  - If the parsing is top-down, and the newly added edge is active, then add further empty active edges at the start of the newly created edge whose categories could match the first category on the 'needs' list of the newly created edge. Any new empty edge, being active, will recursively trigger the creation of further empty active edges.

  - If the parsing is bottom-up, and the newly added edge is inactive, then add empty active edges at its left-hand end that will be able to marry with the inactive edge. Because the empty edges are active rather than inactive, this process will not trigger a recursive creation of further empty active edges.

  - Form all the possible configs that involve the newly created edges, empty or otherwise.

  - If the parsing is breadth-first, add these new configs to the back of the agenda. If it is depth-first, add them to the front.

This algorithm is carefully expressed in terms of categories being matched rather than in terms of categories being equal. Trivial grammars such as the one in Table 8.1 can seduce you into thinking of categories as atoms. If a category is instead represented by a compound term involving variables then you have to be alert to a potential problem. Consider this very simple grammar:

$$s(Plurality) \rightarrow np(Plurality), vp(Plurality)$$
$$np(Plurality) \rightarrow determiner, noun(Plurality)$$
$$\ldots and\ so\ on\ \ldots$$

The Plurality argument in this DCG-like grammar is meant to be an uninstantiated variable. Consider this input:

```
The sheep ate the haggis
```

The word **sheep** can be singular or plural, as can the verb. (Note to the unlucky millions who do not live in Scotland: the word **haggis** is undoubtedly singular. And in case you think that the sentence is far-fetched, the author has witnessed this arcane form of cannibalism.) Thus there are two possible interpretations of this sentence, as being singular or plural. However, suppose that the chart is being built explicitly as a

single huge Prolog list rather than implicitly as a collection of asserted or
recorded terms. If the parsing is proceeding top-down, then the chart will
at some early point contain an edge of the form

```
edge(s(P), [], [np(P), vp(P)], 0, 0)
```

and there may be two edges describing the two interpretations of the initial
noun phrase:

```
edge(np(plural), [noun(plural),determiner], [], 0, 2)
edge(np(singular), [noun(singular),determiner], [], 0, 2)
```

Either of these two inactive edges can be married with the active edge.
Suppose that the first of the inactive edges is married with it. Then if the
Prolog program actually unifies np(P) and np(plural), the existing active
edge (not the new edge) will thereafter be

```
edge(s(plural), [], [np(plural), vp(plural)], 0, 0)
```

so that it has lost its earlier generality! This would prevent the parser from
ever discovering the singular interpretation of the sentence.

This may suggest to you that the chart must be represented implicitly
by a collection of asserted or recorded terms instead. However, this need
not be so. The two terms to be unified can be copied first, and the copies
can be unified instead so that the instantiation state of the original terms
is unaffected. Introductory texts on Prolog often suggest that a term can
be copied like this:

```
copy_term(Term, Copy) :-
    asserta(term_to_copy(Term)),
    retract(term_to_copy(Copy)).
```

It works, but it is very slow in most Prologs. The argument of the as-
serta/1 must not be a variable, and so the presence of the term_to_copy/1
functor is necessary in case Term is a variable. There is also always the
remote danger that the user will manage to interrupt the program just before the retract/1, leaving the database in a dangerous state. Fortunately
there is a much better way to copy an arbitrary term without asserting or
recording, and it is also very much faster in most Prologs. Simply dismantle
the Term recursively, and build the Copy on the way. The method is further
described in Section 8.3.2.

8.2   The data structures

The chart merely grows as parsing proceeds; edges already within the chart
should not be modified or deleted. This means that if the input to be parsed
is of any reasonable size and the grammar is non-trivial, then the chart can

grow to be huge. A chart containing several thousand edges would not be particularly unusual.

A chart could be built implicitly by asserting or recording the individual edges, but – as was mentioned previously – these database-modifying operations are typically slow. This would somewhat counteract the natural benefits of asserting or recording, namely fast access by means of Prolog's database indexing mechanisms. It would also mean that the program had side-effects that would need to be cleaned up at the start of each parse.

Although it is not 100% clear that it is better to build the chart as some sort of explicit monster term, let us adopt this approach. The chart could be kept as a single list of edges, but this would neglect the useful distinction between active and inactive edges. It would be possible to construct the chart as a pair of trees of some sort, with the tree for active edges being keyed on the end vertex of edges and the tree for inactive edges being keyed on the start vertex of the edges instead. For simplicity of explanation, however, we shall take the very simple approach of representing the chart as a term of the form

> `ListOfActiveEdges + ListOfInactiveEdges`

The conversion of the program to use a pair of trees instead, or to use any more efficient term storage mechanism available within a particular Prolog, is left as an exercise.

The agenda must be some kind of ordered sequence of configs. It is necessary to be able to add new configs either to the back or the front of the ordered sequence; this suggests that a difference list is a good choice. The list could consist just of edges, implicitly paired so that (say) an active edge in the list is immediately followed by the inactive edge that it is to be married to (and remember, polygamy is allowed – many edges will eventually marry with several others). This has the disadvantage that it makes the agenda much harder to read should you ever want to print it out, and also makes the program much harder to debug should you make a careless slip in programming somewhere. Therefore, let us suppose that a config is represented by a single term, say of the form

> `ActiveEdge + InactiveEdge`

and that the agenda is also represented as a single term of the form

> `ListOfConfigs - TailVariable`

The decision between top-down and bottom-up parsing will be called the *parsing strategy*, available as a separate argument, which will always be one of the two atoms **td** or **bu**. Similarly, the decision between breadth-first and depth-first will be called the *parsing policy*, which will be either **df** or **bf**. The chosen form of the agenda will make any other kind of search considerably more expensive computationally than these two basic flavours, but it should not be hard to extend the program to cater for others.

How should the lexical data and the grammar rules be represented? Thinking ahead a little, in due course you are likely to have several sets of grammars and lexicons. It is easy to identify each by a tag of some kind, so that a set can be loaded without having to unload another first: just select the set to use by choosing the right tag. If the tag is an arbitrary Prolog term, this also introduces the chance to filter sets by having tags that are suitable compound terms and then choosing to give the parser a tag that matches some but not all of the tags attached to grammar and lexical rules.

The lexical information needed is the set of categories that any particular word belongs to. Therefore, let us suppose that it is represented by a set of unit clauses of the form

```
lexical(Tag, Word, ListOfCategories).
```

The grammar rules can be represented as unit clauses of the form

```
rule(Tag, LHS_Category, RHS_List).
```

When parsing is top-down, it will be useful to know what the top-level category is. It is reasonable to expect that the user can supply it:

```
initial_category(Tag, TopLevelCategory).
```

There may, however, be many rules that have that category as the left-hand side. To make life easy for the initialization routines when parsing top-down, and to help whoever looks at the chart afterwards to spot what the top-level category was, there will be an assumed ersatz rule of the form

```
rule(Tag, user, [TopLevelCategory]).
```

This cheap device ensures that there will be only a single rule for the (fake) top-level category; it simplifies the code slightly as well as being useful to the user. Of course, the penalty is that you could not then have a category called 'user'. To get round this annoying little restriction, let us further suppose that the user can change the name of the ersatz category by providing a unit clause of the form

```
ersatz_category(Tag, ErsatzCategoryName).
```

8.3   The active chart parser

In line with the aim of making this parser a useful experimental tool, free of side-effects at run-time, there will be two top-level goals. One will parse a given input list of words, providing a chart in due course and also printing it. The other will not print it.

Consider for a moment how this parser could be used. It would be possible to use it incrementally, by trying to parse the input sequence even when it is incomplete (or not known to be complete). When more words are available, parsing can continue. This is feasible because a chart merely grows, so any new chart produced as a result of adding new words to the input will just have the old chart as a subset. In order to do this, however, it will be necessary to know the number of the right-hand vertex of the original input, so that new words can be strung onto the end. Therefore the number of the right-most vertex should also be returned, as well as the chart.

The main parsing effort can be done by a tail-recursive loop corresponding to the loop in the algorithm as described above. The arguments needed in this loop are: the grammar rule tag to use, the parsing strategy and policy, the current state of the chart, the current agenda, and a variable to be instantiated to the final state of the chart at the end of parsing. The tail-recursive loop should provide some means for the user to be able to monitor the parsing process; the easiest way to do this is to provide a user-definable hook of some kind, with a default monitoring action that can be turned on or off. The user's monitoring predicate might want access to the tag, strategy and policy, and the current and updated forms of the chart and agenda. The monitoring hook will therefore need to have seven arguments: call it `monitor/7`. The system will need to know whether monitoring is currently on or off; let us suppose that this is determined by whether a predicate `watching(Tag)` succeeds or fails. This is easy to arrange:

```
watch(Tag) :-
    ( watching(Tag)
    ; assert(watching(Tag))
    ).
nowatch(Tag) :-
    ( retract(watching(Tag))
    ; true
    ).
```

The monitoring system can therefore be defined as in Figure 8.3. This allows users to define their own predicate `user_mon/7`. If it succeeds, then `monitor/7` also succeeds and that is the end of the story. If the user's predicate does not exist or if it fails, and if monitoring is turned on, then the default scheme of printing out the old chart and agenda and then waiting for the user to press the return key will be used. In any circumstance, a call of `monitor/7` will definitely succeed.

8.3.1 The top levels

The top levels are described in Figure 8.4. You will need to define the predicate `print_chart/1` to suit yourself; the simplest but least satisfactory answer is to make it just a call to `write/1`. Notice, by the way,

```
% monitor/7: hook for the user to watch what is going
%     on. The user must have turned on 'watching' by
%     using watch/1 (converse nowatch/1) first, and may
%     define user_mon/7 as desired: the arguments are
%         - tag to identify the rule set
%         - strategy    (S )
%         - policy      (P )
%         - old chart   (OC)
%         - old agenda  (OA)
%         - new chart   (NC)
%         - new agenda  (NA)

monitor(T,S,P,OC,OA,NC,NA) :-
    watching(T),
    user_mon(T,S,P,OC,OA,NC,NA),
    !.
monitor(T,_,_,_,_,NC,NA) :-
    watching(T),
    write('Chart:  '),write(NC),nl,nl,
    write('Agenda:  '),write(NA),nl,nl,
    skip(10),
    !.
monitor(_,_,_,_,_,_,_).
```

Figure 8.3   The monitoring hook.

that the (presumed) built-in predicate **prompt/2** is used to change the prompt for user input if monitoring is turned on. This will help to alert the user to the fact that the system will be waiting for the return key to be pressed, or whatever else a user-supplied monitoring scheme is expecting. In the call of **initial_setup/10**, the **[]+[]** is an empty chart and the **Var-Var** is an empty agenda. The call of **chart/7** is the first call of the tail-recursive parsing loop. The loop itself is defined in Figure 8.5. The predicate **stop_parser/6** is a user-redefinable test of whether to stop the parsing process. The default should be merely that the predicate succeeds if the agenda is empty:

```
stop_parser(_,_,_,Chart,Ag-_,Chart) :-
    var(Ag).
```

An easy mistake to make here is to test instead that the agenda matches a term of the form

```
% parse/4: the TOP-LEVEL goal of all this lot.
%    Produces the chart, then prints it

parse(Tag, WordList, MaxVertex, Chart) :-
    make_chart(Tag, WordList, MaxVertex, Chart),
    nl,
    print_chart(Chart).

% make_chart/4: given tag & a WordList, produce the
%    maximum vertex number and a final chart.

make_chart(T, WordList, MaxVertex, FinalChart) :-
    strategy(T,S),     % choices: bu or td
    policy(T,P),       % choices: df or bf
    ( watching(T) ->
        prompt(_, 'monitor:')
    ;   true
    ),
    initial_setup(T,S,P, WordList, 0, MaxVertex,
                  []+[], InitialChart,
                  Var-Var, InitialAgenda),
    monitor(T,S,P,
            InitialChart, InitialAgenda,
            InitialChart, InitialAgenda),
    chart(T,S,P,
          InitialChart, InitialAgenda, FinalChart).
```

Figure 8.4   The top levels.

Variable - Variable

Any agenda, empty or not, would match such a term. The predicate
active/1 is a user-redefinable test of whether a given edge is active or
not. The default form is simple:

```
active(edge(_, _, [_|_] _, _)).
```

This is exactly the definition of an active edge that was given earlier. There
could be reasons, in certain unusual applications, for using a narrower
definition instead, such as having a non-empty 'needs' list that does not
include some special categories.

The predicate apply_fr/3 applies the fundamental rule to produce a
new edge. A user might also be able to find good reasons for redefining this,

```
% chart/6: the main loop (with monitoring hook).
%     This encapsulates the basic control algorithm.

chart(T,S,P, Chart, Agenda, FinalChart) :-
    stop_parser(T,S,P,Chart,Agenda,FinalChart),
    !.
chart(T,S,P, Chart,
        [AEdge+IEdge|Rest]-Var, FinalChart) :-
    apply_fr(AEdge,IEdge,NewEdge),
    ( active(NewEdge) ->
        add_active_edge(T,S,P, NewEdge,
                        Chart, NewChart,
                        Rest-Var, NewAgenda)
    ; add_inactive_edge(T,S,P, NewEdge,
                        Chart, NewChart,
                        Rest-Var, NewAgenda)
    ),
    monitor(T,S,P,
            Chart, [AEdge+IEdge|Rest]-Var,
            NewChart, NewAgenda),
    chart(T,S,P,NewChart,NewAgenda,FinalChart).
```

Figure 8.5   The main parsing loop.

but even the standard definition will need to take account of the dangers that were described earlier, of unifying two terms and so losing generality in either of the parent edges. Figure 8.6 shows a simple definition. In this predicate, there is a need to construct the term that would have resulted if the categories N1 and N2 had been unified. However, N1 might have involved some variables that also figured in the category C and in the remainder of the 'needs' list, Rest. Both of these must therefore be copied, using the same renaming of variables that was involved in constructing N3, so that the copies can appear as genuinely independent subterms in the new edge. It might be possible to get away without copying them, but it would make any chart printed out by the monitoring system very much harder to comprehend. There is also the danger that the user's own monitoring predicate will carelessly instantiate some variable featuring in the chart, and if so this might be very hard to debug if such an instantiation were to ripple through other parts of the chart!

```
apply_fr(edge(C,F,[N1|Rest],SV,MV),
         edge(N2,_,_,MV,EV),
         edge(NewC,[N3=MV|F],NewRest,SV,EV)) :-
     unify_terms(N1, N2, N3, Subst),
     copy_term(C, NewC, Subst, NewSubst),
     copy_term(Rest, NewRest, NewSubst, _).
```

Figure 8.6   The 'fundamental rule'.

8.3.2   Unifying and copying terms

The predicates `unify_terms/4` and `copy_term/4` referred to in Figure 8.6
are not specific to chart parsing, of course; they are generally useful tools.
It was explained earlier that these operations can be done efficiently by dismantling the term(s) involved and building the result along the way. Prolog
provides various metalogical built-in predicates for this kind of task. The
most abused is `=../2`, called 'univ' ever since its first implementation in
the original Marseille Prolog [Roussel 1975], and it is particularly abused
by novices. If the first argument is instantiated, it instantiates its second
argument to a list consisting of the term's functor name and then the term's
arguments in order. However, in nearly all the published cases the list constructed by 'univ' is never needed in its entirety; only selected elements are
needed. So the system effort that went into constructing the list is wasted,
since all the ingredients are otherwise individually obtainable by using either of the built-in predicates `functor/3` and `arg/3`. The former can be
used in mode `functor(+,-,-)` to extract some information about a term,
or in mode `functor(-,+,+)` to construct a new term whose arguments are
all unique new variables. And `arg/3` can be used in mode `arg(+,+,-)` to
access a particular argument or in mode `arg(+,+,+)` to try to instantiate
a particular argument.

Figure 8.7 shows how the unifying and copying operations can be
defined in terms of these two built-in predicates. It also includes a test,
`equiv_terms/4`, that will be used to check whether two terms are the same
up to consistent renaming of variables. In each case, the predicates deal
with a list of variable-variable substitutions of the form

```
NewVariable = OldVariable
```

describing the renamings. You might want to argue that 'univ' is what
is really needed here to copy terms or to test for equivalence, since only
one call of 'univ' is needed for an N-argument term and then the list of
arguments can be processed by recursing down it, whereas N calls of `arg/3`

are needed. However, this depends on how terms are stored internally. If
terms are stored in such a way that the cost of using **arg/3** to get (say)
the fifth argument of a term is just the same as the cost of getting the
first argument, then it is likely to be better to use the 'functor and arg'
approach. If the cost of using **arg/3** to get the Nth argument depends
on N, then it may well be better to use the 'univ' approach. You should
investigate this.

```
% unify_terms/4: takes two terms, constructs as third
%     argument the term that would have resulted if they
%     had been unified (but they are not unified by this
%     procedure). Also returns as fourth argument a list
%     of the variable substitutions made, for possible
%     later use.

unify_terms(Term1, Term2, Result, FinalSubstitution) :-
    copy_term(Term1, Copy1, [], PartSubstitution),
    copy_term(Term2, Copy2, PartSubstitution,
                                    FinalSubstitution),
    Result = Copy1,
    Result = Copy2.


% copy_term/4: takes a term, creates a copy in which
%     the variables have been changed to new ones in a
%     consistent way. Also constructs a list showing
%     the substitutions made.

copy_term(Term, Copy, SubstSoFar, FinalSubst) :-
    var(Term), !,
    subst_member(SubstSoFar, Term, Copy, FinalSubst).
copy_term(Term, Copy, SubstSoFar, FinalSubst) :-
    functor(Term, Functor, Arity),
    functor(Copy, Functor, Arity),
    copy_term(Arity, Term, Copy, SubstSoFar, FinalSubst).

copy_term(0, Term, Copy, SubstSoFar, SubstSoFar) :- !.
copy_term(N, Term, Copy, SubstSoFar, FinalSubst) :-
    arg(N, Term, TermN),
    copy_term(TermN, CopyN, SubstSoFar, FurtherSubst),
    arg(N, Copy, CopyN),
    M is N-1,
    !,
```

```
       copy_term(M, Term, Copy, FurtherSubst, FinalSubst).

subst_member(Subst, Term, Copy, Subst) :-
    subst_member(Subst, Term, Copy), !.
subst_member(Subst, Term, Copy, [Copy = Term|Subst]).

subst_member([New = Old|_], Term, Copy) :-
    Old == Term,
    !,
    New = Copy.
subst_member([_|Rest], Term, Copy) :-
    subst_member(Rest, Term, Copy).

% equiv_terms/4: checks whether two terms are precisely
%     equivalent in structure, modulo change of variables.
%     This is much narrower than checking whether they
%     could be unified, and is only used in the parser
%     recursion checks. Since this test involves structure
%     smashing, so is not cheap, it is only applied after
%     weaker tests have dug up likely equivalences.

equiv_terms(T1, T2, Subst, NewSubst) :-
    var(T1),
    !,
    var(T2),
    ( subst_member(Subst, T1, T3) ->
        T3 == T2,
        NewSubst = Subst
    ;   NewSubst = [T2=T1|Subst]
    ).
equiv_terms(_, T2, _, _) :-
    var(T2),    % If T2 is a variable but T1 is not..
    !,
    fail.       % ... they cannot be equivalent.
equiv_terms(T1, T2, Subst, FinalSubst) :-
    functor(T1, F, N),
    functor(T2, F, N),
    equiv_terms(N, T1, T2, Subst, FinalSubst).

equiv_terms(0, _, _, S, S).
equiv_terms(N, T1, T2, Subst, FinalSubst) :-
    arg(N, T1, A1),
    arg(N, T2, A2),
    equiv_terms(A1, A2, Subst, MidSubst),
    M is N-1,
```

```
        !,
        equiv_terms(M, T1, T2, MidSubst, FinalSubst).
```

Figure 8.7   Unifying, copying and testing terms for equivalence.

8.3.3   Adding edges to the chart

The predicates `add_active_edge/8` and `add_inactive_edge/8` in Figure 8.5 were intended to do all the work of adding an edge to the chart. This includes the creation of new empty active edges when necessary, and adding new configs to the agenda as a result. In fact there will be four main predicates needed:

- `add_active_edge/8` deals with the addition of a new active edge. If the parsing strategy is top-down, this will cause the addition of a list of new empty edges whose category is the first one needed by the new edge.

- `add_active_list/8` will call `add_active_edge/8` for each of a list of active (empty) edges.

- `add_inactive_edge/8` deals with the addition of a new inactive edge. If the parsing strategy is bottom-up, this will cause the addition of a list of new empty edges that can immediately marry with the new inactive edge.

- `add_inactive_list/8` will call `add_inactive_edge/8` for each of a list of active (empty) edges.

In tandem with adding new edges it will be necessary to add new configs to the agenda. How this is done will vary slightly according to whether a new edge is active or inactive, and so it will be simplest to have two further predicates:

- `add_active_configs/5` adds the configs appropriate to a new active edge.

- `add_inactive_configs/5` adds the configs appropriate to a new inactive edge.

Figure 8.8 shows how these can be defined.

```
% add_active_edge/8: arguments are tag, strategy, policy,
%     edge (active), old chart, resulting new chart, old
%     agenda, resulting new agenda. Adds a new active edge
%     and updates the agenda with whatever new configs are
%     created as a result. This is strategy-dependent.

add_active_edge(_,td,_, Edge,
                OldA+OldI, OldA+OldI,
                OldAg-OldV, OldAg-OldV) :-
    Edge = edge(C,[],N,V,V),              % Empty, active?
    member(edge(C1,[],N1,V,V), OldA), % Look for similar,
    equiv_terms(C1,C,[],PartSubst),       % .. test for
    equiv_terms(N1,N,PartSubst,_),        % equivalence.
    !.                    % If so, do not add a duplicate edge
add_active_edge(T,td,P, Edge,
                OldA+OldI, NewA+OldI,
                OldAg-OldV, NewAg-NewV) :-
    Edge = edge(_,_,[N|_],_,EV),
    downward_edge_list(T,N,EV,EdgeList),
    !,                 % Aha ... there are relevant rules!
    add_active_configs(P, Edge, OldI,
                       OldAg-OldV, MidAg-MidV),
    add_active_list(T,td,P, EdgeList,
                    [Edge|OldA]+OldI, NewA+OldI,
                    MidAg-MidV, NewAg-NewV).
add_active_edge(_,_,P, Edge,
                OldA+OldI, [Edge|OldA]+OldI,
                OldAg-OldV, NewAg-NewV) :-
    add_active_configs(P, Edge, OldI,
                       OldAg-OldV, NewAg-NewV).

% add_active_list/8: like add_active_edge/8, but works
%     through a list of active edges.

add_active_list(T,S,P, [Edge|Rest],
                OldA+I, NewA+I,
                OldAg-OldV, NewAg-NewV) :-
    !,
    add_active_edge(T,S,P, Edge,
                    OldA+I, MidA+I,
                    OldAg-OldV, MidAg-MidV),
    add_active_list(T,S,P, Rest,
                    MidA+I, NewA+I,
```

```
                              MidAg-MidV, NewAg-NewV).
add_active_list(_,_,_,[],A+I,A+I,Ag-V,Ag-V).

% add_active_configs/5: given policy, new edge, list of
%    inactive edges, old agenda, then creates a new
%    agenda by adding all possible configurations to the
%    agenda and returning the new agenda.

add_active_configs(df,
           ActiveEdge,
           [InactiveEdge|MoreIs],
           OldAg-OldV,
           NewAg-OldV) :-
    candidate(ActiveEdge,InactiveEdge),
    !,
    MidAg = [ActiveEdge+InactiveEdge|OldAg],
    add_active_configs(df,
                   ActiveEdge,
                   MoreIs,
                   MidAg-OldV,
                   NewAg-OldV).
add_active_configs(bf,
           ActiveEdge,
           [InactiveEdge|MoreIs],
           OldAg-OldV,
           OldAg-NewV) :-
    candidate(ActiveEdge,InactiveEdge),
    !,
    OldV = [ActiveEdge+InactiveEdge|MidV],
    add_active_configs(bf,
                   ActiveEdge,
                   MoreIs,
                   OldAg-MidV,
                   OldAg-NewV).
add_active_configs(P,
           ActiveEdge,
           [_|MoreIs],
           OldAg-OldV,
           NewAg-NewV) :-
    add_active_configs(P,
                   ActiveEdge,
                   MoreIs,
                   OldAg-OldV,
                   NewAg-NewV).
add_active_configs(_,_,[],Ag-V,Ag-V).
```

```
% add_inactive_edge/8: arguments are tag, strategy,
%     policy, edge (inactive), old chart, resulting new
%     chart, old agenda, resulting new agenda. Adds a new
%     inactive edge and updates the agenda with whatever
%     new configs are created as a result. This is
%     strategy-dependent.

% NOTE: you might be tempted to think that a check on
%     whether an inactive edge was duplicated is
%     superfluous. The plausible, but wrong, reason
%     would be that the check against duplicate active
%     edges would clobber the ancestor of any putative
%     duplicate active edge. However, with compound
%     terms for categories and recursive grammars around,
%     it's easily possible for an inactive edge to come
%     from two different combinations of active and
%     inactive edge, if the difference is only to do
%     with which parts are instantiated. To give a
%     non-parser example, the terms
%             a(A,2) and a(1,B)
%     will unify, but so will the terms
%             a(1,2) and a(A,B)
%     to give the same result. The same thing can happen
%     with edges.

add_inactive_edge(_,bu,_, Edge,
                  A+OldI, A+OldI,
                  OldAg-OldV, OldAg-OldV) :-
    Edge = edge(C,F,[],SV,EV),            % If inactive,
    member(edge(C1,F1,[],SV,EV),OldI),  % find similar,
    equiv_terms(C1,C,[],PartSubst),       % .. test for
    equiv_terms(F1,F,PartSubst,_),        % equivalence
    !.                      % in order to avoid a duplicate edge.
add_inactive_edge(T,bu,P, Edge,
                  A+OldI, NewA+[Edge|OldI],
                  OldAg-OldV, NewAg-NewV) :-
    Edge = edge(Cat,_,[],SV,_),
    upward_edge_list(T,Cat,SV,EdgeList),
    !,                      % Aha ... there are relevant rules!
    add_inactive_configs(P, Edge, A,
                         OldAg-OldV, MidAg-MidV),
    add_active_list(T,td,P, EdgeList,
                    A+[Edge|OldI], NewA+[Edge|OldI],
                    MidAg-MidV, NewAg-NewV).
```

```
add_inactive_edge(_,_,P, Edge,
                    A+OldI, A+[Edge|OldI],
                    OldAg-OldV, NewAg-NewV) :-
    add_inactive_configs(P, Edge, A,
                         OldAg-OldV, NewAg-NewV).


% add_inactive_list/8: given tag, strategy, policy,
%    list of inactive edges, old chart, get new chart,
%    given old agenda, get new agenda. This is done by
%    adding each inactive edge in turn.

add_inactive_list(T,S,P, [E|More],
                    Chart, NewChart,
                    Agenda, NewAgenda) :-
    !,
    add_inactive_edge(T,S,P, E,
                      Chart, MidChart,
                      Agenda, MidAgenda),
    add_inactive_list(T,S,P, More,
                      MidChart, NewChart,
                      MidAgenda, NewAgenda).
add_inactive_list(_,_,_, _,
                    Chart, Chart,
                    Agenda, Agenda).


% add_inactive_configs/5: given policy, new edge, list
%    of active edges, old agenda, then creates a new
%    agenda by adding all possible configurations to
%    the agenda and returning the new agenda.

add_inactive_configs(df,
            InactiveEdge,
            [ActiveEdge|MoreAs],
            OldAg-OldV,
            NewAg-OldV) :-
    candidate(ActiveEdge,InactiveEdge),
    !,
    MidAg = [ActiveEdge+InactiveEdge|OldAg],
    add_inactive_configs(df,
                    InactiveEdge,
                    MoreAs,
                    MidAg-OldV,
                    NewAg-OldV).
add_inactive_configs(bf,
            InactiveEdge,
```

```
                [ActiveEdge|MoreAs],
                OldAg-OldV,
                OldAg-NewV) :-
        candidate(ActiveEdge,InactiveEdge),
        !,
        OldV = [ActiveEdge+InactiveEdge|MidV],
        add_inactive_configs(bf,
                        InactiveEdge,
                        MoreAs,
                        OldAg-MidV,
                        OldAg-NewV).
    add_inactive_configs(P,
                InactiveEdge,
                [_|MoreAs],
                OldAg-OldV,
                NewAg-NewV) :-
        add_inactive_configs(P,
                        InactiveEdge,
                        MoreAs,
                        OldAg-OldV,
                        NewAg-NewV).
    add_inactive_configs(_,_,[],Ag-V,Ag-V).
```

Figure 8.8   Adding edges and configs.

The predicate `candidate/2` takes an active and an inactive edge as its arguments, and succeeds if that pair will make a valid config. Normally this test is so simple that it is silly to have it encapsulated as a separate predicate. However, there are possible applications within, say, a plan recognition system in which it is desirable to change this test. For example, it might be desirable to try to marry an active and an inactive edge that do not meet at a common vertex if it turns out that the intervening subsequence of the original input is concerned with a completely different plan. A chart parser can be used in this way to recognize intermixed sequences of actions deriving from completely independent plans, and even to recognize and learn subsequences that are not explicitly represented within the grammar rules but which are semantically equivalent to ones that are.

Figure 8.9 defines `candidate/2`. This clause checks whether two candidates are unifiable, but it must not actually unify them. The `\+(\+(..))` idea is a very cheap and simple way to do this. Recall that `\+/1` is defined as though by the clauses

```
\+(Goal) :-
    Goal,
    !, fail.
\+(_).
```

so that the success of a \+/1 call cannot cause any variables to become
instantiated.

There are two predicates needed for adding edges that are as yet
undefined, namely the two that actually make use of the rules to determine what new empty active edges there will be. The first is **up-
ward_edge_list/4**, which is called when a new inactive edge is being added
and the parsing strategy is bottom-up. In this case, new empty edges are
added at the start vertex of the inactive edge, and they are edges that can
marry with the inactive edge straight away. Thus this predicate needs the
tag, and the inactive edge's category and start vertex as arguments, and
it should return a list of empty active edges to be added to the chart by
add_active_list/8.

The second predicate is **downward_edge_list/4**, which is very similar but is for use when a new active edge is added and the parsing strategy
is also top-down. Its arguments are the tag, the category that the new
active edge needs first and the end vertex of the new active edge, and a
variable to be instantiated to a list of new empty active edges.

These two predicates are defined in Figure 8.10. In both of these
predicates the T^ existential quantifier is needed in the second argument
of the **setof/3** in case the tag T contains free variables. In the definition
of **downward_edge_list/4**, the **setof/3** is made to collect up terms of the
form

    Cat - RHS

rather than just RHS, just in case there are also free variables within the
term that **Cat** is instantiated to. This will then ensure that those free
variables are correctly unified with the variables in the corresponding **RHS**
during the **setof/3** operation.

```
% candidate/2: takes two edges, succeeds if they are
%    candidates for application of the fundamental rule.

candidate(edge(_,_,[N1|_],_,V), edge(N2,_,L,V,_)) :-
    \+(\+(N1=N2)).
```

Figure 8.9   Testing whether two edges make a 'config'.

```
% downward_edge_list/4: given a tag, a category and a
%      vertex, make up a list of new embryo edges.

downward_edge_list(T, Cat, Vertex, EdgeList) :-
    setof(Cat-RHS, T^rule(T,Cat,RHS), CatRHSList),
    rhs_to_edge_list(Vertex, CatRHSList, EdgeList)..

rhs_to_edge_list(V, [Cat-RHS|More],
                 [edge(Cat,[],RHS,V,V)|Rest]) :-
    !,
    rhs_to_edge_list(V,More,Rest).
rhs_to_edge_list(_,[],[]).

% upward_edge_list/4: given a tag, a category and a
%      vertex, make up a list of new embryo edges.

upward_edge_list(T, Cat, Vertex, EdgeList) :-
    setof(Parent=[Cat|Rest],
          T^rule(T,Parent,[Cat|Rest]),
          RuleList),
    rule_to_edge_list(RuleList, Vertex, EdgeList).

rule_to_edge_list([Parent=[Cat|Etc]|More], V,
          [edge(Parent,[],[Cat|Etc],V,V)|Rest]) :-
    !,
    rule_to_edge_list(More,V,Rest).
rule_to_edge_list([],_,[]).
```

Figure 8.10   Determining the new empty active edges.

8.3.4   The initialization stage

All that remains is to define the initial_setup/10 predicate, as used in Figure 8.4. It takes the following arguments:

- The tag, strategy and policy – these will be needed by a call of add_inactive_list/8, which will add the very first edges to the chart.

- A list of the words to be parsed.

- A number representing the first vertex. Usually this will be 0, but if parsing is being done incrementally it will be the maximum vertex found in the partial parse of all the words that preceded these new ones.

- A variable to be instantiated to the number of the rightmost vertex, for later use if parsing is being done incrementally.

- A 'seed' chart, which will normally be []+[] but might be the result of the previous parse in incremental parsing.

- A variable to be instantiated to the result of adding inactive edges to the 'seed chart' for each word's categories.

- A 'seed' agenda, which will normally be Var-Var but could be the previous agenda if parsing is incremental and the user had chosen to halt the previous parse before its agenda was empty.

- A variable to be instantiated to the agenda created by adding new configs to the 'seed' agenda as a result of adding new inactive edges and at least one empty active edge to the chart.

The predicate is defined in Figure 8.11.

```
% initial_setup/10: given tag, strategy, policy,
%    word list, min vertex, return number giving the
%    maximum vertex number, and from a seed chart
%    (typically []+[] if not re-starting) create an
%    initial chart and from a seed agenda (typically
%    Var-Var if not re-starting) create an initial agenda.

initial_setup(T,S,P, WordList, MinVertex, MaxVertex,
        SeedChart, InitialChart,
        SeedAgenda, InitialAgenda) :-
    words_to_edges(T, WordList,
                MinVertex, MaxVertex, EdgeList),
    add_inactive_list(T,S,P, EdgeList,
                SeedChart, TempChart,
                SeedAgenda, TempAgenda),
    initial_category(T, C),
    (ersatz_category(T, EC)
    ; EC = user
    ),
    !,
    add_active_edge(T,S,P,
                edge(EC,[],[C],MinVertex,MinVertex),
                TempChart, InitialChart,
```

```
                   TempAgenda, InitialAgenda).

% words_to_edges/5: given tag, word list, min vertex
%    number, return maximum  vertex number (for later
%    use in inspecting final chart) and list of
%    inactive edges derived from lexical data about
%    each word.

words_to_edges(T, WordList,
                 MinVertex, MaxVertex, EdgeList) :-
    words_to_edges(T, WordList,
                     MinVertex, MaxVertex,
                     [], EdgeList).

words_to_edges(_, [], N, N, Answer, Answer).
words_to_edges(T, [W|More],
                 N, MaxVertex, List, Answer) :-
    !,
    ( lexical(T,W,Categories) ->
        true
    ; write('Word '),
      write(W),
      write(' has no lexical entry under tag '),
      write(T),
      write(' - given not_in_lexicon/2 category'),
      nl,
      Categories = [not_in_lexicon(T,W)]
    ),
    N1 is N+1,
    cats_to_edges(Categories,W,N,N1,List,NewList),
    words_to_edges(T,More,N1,MaxVertex,NewList,Answer).

cats_to_edges([],_,_,_,List,List).
cats_to_edges([C|More],W,N,N1,List,Answer) :-
    cats_to_edges(More,W,N,N1,
                    [edge(C,[word(W)=N],[],N,N1)|List],
                    Answer).
```

Figure 8.11   The initialization of the chart and agenda.

8.4   Further work

An active chart parser like this has many uses. Obviously it can be used in
natural language processing tasks. However, it can be used for many other
sequence analysis jobs too, such as plan recognition [Ross and Lewis 1987]
or automated protocol analysis [van Lehn 1987]. In this case a sequence
of commands or actions is available, possibly not yet complete. Given a
grammar of ways of expanding a set of high-level intentions, it is possible
to parse the sequence so far in order to try to recognize which intention or
intentions lie behind it. There are several complicating factors:

- There may be more than one intention active, and the two sequences
  may be interleaved. However, it is possible to handle this by modifying the fundamental rule so that the edges do not actually have to
  meet at a vertex in order to be combinable. This idea was hinted at
  in Section 8.1.1.

- The user might suspend an intention and resume it later. This is
  handled in just the same way.

- The grammar might not be complete. It is, however, possible to
  search the chart for 'interesting gaps' of various kinds, and test
  whether the subsequence that could not be parsed is in fact semantically equivalent to what was needed by the grammar to plug the gap.
  The parser can even be modified to learn new rules by generalizing
  from such unparsable subsequences.

- The actions may be flawed, because the user has some misconceptions about them. Ways to detect such misconceptions are an active
  topic of research; the problem is that in practice there is very little
  constraint on the kind of misconception that is possible.

Exercise 8.1   Implement such a sequence analysis system. This
is a large and open-ended exercise.

8.5   Thoughts on efficiency

This program clearly shows the need for some kind of user-definable indexing in Prolog in order to make tasks such as the accessing of edge/5 terms
that start or end at a specified vertex efficient. Unfortunately record/3
is not much use, because the key can only usefully be atomic (only the
principal functor name matters) and in some Prologs the key cannot be
an integer; nor is record/3 that fast in most systems. At present all you
really have in many systems is the clause indexing mechanism, so you have
to make do with assert/retract operations and all that that implies if you
want to cut down on searching through big data structures such as long

lists. Proper arrays, hunks, hash tables or other such features now commonplace in the LISP world would be very good to have. Expert Systems International's Prolog-2 does let you specify hash tables for particular predicates, but these are only used by the calling mechanism. It would be nice to have some way of specifying that anything with a given principal functor was to be accessed through a set of hash tables, sub-indexing specifiable by the user in some way. Some systems, such as Arity Prolog, do offer B-trees and hash tables, but it would be useful if such features were more standardized throughout the Prolog world. The semantics of such features can be awkward, however – see Barklund and Millroth [1987] and Eriksson and Rayner [1984], for example.

SUMMARY

- In Prolog, parsing and DCGs are not synonymous.

- You do not actually have to unify two terms to see if they will unify.

- Prolog's metalogical facilities can be used to manipulate terms, for instance to copy them or check whether they unify, very efficiently.

- =../2 is often unnecessary; think carefully about whether you really need to use it.

- Copying terms by assert/retract is unnecessarily slow.

- Prolog is not very good at handling large amounts of data.

ADDITIONAL EXERCISES

8.2 In the program described in this chapter, the chart has been represented as two lists, one of active edges and one of inactive edges. Convert the whole program to use a more efficient representation – for example, as two balanced trees indexed by vertex. Test it to see whether your version is more efficient in practice.

8.3 The program currently handles top-down and bottom-up parsing, either breadth- or depth-first. Extend the range of available strategies and policies.

8.4 Build a set of interactive monitoring tools. For example, it would be useful to be able to see the changes to the chart at any cycle and it would be useful to be able to ask for all the edges that are instances of some named category.

8.5 It was suggested that the fundamental rule could be modified so that an active and an inactive edge need not meet at a vertex: this is useful in sequence analysis. However, it would seem that this would greatly increase the theoretical worst-case complexity of the chart. Do experiments to see whether such a modification does in fact lead to the creation of very many more edges in practice.

8.6 The chart parser as described has explicit parameters for strategy and policy. However, if you are only interested in one particular strategy and policy then it is possible to write a very much smaller chart parser with a much more limited functionality than the one described, based on `bagof/3`. Try to write a version that would fit on a single page if all comments were omitted – it is possible. Test it for speed.

9

A meta-level interpreter

One of the common complaints about Prolog, usually voiced by those who have recently been obliged to learn it for some reason, is that the flow of control is very limited. This chapter explains how the flow of control can easily be modified from the standard one of depth-first search of clauses and purely chronological backtracking. The key idea is *meta-level interpretation* of programs: treating programs as data and executing that data in new ways.

9.1 Meta-level interpretation

A *meta-level interpreter* is an interpreter that treats a given program as data, and that executes instructions according to that data in some specialized way. A *meta-circular* interpreter is such an interpreter that is capable of executing itself – which means that it must be written in the appropriate language, of course. The idea was first discussed in Steele and Sussman [1978]. It is widely agreed that meta-level interpretation is a very useful technique, although it would seem that the extra level of interpretation required must cause programs to execute appreciably more slowly than they would if they were run directly. That is not necessarily so, however; for example, Takeuchi and Furukawa [1985] show how meta-interpretation can be made much more efficient by transforming it by *partial evaluation*. The basic concept of partial evaluation is easy to understand. Suppose, for example, that you have a function in some programming language that returns the Nth root of a given number. The arguments are, presumably, N and the number whose root is to be found. If you happen to know that N is always going to be 2 in some application, then it becomes possible to partially evaluate the text of the function definition to replace it by a one-argument function that is simpler and much faster. If the partial evaluator knew what the function was supposed to do, then in theory it might even be possible to replace the function by an entirely different and much simpler one. Normally such teleological information is not available, and a partial evaluator can only look for optimizations of the code in the light of knowledge about how the function in question will always be called. A form of logic program transformation that does preserve full equivalence between the original and the transformed versions, for programs in a pure subset of Prolog (that is, without side-effects or metalogical features), can be found in Tamaki and Taisuke [1984].

The idea that is described in Takeuchi and Furukawa [1985] is to compile the meta-interpreter and some specific program it is to run into something much more efficient. In doing this, the generality of the meta-interpreter is lost because a partial evaluator has been able to look at the program to be run and has found ways of reconstructing the meta-interpreter to make it run that one program much more efficiently, but perhaps unable to run any other. Even without using such an idea, meta-interpretation can be very powerful. Consider, for example, a program that solves algebraic equations. One algorithm for such a task might look like this:

```
- input the equation
- repeat until solved:
    - is it linear in the unknown? If so,
        apply a linear transformation to
        it to simplify it
    - is it quadratic in the unknown? If
        so, apply the quadratic formula
        to solve it
    - is it factorizable? If so, factorize
        it and solve each factor
    - is it trigonometric? If so, try
        special trig transformations
    - if it is not directly recognizable
        try changing the variable in some
        plausible way
```

A simple-minded algorithm like this might be able to solve an equation such as

$$\cos(x) + \cos(2x) + \cos(3x) = 0$$

by going several times round this loop, making some unnecessary tests on the way. However, the very form of this equation provides the clue to a whole sequence of steps that will solve it, without having to test the form of the transformed equation after each step. For example, a senior high-school student might at once recognize that the first and third terms on the left-hand side can be rewritten as a product involving the second term, and so the left-hand side will become factorizable. An experienced mathematician might well recognize that the entire left-hand side is just the real part of the sum of a geometric series involving e^{ix}, so that it is trivial to solve.

A meta-level algorithm for equation-solving might look for such clues first of all, and invoke a whole series of steps when the right clues are found. This adds the overhead of looking for much more specialized kinds of clue, and saves the overhead of going many times round a simple loop such as the one sketched above. Such a meta-level algorithm is arguably much closer to what a human mathematician does, too. The interested reader is referred to papers on PRESS, a Prolog Equation Solving System developed at the University of Edinburgh – see Bundy and Welham [1981], Sterling *et al.* [1982], Silver [1986].

9.2   Meta-interpretation of Prolog

Many textbooks and manuals contain an example of a very simple Prolog interpreter in Prolog that is some trivial variant of the one shown in Figure 9.1. However, it is a very bad example. First, it is pointless except to suggest how the thing can be done in Prolog. Second, it does not work! To see this, look at how it handles this trivial program:

```
hi :-
    write(hello),
    nl.
```

The goal `solve(hi)` will be handled by clause 3, and within that the variable Body will be instantiated to

```
(write(hello),nl)
```

Clause 2 will be used to run this by calling

```
solve(true)  :-      % clause 1
    !.
solve((A,B))  :-     % clause 2
    !,
    solve(A),
    solve(B).
solve(Goal)  :-      % clause 3
    clause(Goal, Body),
    solve(Body).
solve(Goal)  :-      % clause 4
    call(Goal).
```

Figure 9.1   The standard, bad meta-interpreter.

```
solve(write(hello)),
solve(nl)
```

Since neither `write/1` nor `nl/0` has user-defined clauses available, clause 4 will be used to run both of these goals. So far, the right behaviour seems to be happening. But consider what happens if control backtracks later to the original `solve(hi)` goal. Prolog had used clause 3 for it, and it will now try clause 4 – which will succeed, writing out the message a second time. The problem is, of course, that clause 3 is meant to be used for user-defined goals and clause 4 is meant to be used for built-in goals, but there is nothing in the program to prevent clause 4 from being used for user-defined goals too.

How can this problem be fixed? Some Prologs provide a built-in predicate that tests whether a given functor corresponds to a built-in predicate. All Prologs should provide `clause/2` at least. Clause 4 could be modified to read:

```
solve(Goal) :-
    \+(clause(Goal,_)),
    call(Goal).
```

so that the goal is only called if there is no clause whose head matches the goal. This can still go wrong if you have a Prolog compiler and are running compiled code. In this case, the original terms that were the source of the clauses for the goal may no longer be around to be found by `clause/2`, but the compiled versions may exist to be called by `call/1`. Thus clause 4 would again be used instead of clause 3 to run some user-defined goal, but at least clause 3 would not have succeeded in the first place.

The trivial interpreter in Figure 9.1 also fails to handle cuts, disjuncts and other control constructs properly. Consider this program:

```
trash :-
    !, fail.
trash :-
    write('You will never see this message'),
    nl.
```

The goal `solve(trash)` will print out the unwanted message, because clause 3 will first pick up the body (`!,fail`), clause 2 will be used to run this body, clause 4 will be used for each of the two goals involved. In particular, the goal

```
solve(!)
```

will lead to a `call(!)` goal, which will have no effect since it will merely cut the final clause for `solve/1`. The subsequent goal of

```
solve(fail)
```

will cause backtracking within clause 3 to find a further clause body for
`trash`.

It is possible to amend this interpreter so that it handles a cut in a
clause properly. The key idea (due, I think, to Fernando Pereira) is mildly
ingenious and is best explained by means of an example. Suppose that
you wish to design a meta-intepreter that runs Prolog as normal, but also
writes out useful tracing messages. You need it to handle cuts properly.
Consider a clause such as

```
junk :-
    alpha, !, beta, gamma, delta.
```

In the trivial interpreter above, clause 2 would be used to run the body of
this, by calling

```
solve(alpha),
solve((!,beta,gamma,delta))
```

and the second of these goals would again be handled by clause 2, by calling

```
solve(!),
solve((beta,gamma,delta))
```

Now suppose that control backtracks to the `solve(!)` because of some
failure. What should happen? Clearly the call of `solve(junk)` must be
made to fail, but how? Not, clearly, by simple backtracking, for then the
information about why the backtracking is happening will have been lost by
the time control backtracks to the `solve(junk)` call. There must be some
information made available to *show the outcome of the call*. So, another
argument is needed: `solve/1` must become `solve/2`. Here is a first attempt
at a new version of clause 2:

```
solve((A,B), Outcome) :-
    solve(A, OutcomeOfA),
    solve(B, Outcome).
```

What is `OutcomeOfA` doing here? Consider `junk` again: it leads to the goals

```
solve(!, OutcomeOfCut),
solve((beta,gamma,delta), OutcomeOfWholeClause)
```

Suppose control backtracks to the `solve(!,..)` goal. Then it will be easy
to arrange that `OutcomeOfCut` becomes instantiated to some suitable term,
to mark the fact that there was a backtrack to a cut. But at this point, the
`solve(!,..)` goal should succeed again, and in this case the remainder of
the clause for `junk` should not be run at all, and the outcome of the whole
clause should be that it was cut. The meta-interpreter can pick up this
information about the outcome and take appropriate action.

Thus clause 2 should look something like this:

```
solve((A,B), Outcome) :-
   solve(A, OutcomeOfA),
   ( cut_happened(OutComeOfA) ->
       Outcome = OutcomeOfA
   ;   solve(B, Outcome)
   ).
```

Imagine that clause 2 was called from clause 3. What should clause 3 now look like? It needs to react to the outcome, like this:

```
solve(Goal, Outcome) :-
   clause(Goal, Body),
   solve(Body, OutcomeOfBody),
   ( cut_happened(OutcomeOfBody) ->
       !, fail
   ;   successful(Outcome)  % or whatever
   ).
```

Here the cut–fail combination ensures that it is the call of `solve(Goal,..)` that fails.

The 'outcome' argument, in this simple interpreter, merely needs to register whether a call was cut or not. The simplest way to do this is to leave it alone, uninstantiated, if the call succeeded and to instantiate it to something when the meta-interpreter has a second go at a cut. However, that something can carry further information. In particular, it can carry information about *which ancestor goal is to be cut*. Then clause 3 would look something like this:

```
solve(Goal, Outcome) :-
   clause(Goal, Body),
   solve(Body, OutcomeOfBody),
   ( ( cut_happened(OutcomeOfBody),
       is_it_this_one(Goal,OutcomeOfBody) ) ->
           !, fail
   ;       Outcome = OutcomeOfBody
   ).
```

Thus it is possible to provide an 'ancestor cut'. A few Prologs already provide something like this. If yours does not, you now know how to create it for yourself.

In order to spell out some details, the next section describes such a meta-interpreter that also provides some further features. It offers a very useful form of the predicate `ancestors/1` that supplies information about the calling goals, and builds a list of the goals on the successful proof path.

9.3   A practical meta-interpreter

This meta-interpreter provides a predicate `ancestors/1` that instantiates its argument to a list of terms of the form

```
ParentGoal = [Body1, Body2, ...]
```

where the list contains all those bodies of clauses for the named parent goal that have not yet been tried. It also provides a predicate `fail(Goal)` that behaves like a cut, but doesn't just fail the parent goal. It fails all the ancestor goals back to and including the most recent one that matches the argument. Thus `fail(_)` will behave exactly like a cut, since the immediate parent goal will match the argument. Between them, these two predicates provide an easy way to escape from purely chronological backtracking: `ancestors/1` provides the information needed to decide which ancestor to cut with the aid of `fail/1`.

The meta-interpreter also builds a list of terms of the following types:

- `Goal/called`, indicating when the user-defined `Goal` was called.

- `Goal/done`, indicating the point where the user-defined `Goal` finally succeeded.

- `Goal`, indicating that the `Goal` was a built-in goal.

These terms describe the successful proof path, hence there are no terms to describe failures of any sort.

The meta-interpreter is shown in Figure 9.2. There are three top-level goals. The simplest, `run/1`, just runs its argument. If you want a list describing the successful proof path as well, use `run/2`. Both of these call `run/5`, whose arguments are as follows:

- The goal(s) to be run.

- An argument used to convey the information about backtracking and cuts. Normally it is uninstantiated, but a `fail/1` goal or backtracking to a cut will cause it to be instantiated to a term

  ```
  backing_up(Ancestor)
  ```

  where `Ancestor` is a term meant to match the ancestor that is to be failed.

- A list giving the data about the ancestor goals that will be needed by a call of the goal `ancestors/1`.

- A list giving the proof path so far.

- A variable to be instantiated to the final proof path.

```
run(Goal) :-
    run(Goal, backing_up(_), [], [], _).

run(Goal, List) :-
    run(Goal, backing_up(_), [], [], List).

run(!, backing_up(_), _, G, [!|G]).
run(!, backing_up(Goal), [Goal=_|_], G, G).
run(fail(Goal),
        backing_up(Goal), _, G, [fail(Goal)|G]) :-
    !. % Cut here in case user tries to redefine fail/1.
run((P,Q), backing_up(To), L, G1, G3) :-
    !, % This is the only clause for a conjunction
    run(P, backing_up(Goal), L, G1, G2),
    ( nonvar(Goal),
      G3 = G2,
      To = Goal
    ; run(Q, backing_up(To), L, G2, G3)
    ).
run((P;Q), backing_up(To), L, G1, G2) :-
    !, % This is the only clause for a disjunction
    ( run(P, backing_up(To), L, G1, G2)
    ; run(Q, backing_up(To), L, G1, G2)
    ).
run(ancestors(L), _, L, G, [ancestors(L)|G]) :-
    !. % Cut here in case user redefines ancestors/1.
run(P, backing_up(To), L, G1, [P/done|G2]) :-
    functor(P, Func, ArgCount),
    functor(Pgeneral, Func, ArgCount),
    findall(Q=Ref, clause(Pgeneral,Q,Ref), BodyList),
    \+(BodyList = []),
    !, % The only clause for a user-defined predicate.
    select(Body=Ref, BodyList, Outstanding),
    clause(P, Body, Ref),
    run(Body, backing_up(To),
        [P=Outstanding|L], [P/called|G1], G2),
    ( nonvar(To),
      To = P,
      !, fail
    ; true
    ).
run(P, backing_up(_), _, G, [P|G]) :-
```

```
      % If you want a 'query the user' facility,
      % or if you want the system to gripe about
      % non-existent predicates, put it here!
   call(P).

select(Item, [Item|Rest], Rest).
select(Item, [_|Rest], Tail) :-
    select(Item, Rest, Tail).
```

Figure 9.2   A practical meta-interpreter.

The second-to-last clause for `run/5` needs a little explanation. The two `functor/3` goals serve to instantiate `Pgeneral` to the most general form of the goal P, so that all clauses for the goal can be found – even those that will not match the specific goal. This information is useful if you want to extend the meta-interpreter to be a fancy debugger that will show even those clauses which are not tried for a given goal. You may also wonder why `findall/3` is used here instead of, say, `bagof/3`. The reason is that `Pgeneral` may contain free variables, and these ought to be treated as existentially quantified. If `bagof/3` were used instead, then it might not pick up all the clause bodies first time.

The goal

```
\+(BodyList=[])
```

is the test that P is a user-defined predicate. The `BodyList` contains terms of the form

```
Body = DatabaseReference
```

because the clause bodies are currently in their most general form. When P is matched with the head of a clause, some variables in that head may become instantiated, and so the same variables in the body must also be instantiated. The match between P and a clause head, to cause the body to be instantiated as necessary, happens in the goal

```
clause(P, Body, Ref)
```

The following example shows what the proof path list looks like. Imagine that the following program is run:

```
try(X) :-
    p(X), q(X).

p(X) :-
```

```
        get_example(X).

    q(X) :-
        number(X),
        0 is X mod 2.
    q(X) :-
        atom(X).

    get_example(12).
    get_example(twelve).
```

In response to the goal

```
    | ?- run(try(A), L).
```

you will get first the following answer (where the list L has been laid out in a form more convenient for understanding its contents):

```
    L = [try(12)/done,
        q(12)/done,
            0 is 12 mod 2,
            number(12),
        q(12)/called,
        p(12)/done,
            get_example(12)/done,
            true,
            get_example(12)/called,
        p(12)/called,
        try(12)/called]
    A = 12
```

and on backtracking you will get the second answer:

```
    L = [try(twelve)/done,
        q(twelve)/done,
            atom(twelve),
        q(twelve)/called,
        p(twelve)/done,
            get_example(twelve)/done,
            true,
            get_example(twelve)/called,
        p(twelve)/called,
        try(twelve)/called]
    A = twelve
```

Notice that, for example, in this second answer p(X) was called, but the X was instantiated later, at the time that the call of **get_example/1** succeeded. If you want the path list to contain

```
p(X)/called
```

rather than the misleading

```
p(twelve)/called
```

you will need to insert some kind of term copying operation. See the chart parser program in Chapter 8 for how to do this.

9.3.1   An example of an ancestral cut

The following simple example may help to explain how the meta-interpreter handles a `fail/1` goal. Consider this trivial program:

```
test(X) :-
    a(X), b(X).

a(X) :- g(X), h(X).
b(_).

g(X) :- p(X), fail(a(_)).
g(_).
h(_).

p(5).
```

The goal

```
?- run(test(5), backing_up(A), ...).
```

leads to the following calling sequence:

```
run(test(5), backing_up(A), ..) calls
. run((a(5),b(5)), backing_up(A), ..), which calls
.. run(a(5), backing_up(B), ..), which calls
... run((g(5),h(5)), backing_up(B), ..), which calls
.... run(g5), backing_up(C), ..), which calls
..... run((p(5),fail(a(_))), backing_up(C), ..) calls
...... run(p(5), backing_up(D), ..), which succeeds
...... with D not instantiated, so on to
...... run(fail(a(_)), backing_up(C), ..), which
..... succeeds with C instantiated to a(_)
..... and this succeeds with C instantiated
.... so this succeeds with C instantiated
... so h(5) is not tried, and B is instantiated to a(_)
.. and since B matches a(5) this fails
. and so this fails before it can call b(5)
and so this fails.
```

Note that `b(5)` and `h(5)` were never even called, because of the `fail/1` goal.

SUMMARY

- Meta-level interpreters in Prolog can be small and yet very powerful.

- Partial evaluation can be used to speed up programs.

- Meta-level interpreters can be used to extend the range of metalogical features available to the programmer.

- Meta-level interpreters can be used for debugging, explanation, proof analysis and many other tasks.

EXERCISES

9.1   The meta-interpreter is not complete. As yet it does not handle ->/2, for instance. You should be able to extend it easily.

9.2   This meta-interpreter can be used as part of a reasoning maintenance system, in determining which assumptions support a particular conclusion. Information about which of a given set of facts were actually used in the proof can be extracted from the proof path information. Implement such a reasoning maintenance system – but design it first!

9.3   Modify the interpreter so that the proof tree it builds also contains information (of some kind) about which clauses for each goal had been tried but failed before finding a successful clause.

9.4   The data returned by **run/5** could be used as the basis of a tutorial debugger or tracer. Design and implement such systems. Shapiro [1983] describes a Prolog meta-interpreter for systematically debugging a program, and Huntbach [1986] describes an improved version. Other examples of debugging with the aid of meta-interpreters can be found in Takahashi and Shibayama [1985], Pereira [1986] and Eisenstadt and Brayshaw [1987]. Sterling [1985] describes how a meta-interpreter can be used to construct explanations of a program's behaviour.

9.5   The interpreter is significantly slower than the real one. It is possible to speed up the execution of code by declaring certain goals or the remainder of the body of a clause to be 'safe' – that is, can be safely executed by the real interpreter without loss of information of interest to the user. Implement such a feature.

9.6   The predicate `select/3` is used in the second-to-last clause of `run/5` to select a body of a clause for P to be run. As it stands it behaves very like `member/2` and just chooses the next clause. Experiment with dynamically reordering the clause bodies, and the goals within a single clause body too. For example, an interesting control regimen to try is one in which the goals containing fewest uninstantiated variables are run first.

9.7   A meta-interpreter such as this can be used to implement a simple form of proof analyser, in order to find useful generalizations in proofs of 'similar' goals. It can also be used to find new efficient clauses by analysis of a single proof. The example given in Kedar-Cabelli and McCarty [1987] is as follows. Consider this program:

```
kill(A,B) :-
    hate(A,B),
    possesses(A,W),
    weapon(W).

hate(Person,Person) :-
    depressed(Person).

possesses(Person,Thing) :-
    buy(Person,Thing).

weapon(G) :-
    gun(G).

depressed(john).
buy(john,gun1).
gun(gun1).
```

Suicide, in the form `kill(john,john)`, follows at once. From the proof tree it is possible to extract a more efficient program for the case of suicide, namely:

```
kill(X,X) :-
    depressed(X),
    buy(X,W),
    gun(W).
```

This particular case is essentially an example of partial evaluation. Experiment with these ideas – this can become a large, open-ended research exercise.

Appendix A
Quintus Prolog

Quintus Prolog is supplied by Quintus Computer Systems Inc. of Mountain View, California and by their authorized distributors.

A.1 Built-in predicates

The table on the following pages describes what Quintus Prolog offers, in version 2.0 or later. Most good Prologs offer much of this – leaving out some of the more system-specific ones – and offer others besides. Nearly all Prolog suppliers start with what DEC-10 Prolog offered and then add to that set. However, DEC-10 Prolog had a number of what would now be regarded as serious omissions. For example, DEC-10 Prolog did not handle real numbers, only integers. Most 'compatible' Prologs extend the definitions below to handle real numbers too, and provide further useful functions for use in expressions.

Predicate	Brief description
abolish(F)	abolish predicates specified by F
abolish(F,N)	abolish procedure named F arity N
abort	abort; return to toplevel
absolute_file_name(R,A)	A is absolute name of file R
ancestors(L)	L is list of (interpreted) ancestors
arg(N,T,A)	Nth argument of T is A
assert(C)	assert clause C (for dynamic predicate)
assert(C,R)	assert clause C; return reference R
asserta(C)	assert clause C before existing ones
asserta(C,R)	assert clause C before existing ones: ref R
assertz(C)	assert clause C after existing ones
assertz(C,R)	assert clause C after existing ones: ref R
atom(T)	T is an atom
atom_chars(A,L)	A is atomic representation of list of chars L
atomic(T)	T is an atom or number
bagof(X,P,B)	bag of instances of X such that P is B
break	break at next procedure call
'C'(S1,T,S2)	(DCGs) S1 connected by terminal T to S2
call(P)	call P
character_count(S,N)	N is no. of chars read/written on stream S
clause(P,Q)	dynamic predicate clause, head P, body Q
clause(P,Q,R)	like clause/2 but returns ref R too
close(F)	close file F
compare(C,X,Y)	C is result of comparing X and Y
compile(F)	add compiled procs from F (file/list) to d.b.
consult(F)	add interp'd procs from F (file/list) to d.b.
current_atom(A)	A is a current atom (non-determinate)
current_input(S)	S is current input stream
current_key(N,K)	N is name and K is key of a recorded term
current_module(M)	M is name of a current module
current_module(M,F)	module M's declaration is in file F
current_op(P,T,A)	atom A is an operator type T precedence P
current_output(S)	S is current output stream
current_predicate(A,P)	A is name of a predicate, m. g. goal P
current_stream(F,M,S)	S is a stream open on file F in mode M
debug	switch on debugging
debugging	output debugging information
depth(D)	current interpreted calling depth is D

Figure A.1   Quintus Prolog evaluable predicates: part 1 of 5.

Predicate	Brief description
display(T)	write T (prefix notation) to user stream
ensure_loaded(F)	compile F if not already loaded
erase(R)	erase clause or record, reference R
expand_term(T,X)	T expands to X by term_expansion/2 or DCG
fail	backtrack immediately
false	backtrack immediately
fileerrors	enable reporting of file errors
float(N)	N is a floating point number
flush_output(S)	flush output buffer for stream S
foreign(F,P)	(user); C function F is attached to predicate P
foreign(F,L,P)	(user); function F in language L attached to P
foreign_file(F,L)	(user); file F defines C functions in list L
format(C,A)	write args A according to control string C
format(S,C,A)	like format/2 but on stream S
functor(T,F,N)	principal functor of T has name F, arity N
garbage_collect	force a garbage collection
gc	enable garbage collection (no effect at present)
gcguide(F,O,N)	(VMS) change GC parameter F from O to N
get(C)	C is next non-blank char on current input
get(S,C)	C is next non-blank char input on stream S
get0(C)	C is next char input on current input
get0(S,C)	C is next char input on stream S
halt	exit from Prolog
help	display a help message
help(T)	give help on topic T
incore(P)	same as call/1
instance(R,T)	instance of clause/term referenced by R is T
integer(T)	T is an integer
Y is X	Y is value of arithmetic expression X
keysort(L,S)	list L sorted by key yields S
leash(M)	set debugger's leashing mode to M
length(L,N)	length of list L is N
library_directory(D)	D is a library directory that will be searched
line_count(S,N)	N is no. of lines read/written on stream S
line_position(S,N)	N is current position on current line of S
lisp_apply(F,L,R)	(Xerox) apply LISP fn F to L, return R
lisp_predicate(F,P)	(Xerox) link predicate P to LISP fn F
listing	list all interpreted procedures

Figure A.2   Quintus Prolog evaluable predicates: part 2 of 5.

Predicate	*Brief description*
listing(P)	list interpreted procedure(s) specified by P
load_foreign_files(F,L)	load object files from list F using libraries L
manual	access top level of on-line manual
manual(X)	access specified manual section
maxdepth(D)	limit calling depth (interpreted code) to D
name(A,L)	list of chars of atom or number A is L
nl	output a new line to current output
nl(S)	output a newline on stream S
no_style_check(A)	switch off style checking of type A
nodebug	switch off debugging
nofileerrors	disable reporting of file errors
nogc	garbage collection off (no effect at present)
nonvar(T)	T is a non-variable
nospy(P)	remove spy-points from proc(s) specified by P
nospyall	remove all spypoints
notrace	same as nodebug/0
number(N)	N is a number
number_chars(N,L)	N is numeric representation of list of chars L
numbervars(T,M,N)	number variables in T from M to N-1
op(P,T,A)	make atom A operator type T prec P
open(F,M,S)	open file F in mode M returning stream S
open_null_stream(S)	output stream S goes nowhere
otherwise	same as true/0
phrase(P,L)	list L can be parsed as a phrase of type P
phrase(P,L,R)	L starts with phrase type P; R is remnant
portray(T)	(user); tells print what to do
portray_clause(C)	write clause C to current output stream
predicate_property(P,Q)	Q is a property of loaded predicate P
print(T)	portray or else write T on current output
print(S,T)	portray or else write T on stream S
prolog_flag(F,V)	V is current value of Prolog flag F
prolog_flag(F,O,N)	O is old value of flag F, N is new
prompt(A,B)	change prompt from A to B
put(C)	output char C on current output
put(S,C)	output char C on stream S
read(T)	read T from current input
read(S,T)	read T from stream S
recorda(K,T,R)	make T first record under key K, ref R

Figure A.3   Quintus Prolog evaluable predicates: part 3 of 5.

Predicate	Brief description
recorded(K,T,R)	T is recorded under key K, ref R
recordz(K,T,R)	make T last record under key K, ref R
reinitialise	abort and consult user's prolog.ini file
repeat	succeed repeatedly
restore(S)	restore state saved in file S
retract(C)	erase first interpreted clause of form C
retractall(H)	erase interp'd clauses with head H
save(F)	save current state of Prolog in file F
save(F,R)	as save/1: R = 1 after 'restore' else 0
save_program(F)	save current state of Prolog d.b. in file F
see(F)	make file F be current input stream
seeing(F)	current input stream is named F
seen	close current input stream
set_input(S)	set S to be current input stream
set_output(S)	set S to be current output stream
setof(X,P,S)	set of instances of X such that P is S
skip(C)	skip input on current stream till past C
skip(S,C)	skip input on stream S till past char C
sort(L,S)	list L sorted into order yields S
source_file(F)	F is a loaded file
source_file(P,F)	P is a predicate defined in loaded file F
spy(P)	set spy-points on procedure(s) specified by P
statistics	output various execution statistics
statistics(K,V)	execution statistic key K has value V
stream_code(S,U)	U is unique integer associated with stream S
stream_position(S,P)	P is current position in stream S
stream_position(S,O,N)	O is old position of stream S, N is new
style_check(A)	turn on style checking of type A
subgoal_of(G)	an interpreted ancestor of current clause is G
tab(N)	output N spaces to current output
tab(S,N)	output N spaces on stream S
tell(F)	make file F current output stream
telling(F)	current output stream is named F
term_expansion(T,N)	(user); see expand_term/2
told	close current output stream
trace	switch on debugging, trace immediately
trimcore	reduce free stack space to a minimum
true	succeed

Figure A.4   Quintus Prolog evaluable predicates: part 4 of 5.

Predicate	Brief description
ttyflush	transmit all outstanding terminal output
ttyget(C)	next non-blank char input from terminal is C
ttyget0(C)	next char input from terminal is C
ttynl	output a new line on terminal
ttyput(C)	next char output to terminal is C
ttyskip(C)	skip over terminal input until after char C
ttytab(N)	output N spaces to terminal
unix(T)	(UNIX) gives access to UNIX facilities
unknown(A,B)	change action on unknown procs from A to B
use_module(F)	import module files F, loading if necessary
use_module(F,P)	import procedures P from module file F
user_help	(user); tells help what to do
var(T)	T is a variable
version	displays system identification messages
version(A)	adds atom A to list of introductory messages
write(T)	write T on current output
write(S,T)	write T on stream S
write_canonical(T)	write T so it can be read back in
write_canonical(S,T)	write T on stream S so it can be read back in
writeq(T)	write T, quoting names where necessary
writeq(S,T)	write T on S, quoting atoms where necessary
!	cut any choices taken in current procedure
\+ P	goal P is not provable
X^P	there exists an X such that P is provable
X =:= Y	results of evaluating X and Y are equal
X =\= Y	results of evaluating X and Y are not equal
X < Y	after evaluation, X is less than Y
X =< Y	after evaluation, X is less than or equal to Y
X > Y	after evaluation, X is greater than Y
X >= Y	after evaluation, X is greater than or equal to Y
X = Y	X and Y are equal (i.e. unified)
T =.. L	list L holds functor and arguments of T
X == Y	X and Y are strictly identical
X \== Y	X and Y are not strictly identical
X @< Y	X precedes Y in standard order
X @=< Y	X precedes or is identical to Y
X @> Y	X follows Y in standard order
X @>= Y	X follows or is identical to Y

Figure A.5   Quintus Prolog evaluable predicates: part 5 of 5.

A.1.1   Obsolete DEC-10 Prolog predicates

A few of the original DEC-10 Prolog predicates are now obsolete, and many suppliers omit them or provide something better. These include:

- The predicates concerned with compilation, namely `compile/1`, `in-core/1` and `revive/1`. Those systems that offer a user-controllable compiler (as opposed to automatic incremental compilation) usually provide their own style of hooks.

- Those related to the actual implementation, such as `depth/1`, `gc`, `nogc`, `gcguide/3`, `log`, `nolog`, `maxdepth/1`, `reinitialise/0`, `trim-core/0` and `subgoal_of/1`. Control of garbage collection and internal spaces is obviously a matter for the designers.

- `restore/1` is often omitted for technical reasons – after all, what does it really mean to restore a saved state in the middle of the execution of a procedure? On the other hand, `save/2` is very useful, and usually it can only be simulated in clumsy ways.

- `close/1`, `plsys/1` and `rename/2` are often replaced by some more convenient form of access to the operating system.

- `version/0` and `version/1` can be trivially simulated.

Note that DEC-10 Prolog *did not* provide `not/1`, a frequently provided synonym for `\+/1`, because the name is too suggestive of true logical negation. Quintus Prolog also omits `not/1`. The predicate name `\+` is the closest that a standard keyboard can provide to the logical operator ⊬.

A.1.2   Quintus Prolog operator declarations

In Quintus Prolog precedences can range from 0 to 1200 inclusive, although because of the standard declarations below it is wise to stay strictly below 1000. A precedence of 0, in many of the 'DEC-10-compatible' Prologs, disables a previous declaration for the given operator name and associativity.

```
:- op(1200, xfx, [ :-, --> ]).
:- op(1200,  fx, [ :-, ?- ]).
:- op(1150,  fx, [ mode, public, dynamic,
                   multifile, meta_predicate ]).
:- op(1100, xfy, [ ; ]).
:- op(1050, xfy, [ -> ]).
:- op(1000, xfy, [ ',' ]).    % Ersatz - see below
:- op( 900,  fy, [ \+, spy, nospy ]).
:- op( 700, xfx, [ =, is, =.., ==, \==,
                   @<, @>, @=<, @>=, =:=,
                   =\=, <, >, =<, >= ]).
```

```
:- op( 600, xfy, [:]).
:- op( 500, yfx, [ +, -, /\, \/ ]).
:- op( 500,  fx, [ +, - ]).
:- op( 400, yfx, [ *, /, <<, >> ]).
:- op( 300, xfx, [ mod ]).
:- op( 200, xfy, [ ^ ]).
```

In many 'DEC-10-compatible' Prologs the comma, when used as a separator between arguments, behaves as though it were an operator defined as above. For instance,

```
?- (A,B) =.. [H|T].
```

will instantiate H to (,).

Appendix B
Some Prolog suppliers

This appendix lists some suppliers of Prolog systems. But, to quote the Greek philosopher Heraclitus, 'nothing is permanent except change'. The details given here are bound to change as suppliers provide new products, improve or discontinue old ones, move or go out of business, and as new suppliers start up. Perhaps, by the time you read it, this appendix will be just a historical curiosity. In any event, you should try to contact these or other suppliers for yourself rather than relying on the scanty information here. Who knows, perhaps that supplier of low-cost systems for IBM PCs now also sells the best supercomputer version in the world – or vice versa? The list does not mention prices or features, as these also change all too rapidly.

If you are a major supplier of Prolog and you have been omitted from this list, then I can only apologize to you for my oversight. Take comfort from the fact that other readers may believe that your product is too new to have featured in this list: since the general quality of available Prologs has been rising rapidly, they may feel that your absence from the list reflects well upon you.

Various universities that are not mentioned in this list supply their own versions of Prolog for academic or research purposes, but do not wish to run a distribution service or have other reasons for not widely publicizing their software.

Name:	**AAIS Prolog**
For:	Apple Macintosh
Source:	Advanced AI Systems
	PO Box 39-0360
	Mountain View, California 94039-6360
	(415) 948-8658

Name: **ADA Prolog** (five versions)
For: IBM PCs and compatibles
Source: Automata Design Associates
            1570 Arran Way
            Drescher, Pennsylvania 19025
            (215) 335-5400

Name: **ALS Prolog**
For: SUN, Apple Macintosh, IBM PCs and compatibles
Source: Applied Logic Systems
            PO Box 90
            University Station
            Syracuse, New York 13210-0090
            (315) 471-3900

Name: **Arity Prolog**
For: IBM PCs and compatibles
Source: Arity Corporation
            30 Domino Drive
            Concord, Massachusetts 01742
            (617) 371-1243

Name: **Basser Prolog**
For: UNIX and VMS
Source: Andrew Taylor
            Department of Computer Science
            Sydney University
            Sydney, New South Wales 2006
            Australia

Name: **BIM Prolog**
For: UNIX on VAX and SUN
Source: Raf Venken
            Belgian Inst. of Management
            Kwikstraat 4
            B-3047 Belgium
            (02) 759-5925
                or
            The SHURE Group
            1514 Pacific Ranch Drive
            Encinitas, California 92024
            (619) 944-0320

Name: **Chalcedony Prolog (i, V, V Plus)**
For: IBM PCs and compatibles
Source: Chalcedony Software

5580 La Jolla Blvd., Suite 126
La Jolla, California 95066
(619) 483-8513

Name: **Coder's Prolog in C**
For: IBM PC and compatibles
Source: Austin Code Works
            11100 Leafwood Lane
            Austin, Texas 78750-3409
            (512) 258-0785

Name: **C-Prolog**
For: UNIX, VMS and others
Source: Dept. of Architecture
            Edinburgh University
            Chambers Street
            Edinburgh EH1 1GZ
            Scotland
            (31) 667-1011
                    or
            SRI International
            333 Ravenswood Ave.
            Menlo Park, California 94025

Name: **Edinburgh Prolog** (NIP)
For: various UNIX systems
Source: AI Applications Institute
            University of Edinburgh
            80 South Bridge
            Edinburgh EH1 1HN
            Scotland
            (31) 225-4464

Name: **ExperProlog**
For: IBM PCs and compatibles, Apple Macintosh
Source: Expertelligence
            559 San Ysidro Road
            Santa Barbara, California 93108
            (800) 828-0113

Name: **IF/Prolog**
For: Apple Macintosh, UNIX on Apollo/SUN/PC, VMS,
            Data General AOS/VS, and others
Source: InterFace Computer GmbH
            Garmischer Strasse
            D-8000 Munich 2

West Germany
(089) 510-86-55

Name: **LISPLOG**
For: Symbolics and UNIX Franz and Common LISP systems
Source: LISPLOG-Büro, AG Richter
             FB Informatik
             Postfach 3049
             Univ. Kaiserslautern
             6750 Kaiserslautern
             West Germany

Name: **LM-Prolog**
For: ZetaLisp and LMI Lambda
Source: Mats Carlsson
             SICS, PO Box 1263
             S-16313 SPANGA
             Sweden

Name: **The Logic Workbench**
For: various 68000 UNIX systems
Source: Silogic Inc.
             6420 Wilshire Blvd.
             Los Angeles, California 90048
             (213) 653-6470

Name: **LOGLISP**
For: UCI LISP, ZetaLisp and LMI Lambda
Source: K. J. Greene
             313 Link Hall
             School of Computer and Information Sciences
             Syracuse University
             Syracuse, New York 13210

Name: **micro-Prolog**
For: IBM PCs and compatibles and CP/M-80
Source: Logic Programming Associates
             Studio 4
             Royal Victoria Patriotic Building
             Trinity Road
             London SW18 6SX
                  or
             Programming Logic Systems
             31 Crescent Drive
             Milford
             Connecticut 06460

Name:	**MProlog**
For:	UNIX and VMS systems, IBM PCs and others
Source:	Logicware Inc.
	5915 Airport Road
	Toronto, Ontario
	Canada

or

Systems, Computers and Informatics Lab
SZKI
1368 Budapest POB 224
Hungary

Name:	**MacProlog**
Source:	Logic Programming Associates
	Studio 4
	Royal Victoria Patriotic Building
	Trinity Road
	London SW18 6SX

or

Programming Logic Systems
31 Crescent Drive
Milford
Connecticut 06460

Name:	**MU- and NU-Prolog**
For:	UNIX systems
Source:	Prolog Distribution
	Department of Computer Science
	University of Melbourne
	Parkville, Victoria 3052
	Australia

Name:	**POPLOG Prolog**
For:	VAX VMS and SUNs
Source:	AI Business Centre
	SD Scicon plc
	Pembroke House
	Pembroke Broadway
	Camberley, Surrey QU15 3XD
	England
	(0)276 686200

or

Prof. R. Popplestone
Computable Functions Inc.
35 South Orchard Drive
Amherst, Massachusetts 01002

(413) 253-7637

Name:	**Prolog-1 and -2**
For:	IBM PCs and compatibles
Source:	Expert Systems International
	34 Alexandra Road
	Oxford OX2 0DB
	England
	or
	ESI
	1700 Walnut Street
	Philadelphia, Pennsylvania 19103
	(215) 735-8510

Name:	**Prolog-10 and -20**
For:	TOPS-10 and -20
Source:	Quintus Computer Systems Inc.
	1310 Villa Street
	Mountain View, California 94041
	(415) 965-7700

Name:	**Prolog-86 Plus**
For:	IBM PCs and compatibles
Source:	Micro-AI
	PO Box 91
	Rheem Valley, California 94570
	(415) 376-1146

Name:	**Personal Prolog**
For:	Apple Macintosh
Source:	Optimized Systems Software
	1221B Kentwood Ave.
	San Jose, California 95129
	(408) 446-3099

Name:	**Prolog-II**
For:	many systems
Source:	M. van Canegham
	PrologIA
	278 Rue St. Pierre
	13005 Marseille
	France

Name:	**Prolog-CRISS**
For:	UNIX, VMS, HB 68, ICL 2900, IBM PCs
Source:	CRISS - BP 47X
	38040 Grenoble Cedex
	France

Name: **Prolog/P**
For: many systems
Source: CRIL
12 bis, Rue Jean-Jaures
92807 Puteaux
France

Name: **Quintus Prolog**
For: SUN, Apollo, NCR Tower, PC/RT
Source: Quintus Computer Systems Inc.
1310 Villa Street
Mountain View, California 94041
(415) 965-7700

Name: **SD Prolog**
For: IBM PCs and compatibles
Source: AI Business Centre
SD Scicon plc
Pembroke House
Pembroke Broadway
Camberley, Surrey QU15 3XD
England
(0)276 686200
or
Systems Designers International
5203 Leesburg Pike suite 1201
Falls Church, Virginia 22041
(800) 888-9988

Name: **Salford University Prolog**
For: Prime computers
Source: Salford University Industrial Centre Ltd
Salford University
Salford M5 4WT
England
or
Mitchell Associates
PO Box 6189
San Rafael, California
(415) 435-2024

Name: **SB-Prolog**
For: various UNIX systems
Source: Department of Computer Science (only by FTP)
University of Arizona
Tucson, Arizona 85721
(602) 621-4527

Name: **Sicstus Prolog**
For: UNIX systems
Source: Mats Carlsson
            SICS
            PO Box 1263
            S-16313 SPANGA,
            Sweden

Name: **Turbo Prolog**
For: IBM PCs and compatibles
Source: Borland International
            4585 Scotts Valley Drive
            Scotts Valley, California 95066
            (408) 438-8400

Name: **UNH Prolog**
For: UNIX and VMS
Source: Department of Computer Science
            University of New Hampshire
            Durham, New Hampshire 03824

Name: **UNSW Prolog**
For: UNIX systems (education/research only)
Source: School of EE and CS
            University of New South Wales
            PO Box 1
            Kensington, New South Wales 2033
            Australia

Name: **VPI Prolog**
For: VMS
Source: Dept. of Computer Science
            Virginia Polytechnic Institute
            Blacksburg, Virginia
            (703) 961-5368

Name: **Waterloo Prolog**
For: IBM VM/370
Source: WATCOM Products Inc.
            415 Philip Street
            Waterloo, Ontario N2L 3X2
            Canada
            (519) 886-3700

Name: **XPRO**
For: Atari ST

Source: Rational Visions
7111 W. Indian School
Phoenix, Arizona 85033
(415) 965-7700

Name: **York Portable Prolog**
For: many systems (in Pascal)
Source: Department of Computer Science
University of York
York Y01 5DD
England
(0904)

References

[**Aho and Ullman 1972**] Aho A.V. and J.D.Ullman, *The Theory of Parsing, Translation and Compiling*, Vol. 1, Prentice-Hall, Englewood Cliffs, NJ, 1972

[**Baldwin 1983**] Baldwin J., FRIL – an inference language based on fuzzy logic,in *Proceedings of Expert Systems 83 Conference*, Brighton, BCS Specialist Group on Expert Systems, pp.163–172, 1983

[**Barklund and Millroth 1987**] Barklund J. and H.Millroth, Hash tables in logic programming, in *Proceedings of the Fourth International Logic Programming Conference* (ed. J-L.Lassez), Melbourne, pp.411–427, MIT Press, Cambridge, Mass., 1987

[**Berlekamp et al. 1982**] Berlekamp E.R., J.H.Conway and R.K.Guy, *Winning Ways for your Mathematical Plays*, 2 vols, Academic Press, New York, 1982

[**Bradshaw 1986**] Bradshaw G., Learning by disjunctive spanning, in *Machine Learning: a Guide to Current Research* (eds. T.Mitchell, J.Carbonell and R.Michalski), Kluwer Academic Publishers, Boston, Mass., pp.11–14, 1986

[**Bratko 1986**] Bratko I., *Prolog Programming for Artificial Intelligence*, Addison-Wesley, Reading, Mass., USA, 1986

[**Buchanan and Shortliffe 1984**] Buchanan B. and E.H.Shortliffe, *Rule-based Expert Systems*, 748pp, Addison-Wesley, Reading, Mass., USA, 1984

[**Bundy 1985**] Bundy A., *The Computer Modelling Of Mathematical Reasoning*, Harvester Press, Brighton, UK, 1985

[**Bundy and Welham 1981**] Bundy A. and R.Welham, Using meta-level inference for selective application of multiple rewrite rules in algebraic manipulation, *Artificial Intelligence*, 16, pp.189–212, 1981

[**Clark and McCabe 1984**] Clark K.L. and F.G.McCabe, *micro-Prolog: Programming in Logic*, Prentice-Hall, Englewood Cliffs, NJ, USA, 1984

[**Clark and Tärnlund 1977**] Clark K. and S.-A.Tärnlund, A first-order theory of data and programs, *Information Processing* 77 (Proceedings of the IFIP Congress, ed. B.Gilchrist), pp.933–944, North-Holland, Amsterdam, 1977

[**Clark et al. 1988**] Clark, K., F.McCabe, N.Johns and C.Spenser, *LPA MacPROLOG Reference Manual*, Logic Programming Associates, London, England, 1988

[**Clocksin and Mellish 1987**] Clocksin W.F. and C.S.Mellish, *Programming in Prolog*, third edition, Springer-Verlag, Berlin, 1987

[**Cohn 1985**] Cohn A.G., On the solution of Schubert's Steamroller in many-sorted logic, in *Proceedings of IJCAI-85*, pp.1169–1174, Morgan Kaufmann, 1985

[**Colmerauer 1975**] Colmerauer A., Les grammaires de metamorphose, Technical Report from Groupe d'Intelligence Artificielle, Marseille-Lumin, November 1975, and as Metamorphosis grammars, in *Natural Language Communication With Computers* (ed. L.Bolc), Springer-Verlag, Berlin, 1978

[**Colmerauer et al. 1974**] Colmerauer A., H.Kanoui, R.Pasero and P. Roussel, Un système de communication homme–machine en français, Research Report, Groupe d'Intelligence Artificielle, Université Aix-Marseille II, 1973

[**CRI 1987**] *The CRI Directory of Expert Systems*, Learned Information, Oxford/New York, 364pp, 1987

[**Earley**] 1970 Earley J., An efficient context-free parsing algorithm, Communications of the Association for Computing Machinery, **13**, 2, pp.94–102, 1970

[**Eisenstadt and Brayshaw 1987**] Eisenstadt M. and M.Brayshaw, Graphical debugging with the Transparent Prolog Machine (TPM), *Proceedings of IJCAI-87*, Milan, pp.83–86, Morgan Kaufmann, San Mateo, California, 1987

[**Eriksson and Rayner 1984**] Eriksson L-H. and M.Rayner, Incorporating mutable arrays into Prolog, in *Proceedings of the Second International Logic Programming Conference* (ed. S-A.Tärnlund), pp.101–104, Uppsala University, Uppsala, Sweden 1984

[**Genesereth and Nilsson 1987**] Genesereth M. and N.J.Nilsson, *Logical Foundations of Artificial Intelligence*, Morgan Kaufmann, San Mateo, California, 1987

[**Harmon and King 1985**] Harmon P. and D.King, *Expert Systems: Artificial Intelligence In Business*, 283pp, Wiley, New York, USA, 1985

[**Hughes and Cresswell 1969**] Hughes G.E. and M.J.Cresswell, *Introduction to Modal Logic*, Methuen, London, 1969

[**Huntbach 1986**] Huntbach M., An improved ersion of Shapiro's model inference system, in *Proceedings of the Third International Logic Programming Conference* (ed. E.Shapiro), London, pp.180–187, Springer-Verlag, Berlin, 1986

[**Kay 1973**] Kay M., The MIND System, in *Natural Language Processing* (ed. R.Rustin), Prentice-Hall, Englewood Cliffs, NJ, USA, 1973

[**Kedar-Cabelli and McCarty 1987**] Kedar-Cabelli, S.T. and L.T.McCarty, Explanation-based generalization as resolution theorem proving, in *Proceedings of the Fourth International Workshop on Machine Learning* (Irvine, California), pp.383–389, Morgan Kaufmann, Los Altos, California, 1987

[**Kowalski 1974**] Kowalski R., Predicate logic as a programming language, in *Proceedings of the IFIP Congress*, Stockholm, North-Holland, Amsterdam, Holland, 1974

[**Kowalski and Kuehner 1971**] Kowalski R. and D.Kuehner, Linear Resolution with selection functions, *Artificial Intelligence*, 22, pp.227–260, 1971

[**Kripke 1963**] Kripke S., Semantical considerations on modal logic, *Acta Philosophica Fennica*, 16, pp.83–94, 1963

[**Littleford 1984**] Littleford A., A MYCIN-like expert system in Prolog, in *Proceedings of the Second International Logic Programming Conference* (ed. S-A.Tärnlund), pp.289–300, Uppsala University, Uppsala, Sweden 1984

[**Lloyd 1984**] Lloyd J.W., *Foundations of Logic Programming*, Springer-Verlag, Berlin, 1984

[**Loveland 1978**] Loveland D.W., *Automated Theorem Proving: A Logical Basis*, North-Holland, Amsterdam, Holland, 405pp, 1978

[**Mamdani and Gaines 1981**] Mamdani E. and B.Gaines, *Fuzzy Reasoning and Its Applications*, Academic Press, New York, 1981

[**Michalski et al. 1983**] Michalski R.S., J.G.Carbonell and T.M.Mitchell, *Machine Learning: an Artificial Intelligence Approach*, Morgan Kaufmann, San Mateo, California, 1983

[**Michalski et al. 1986**] Michalski R.S., J.G.Carbonell and T.M.Mitchell, *Machine Learning: an Artificial Intelligence Approach*, Vol. 2, Morgan Kaufmann, San Mateo, California, 1986

[**Monti 1987**] Monti G., Efficiency considerations of built-in taxonomic reasoning in Prolog, *Proceedings of IJCAI-87*, Milan, pp.68–75, Morgan Kaufmann, San Mateo, California, 1987

[**Morris 1969**] Morris J.B., E-resolution: extension of resolution to include the equality relation, Proceedings of IJCAI-69, pp.287–194, Morgan Kaufmann, San Mateo, California, 1969

[**Moss 1986**] Moss C.D.M., CUT and PASTE – defining the impure primitives of Prolog, Proceedings of the Third International Conference on Logic Programming, Springer-Verlag, Berlin, Germany, pp.686–694, 1986

[**Murray 1987**] Murray K., Multiple convergence: an approach to disjunctive concept acquisition, in *Proceedings of the International Joint Conference on AI 1987*, Morgan Kaufmann, Los Altos, California, pp.297–300, 1987

[**Mycroft and O'Keefe 1984**] Mycroft A. and R.A.O'Keefe, A polymorphic type system for Prolog, *Artificial Intelligence*, 23, pp.295–307, 1984

[**Numao and Mariyama 1985**] Numao M. and H.Mariyama, PROEDIT – a screen oriented Prolog programming environment, *Logic programming 1985* (ed. E.Wada), Tokyo, pp.100–109, Springer-Verlag, Berlin, 1985

[**O'Keefe 1983**] O'Keefe R.A., Updatable arrays in Prolog, Dept. of AI Working Paper 150, University of Edinburgh, 1983

[**O'Keefe 1985**] O'Keefe R.A., On the treatment of cuts in Prolog source-level code, *IEEE Symposium on Logic Programming*, Boston, Mass., pp.68–72, IEEE, 1985

[**Paterson and Wegman 1978**] Paterson M. and M.Wegman, Linear resolution, *Journal of Computer and System Science*, 16, pp.158–167, 1978

[**Pereira and Sheiber 1987**] Pereira F.C.N. and S.M.Sheiber, *Prolog and Natural Language Analysis*, CSLI Lecture Notes 10, Center for the Study of Language and Information, Stanford University/SRI International, California, 1987

[**Pereira and Warren 1980**] Pereira F.C.N. and D.H.D.Warren, Definite-clause grammars for language analysis – a survey of the formalism and a comparison with augmented transition networks, *Artificial Intelligence*, 13, pp.231–278, 1980

[Pereira 1986] Pereira L.M., Rational debugging in logic programs, in *Proceedings of the Third International Logic Programming Conference* (ed. E.Shapiro), London, pp.203–210, Springer-Verlag, Berlin, 1986

[Pique 1984] Pique J-F., Drawing trees and their equations in Prolog, in *Proceedings of the Second International Logic Programming Conference* (ed. S-A.Tärnlund), pp.23–33, Uppsala University, Uppsala, Sweden 1984

[Poole et al. 1986] Poole D., R.Goebel and R.Aleliunas, Theorist: a logical reasoning system for defaults and diagnosis, University of Waterloo Computer Science Research Report CS-86-06, 16pp, University of Waterloo, Canada, 1986

[Robinson 1965] Robinson J.A., A machine-oriented logic based on the resolution principle, *Journal of the ACM*, 12, pp.23–41, 1965

[Ross and Lewis 1987] Ross P.M. and J.M.Lewis, Plan recognition in intelligent tutoring systems, in *Artificial Intelligence Tools in Education* (eds. R.Lewis and P.Ercoli), pp.29–39, North-Holland, Amsterdam, 1987

[Roussel 1975] Roussel P., Prolog: manuel de référence et utilisation Technical Report, Groupe d'Intelligence Artificielle, Université Aix Marseille II, 1975

[Russell 1985] Russell S., The Compleat guide to MRS, Stanford Memo KRL-85-12, Stanford University Dept. of Computer Science, 1985

[Searls 1988] Searls D.B., Representing genetic information with formal grammars, *Proceedings of AAAI-88*, St.Paul, Missouri, pp.386–391, Morgan Kaufmann, San Mateo, California, 1988

[Shapiro 1983] Shapiro E., *Algorithmic Program Debugging*, MIT Press, Cambridge, Mass., 1983

[Silver 1986] Silver B., *Meta-level Inference*, Springer-Verlag, Berlin, 1986

[Smullyan 1981] Smullyan R., *What is the Name of this Book?*, Penguin Books, Harmondsworth, UK, 1981

[Steele and Sussman 1978] Steele G.L. and G.Sussman, The art of the interpreter, Technical memo AIM-453, MIT AI Laboratory, 1978

[**Sterling 1985**] Sterling L., Expert system = knowledge + meta-interpreter, Technical report CS-84-17, Weizmann Institute of Science, Rehovot, Israel, 1985

[**Sterling and Nygate 1987**] Sterling L. and Y.Nygate, PYTHON: an expert squeezer, in *Proceedings of the Fourth International Logic Programming Conference* (ed. J-L.Lassez), Melbourne, pp.654–674, MIT Press, Cambridge, Mass., 1987

[**Sterling and Shapiro 1986**] Sterling L. and E.Shapiro, *The Art of Prolog*, MIT Press, Cambridge, Mass., 1986

[**Sterling et al. 1982**] Sterling L., A.Bundy, L.Byrd, R.O'Keefe and B. Silver, Solving equations with PRESS, in *Computer Algebra*, pp.109–116, Springer-Verlag Lecture Notes in Computer Science, Springer-Verlag, Berlin, 1982

[**Takahashi and Shibayama 1985**] Takahashi H. and E. Shibayama, PRESET – a debugging enironment for Prolog, in *Logic Programming 1985* (ed. E.Wada), Tokyo, pp.90–99, Springer-Verlag, Berlin, 1985

[**Takeuchi and Furukawa 1985**] Takeuchi A. and K.Furukawa, Partial Evaluation of Prolog Programs and its Application to Meta-programming, Technical Report TR-126, Institute for New Generation Computer Technology (ICOT), Tokyo, Japan, 1985

[**Tamaki and Taisuke 1984**] Tamaki H. and S.Taisuke, Unfold/fold transformations of logic programs, in *Proceedings of the Second Logic Programming Conference*, pp.127–138, Uppsala University, Uppsala, Sweden, 1984

[**van Lehn 1987**] van Lehn K., Cirrus: an automated protocol analysis tool in *Proceedings of 4th International Workshop on Machine Learning*, pp.205–217, Morgan Kaufmann, San Mateo, California, 1987

[**Warren 1977**] Warren D.H.D., Implementing Prolog – compiling logic programs, Research Reports 39 and 40, Dept. of AI, University of Edinburgh, 1977

[**Warren et al. 1979**] Warren D.H.D., F.Pereira and L.M.Pereira, User's guide to DECsystem-10 Prolog, Occasional Paper 15, Dept. of AI, University of Edinburgh, 1979

[**Weizenbaum 1966**] Weizenbaum J., ELIZA – A computer program for the study of natural language communication between man and machine, *Communications of the ACM*, 9, pp.36–45, 1966

[**Wos and Robinson 1970**] Wos L. and J.A.Robinson, Paramodulation and set of support, *Symposium on Automatic Deduction*, Lecture Notes in Mathematics 125, pp.276–310, Springer-Verlag, Berlin, 1970

Index

This index is in two parts. The first part is a conventional index including authors mentioned in the text. The second part is an index to all the predicates defined in the text.

The index below tells you where to find each predicate which has been defined somewhere in the book. The page number given is the page on which the head of the first clause of the definition appears. If there is more than one version of a predicate, then a page number is given for each version.